PRAISE FOR *RESISTING NAZISM*

"A poignant, powerful, and personal portrait of diverse ways in which people resisted Nazism during the Holocaust and in its aftermath. Many ways of resisting are depicted in this moving work, which has a special meaning in our time when nonviolent resistance to authoritarian rule may well determine much of the future. I think that each reader can find in these portraits a model of a person to emulate, someone who challenges our complacency and shows us how we should act, how we must act!"

Michael Berenbaum, *Director, Sigi Ziering Institute*

"Resistance comes in many forms, especially when the trigger is Nazism. A stroke of the pen, a searing speech, an outreached hand can do more to fight back than a shower of bullets. Luke Berryman presents extraordinary stories of such resistance, meanwhile giving lie to one of the most pernicious myths of all: that Jews didn't resist during the Holocaust."

Howard Reich, Emmy-winning author of *The Art of Inventing Hope: Intimate Conversations with Elie Wiesel* and *Prisoner of Her Past: A Son's Memoir*

"Resisting Nazism by Luke Berryman should serve as a central text in teaching the Holocaust and enlightening readers about how Nazism has been thoughtfully confronted. This book is comprised of a discerning selection of texts toward the aim of understanding challenges to Hitler and his legacy of tyranny and genocide—which is more timely than ever."

Michael Berkowitz, Professor of Modern Jewish History at University College London and the author of *The Crime of My Very Existence: Nazism and the Myth of Jewish Criminality*

"In these contentious times, this book illuminates our personal responsibility to become informed and resist propaganda and hatred prevalent today."

Liza Wiemer, author of *The Assignment*

"In Resisting Nazism, Luke Berryman introduces us to ordinary people who became extraordinary resisters. He reminds us that resistance—spiritual, physical, and political—is both possible and necessary, even when we feel powerless to effect change. This book offers not only a record of the past but a blueprint for dignity and courage today."

Dave Reckess, Executive Director, 3GNY—Descendants of Holocaust Survivors

"This book is a tribute to those who have and are resisting the Nazi movement. Knowing history is essential and this is a reminder that it is not only the great acts of defiance that shape our future, but the small, everyday choices we make to stand against hate."

Mark Schonwetter, founder Mark Schonwetter Holocaust Education Foundation/Holocaust Survivor

RESISTING NAZISM

RESISTING NAZISM

True Stories of Resistance to the World's Most Dangerous Ideology, from 1920 to the Present

LUKE BERRYMAN

BLOOMSBURY ACADEMIC
NEW YORK • LONDON • OXFORD • NEW DELHI • SYDNEY

BLOOMSBURY ACADEMIC
Bloomsbury Publishing Inc
1359 Broadway, New York, NY 10018, USA
50 Bedford Square, London, WC1B 3DP, UK
29 Earlsfort Terrace, Dublin 2, Ireland

BLOOMSBURY, BLOOMSBURY ACADEMIC and the Diana logo are trademarks of Bloomsbury Publishing Plc

First published in the United States of America 2025

Copyright © Luke B. Berryman

Cover design: Chloe Batch
Cover image © iStock.com/bymuratdeniz

All rights reserved. No part of this publication may be reproduced or transmitted in any form or by any means, electronic or mechanical, including photocopying, recording, or any information storage or retrieval system, without prior permission in writing from the publishers.

Bloomsbury Publishing Inc does not have any control over, or responsibility for, any third-party websites referred to or in this book. All internet addresses given in this book were correct at the time of going to press. The author and publisher regret any inconvenience caused if addresses have changed or sites have ceased to exist, but can accept no responsibility for any such changes.

Library of Congress Cataloging-in-Publication Data
Names: Berryman, Luke B. author
Title: Resisting Nazism: true stories of resistance to the world's most dangerous ideology, from 1920 to the present / Luke B. Berryman.
Description: New York: Bloomsbury Academic, 2025. | Includes bibliographical references and index.
Identifiers: LCCN 2025022920 (print) | LCCN 2025022921 (ebook) | ISBN 9798881800697 hardback | ISBN 9798881800703 epub | ISBN 9798881857370 pdf
Subjects: LCSH: Anti-Nazi movement–History | Human rights workers–Biography | Jews–Persecutions–History–20th century | Holocaust, Jewish (1939-1945)–Influence
Classification: LCC DD256.3 .B445 2025 (print) | LCC DD256.3 (ebook)
LC record available at https://lccn.loc.gov/2025022920
LC ebook record available at https://lccn.loc.gov/2025022921

ISBN: HB: 979-8-8818-0069-7
ePub: 979-8-8818-0070-3
ePDF: 979-8-8818-5737-0

Typeset by Deanta Global Publishing Services, Chennai, India
Printed and bound in the United States of America

To find out more about our authors and books visit www.bloomsbury.com and sign up for our newsletters.

This book is dedicated to
Edward Tuffnell
of Cambridgeshire, England
without whom it would never have been written

Even in the darkest of times we have the right to expect some illumination [...] from the uncertain, flickering, and often weak light that some men and women, in their lives and their works, will kindle under almost all circumstances.

Hannah Arendt

When the state takes iniquitous decisions and engages in unjust policies, the individual cannot rest content with complaining before going off to sleep. He or she is not merely "authorized" to disobey, as if this were a right that might or might not be taken up in the name of conscience. Rather I have a duty to disobey, if I am to remain faithful to myself.

Frédéric Gros

CONTENTS

Guide to Common Abbreviations xi
Acknowledgments xiii

Introduction: In Search of My Grandfather 1

1. Cartoons: The Satirists Who Sounded the Alarm on Nazism in the 1920s 7

2. Sebastian Haffner: The Lost Book by the German Who Fled the Nazis and Helped the Allies 31

3. The Edelweiss Pirates: The Working-Class German Children Who Resisted Nazism 49

4. Kurt Gerstein: The SS Man Who Tried to Blow the Whistle on the Nazis' Extermination Camps 69

5. Alexander Pechersky: The Jewish Soldier Who Led an Uprising in a Nazi Extermination Camp 87

6. Field Security Sections: Finding and Arresting War Criminals in the Ruins of Nazi Germany 105

7. Leon Bass: The Black American Soldier Who Told the World about Buchenwald 123

8. Emmi Bonhoeffer: The German Activist Who Helped Holocaust Survivors in the Frankfurt Auschwitz Trial 143

9. Gitta Sereny: The Journalist Who Interviewed a Nazi Mass Murderer 161

10. Shoah: The People Who Got Nazi War Criminals to Discuss Their Crimes on Camera 177

11 The Holtzman Amendment: The People Who Expelled Nazi War Criminals from the United States 197

12 Formers: The American Neo-Nazis Who Turned on Their Beliefs 215

Conclusion 231
Notes 237
Further Reading 256
Works Cited 263
Index 270

GUIDE TO COMMON ABBREVIATIONS

The Nazi Party contained a labyrinth of organizations. These organizations all had their own names and jargon, and they often overlapped or were in direct competition with each other. The five mentioned most often in this book are the SA, the SD, the SS, and the Gestapo, as well as the NSDAP. This section briefly explains what each abbreviation stands for and what each organization did.

> NSDAP: *Nationalsozialistische Deutsche Arbeiterpartei*, "National Socialist German Workers' Party," or the "Nazi Party"

The Nazi Party ruled Germany in a one-party dictatorship between 1933 and 1945. Its governing ideology was National Socialism—or Nazism (*Nazismus*)—a type of far-right extremism born in Munich, Germany, in 1920.

> SA: *Sturmabteilung*, "Storm Division"

The SA was one of the Nazi Party's paramilitary groups. It played a significant role in the Party's development in the 1920s and early 1930s. By the end of 1933, its membership was well into the millions. However, its leader, Ernst Röhm, was arrested for treason and murdered in 1934, in a purge known as the "Night of the Long Knives." Röhm and the SA had fallen foul of too many people in the regime, including Hitler. This was down to the SA's continued desire for revolution after the Nazis had seized power through more traditional political channels, and to its sheer size, which meant that it posed a threat to the German Army. While the SA was never formally disbanded, it was quickly overshadowed by the SS after Röhm's death.

> SS: *Schutzstaffle*, "Protection Squadron"

Like the SA, the SS was another of the Nazi Party's paramilitary groups. It began in the early 1920s as a small unit of bodyguards. Under the leadership of Heinrich Himmler, who took over in 1929, it ballooned into an enormous security organization. It was responsible for mass surveillance of civilians, and for the Nazis' penal system, including its network of concentration and extermination camps. As such, it played a decisive role in the Holocaust. There were multiple subdivisions within it, with responsibility for camps, combat, and policing, among many other things, carved up between them.

SD: *Sicherheitsdienst des Reichsführers-SS*, or "The Security Service of the Leader of the SS"

The SD was an intelligence-gathering organization within the SS—so, a security organization within a security organization. The intelligence concerned was on the Nazi Party's perceived enemies and opponents, domestically and internationally. It was given to other organizations that were responsible for acting on it, like the *Einsatzgruppen*, the shooting squads that went into Poland behind the army in 1939, initially to exterminate Polish political and civil leaders, and, later, Jewish people. Its head, Reinhard Heydrich, also chaired the infamous Wannsee Conference in January 1942, at which the plan to murder all Jewish people in Europe was unveiled to several branches of the Nazi government.

Gestapo: ***Geh**eime **Sta**atspolizei*, or "Secret State Police"

The Gestapo was a relatively small organization that worked in tandem with the SD. From 1934, it too was led by Heydrich, and, like the SD, it was under the jurisdiction of the SS. Unlike the SD, most of its staff were career policemen, and its work focused exclusively on the Nazis' domestic enemies and opponents. The Gestapo was also an enforcement agency. As such, its members handled arrests, interrogations, and torture—hence its lasting association with brutality.

ACKNOWLEDGMENTS

I'd like to thank everyone who agreed to be interviewed for *Resisting Nazism*. Beyond taking the time to speak, they all helped me by sending additional resources, or by putting me in touch with other experts, or just by their willingness to answer more questions as they came up. (Though of course, any errors of fact or translation that remain are my own.)

The Board of the Ninth Candle built the organization into the force that it's become. Along with the schools that have done our programs (and especially the students who've grilled me at the end of them), they helped to bring this book into being. I'd like to thank Rita Rosenkranz for championing it from the start and for everything that she did to carve my initial bundle of ideas into a strong proposal. The people who read the manuscript as it was being written and who gave feedback, or who ran to archives, libraries, and museums on my behalf, are too numerous to mention individually. But I would like to offer special thanks to James Belassie, and to my parents, Tessa and Melvin.

Owen Fullarton left the Military Intelligence Museum in the months after our interview. His successor, Cameron Dewson, picked up the baton and generously assisted with my research into the British Field Security Sections and Rudolf Höss's arrest. Over the course of more than a year, Connie James-Jenkin and Angela Richardson patiently acquired more books for me at the Library and Information Resource Center of the Illinois Mathematics and Science Academy than I can remember. Dr. Evan Cortens, Dr. Emily Gauld, and Selina Kemper kindly helped me with my German translations.

In this book, I share the stories of many other people. To explain its dedication, I must share a part of my own. The year 2013 was indescribably difficult for me, for both personal and professional reasons. Reluctantly, but with some encouragement from friends and family (perhaps in the form of an elbow or two), I began to speak with Edward Tuffnell, a therapist in Cambridgeshire, England. Despite my initial reluctance, Ed found a way to help me rebuild my life. At the heart of that rebuilding was the love of writing that he kindled. When we said goodbye at the end of our last meeting in spring 2014, I promised that if I ever ended up writing a book, then I'd dedicate it to him. Over a decade later, I'm glad to finally be able to honor that promise. I also hope that by sharing this part of my story, I might encourage others to seek the help that they need—especially if they're as reluctant as I was to go and get it.

Last, and most of all, I'd like to thank my wife, Sarah. Living with any writer must be a challenge. Living with a writer who leaves piles of books about the Third Reich scattered all over the house, doubly so. But in addition to her ceaseless support, Sarah gave invaluable, insightful feedback on every aspect of this project as it unfolded. She and our baby son Isaac have been my guiding stars—and for that, I will be forever grateful.

LB | Chicago, 2025

Introduction
In Search of My Grandfather

The email came out of the blue one day in 2018.[1] It was from a relative so distant that no one in my immediate family had heard of him. He said that he was working on a family tree begun by his father. It started in the late 1700s, and it was over twenty pages long.

My grandfather, Samuel Mindel, had died in 2006, over a decade earlier. I already knew that he was born in Lithuania, that his parents moved their family to South Africa in the 1920s when he was just a toddler, and that he and my grandmother moved their own family to England in the 1960s.

I read through the tree until I found him. His relatives' names sounded distant and alien. Names like Etel, Frade, and Shlomo. He had an Aunt Riva on his mother's side. The word *Shoah* was next to her name—the Hebrew term for the Holocaust. It was next to his Aunt Chaia, too. I continued reading. Next to one relative after another, *Shoah*. Apparently, most of them had died in 1941 in a place called Anyksciai.

My grandfather had never spoken about the Holocaust to anyone. He never showed any sign of being burdened by it, either. He'd just found a way to separate himself from it, quietly allowing me and everyone else in his family to reach the same conclusion: our ancestors left Lithuania well before the Nazis came.

I stared at the screen for what must have been a long time. Eventually, I got a piece of paper from a drawer and scribbled out names and branches again and again, trying to be certain that I'd understood correctly. There was no mistake. More than a dozen of my grandfather's relatives were murdered in the Holocaust.

I knew that he wouldn't have remembered them. He probably wouldn't even have remembered Lithuania. He had six older siblings, though. It must have been different for some of them. And what about his mother and father, who lost brothers and sisters, nieces and nephews? The dark cloud of death must have hung over their home in Johannesburg.

I called my mom. Had she seen what was in this family tree? Had she known? She said no. She asked my elderly grandmother the same questions. She hadn't known either.

I started visiting a Jewish research room in the New York City Public Library. Slowly, I pieced together what had happened in Anyksciai. The Nazis arrived soon after invading the Soviet Union on June 22nd, 1941. The Jewish population there lived in a shtetl of about 2,000 people. Lithuanian nationalists detained them in local synagogues, torturing them while others robbed their homes. Eventually, they moved them to an improvised, open-air camp in a nearby forest, where farmers used them for slave labor. On July 28th, the Nazis and their Lithuanian collaborators took the men from the group to a hill less than a mile outside Anyksciai and shot them into a ditch. On August 29th, Anyksciai's Jewish women and children were also taken, starving and defenseless, and shot into ditches on the same hill.

My grandmother died in 2022 at the age of ninety-four. While clearing her house, my mom found a small brown-leather satchel that had belonged to my grandfather. It was filled with documents, like passports and professional certificates. Sandwiched somewhere in the middle were two numbered pieces of paper, both yellowed and crumpled.

At the top of the first one, typed in capital letters, were the words, "Early Days in South Africa." The text went on to describe childhood memories of Johannesburg in the 1920s. There were a few handwritten corrections, but it read smoothly, like a large-scale project that had already been edited more than once. The last sentence of the second page broke off as if it should flow into a third. My grandfather had been dead for over fifteen years, but these pages sang with his voice. Whatever the project was, we never found the rest of it. To this day, it's the closest we've come to hearing his story.

*

I wrote a PhD about Nazi Germany and became a university and high-school teacher afterward. I often dreamed about starting an organization to improve Holocaust education. There had to be a way, I thought, to combine my research with the experiences that I'd had in the classroom. For a long time, this dream was just that—a dream. "Maybe one day," I'd tell myself. But when I discovered the truth about my grandfather's family, the idea began to burn with an urgency that didn't belong to a dream. Within two years, I'd founded a nonprofit organization called The Ninth Candle. It runs educational programs for students and professional development programs for teachers in middle and high schools across the United States. This book was inspired by the question that I'm asked most in The Ninth Candle's programs: "Why didn't more people resist Nazism?"

The answer is that it depends on your definition of the word "resistance" and on your time frame.

"Resistance" is generally used to describe organized efforts to overthrow or at least to undermine Adolf Hitler and the Nazi Party. Only a handful of Germans engaged in such resistance. They include dramatic examples like Oskar Schindler, a member of the Nazi Party and an industrialist who saved around 1,200 Jewish people during the Holocaust through subterfuge and bribery; Claus von Stauffenberg, a colonel who led an attempt to assassinate Hitler in July 1944; and the "White Rose" student group, some of whom were executed after two members were caught distributing anti-Nazi leaflets at the University of Munich in February 1943. One reason that so few Germans resisted like this is that many of them supported the Nazis, acquiesced to them, or just learned to tolerate them. Another reason is that it was simply too dangerous. As the historian Richard Evans wrote, the Nazis always "operated extra-legally." They ignored common principles about destruction and murder being wrong because "they believed that history and the interests of the German ('Aryan') race justified extreme measures."[2] This meant that even minor acts of resistance could end in a death sentence. As for Jewish people, they were a tiny minority in Germany, and the Nazis continuously lied to them while stripping them of everything needed to mount any organized efforts to undermine or overthrow the regime.

But "resistance" can be defined in other ways. As long ago as the 1980s, the historian Detlev Peukert divided it into levels. "Active political resistance" (which would describe the actions of Schindler, Stauffenberg, or the White Rose) was at the top, but there were three other levels beneath it.[3] The first was "nonconformity." It consisted of any behavior that contradicted Nazi ideals, even if it was only in private. If nonconformist behavior continued despite harassment from the Nazis, then it entered the second level, "refusal." And if refusal continued despite intimidation from the Nazis, and especially if it began to provoke them, then it entered the third level, "protest." Historians still use these categories, but they often escape the public's attention. Perhaps they were lower stakes and less spectacular than "active political resistance," but they were types of resistance nevertheless. It's also possible to look beyond the twelve years of the Nazi dictatorship. Nazism is an ideology. It was born in 1920, and it's survived up to the present. There were nonconformists, refusers, protestors, and active political resistors who resisted it before Hitler seized power in 1933, and there were others who continued to resist it after the Second World War ended in 1945.

This combination—of a broader definition of "resistance" on the one hand with a wider time frame on the other—can lead us to another answer to the question. Namely, that Nazism has *always* faced resistance. This resistance has taken many forms, and it's come from people of all faiths, nationalities, and political affiliations, but many of them have been forgotten. My book collects twelve such stories and augments them with interviews with experts and eyewitnesses.

In part, the goal is simply to deepen our understanding of the past. But I also want to help us address a catastrophe that's unfolding in the present. That catastrophe is the new far-right extremism that's plagued the United States, Europe, and other parts of the world since the mid-2010s. Labeled variously as nativism, neofascism, populism, and the alt-right, it isn't always the same thing as Nazism—but it has enough points of overlap to give the stories in this book fresh relevance. Those points include nationalist racism; sexism and misogyny; a disdain for democracy, the law, and the state; a willingness to use violence for political gain; and a fundamental disregard for facts and truth.

The new far-right extremism has gifted some of the world's most important political offices to charlatans and criminals. Under them, the poor, the vulnerable, and minorities of every description are scapegoated and brutalized. The rich are idolized, and the very richest are given unbridled political power, no matter how unqualified they are to hold it. The public is encouraged to ignore the earth's destruction from climate change, not to mention the innocent people being murdered in illegal wars of aggression around the world. What's more, every attempt to resist the new far-right extremism has failed. No matter how corrupt or outrageous it becomes, it continues to go from strength to strength. The philosopher Frédéric Gros wrote that, under such circumstances, "Talk of 'injustice' has become obsolete. We are in an age of indecency."[4]

Most of the stories in this book are about ordinary folks in extraordinary circumstances who heard the call of their conscience and resolved to *do something*. They weren't trying to be heroes, and their stories are often complicated, sometimes contradictory. By sharing them, I don't want to uplift you or call you to arms. I don't want to warm your heart or to convince you that goodness always wins in the end. I want to challenge you—to treat history as a tool for carving out a better future.

1

Cartoons

The Satirists Who Sounded the Alarm on Nazism in the 1920s

March 1933, Munich, Germany

Franz Schoenberner went into hiding at a friend's place after his office got trashed.[1] He planned escape routes from the roof in case he needed to make a quick getaway, and he wore an oversize windbreaker to disguise himself whenever he went out. He only held meetings in a cemetery. It was the most isolated place that he could find in bustling Munich. All through this, though, he saw a funny side. To him, Hitler and the Nazis had always been a bad joke that couldn't be taken too seriously. He thought that they always would be.

He changed his mind when Stefan Lorant, the editor of *The Munich Illustrated Times*, was taken into "protective custody"—the Nazis' euphemistic term for indefinite detention. Then the entire staff of the publisher Knorr and Hirth was taken in as well. Franz finally realized that the Nazis' "war of extermination against every trace of democratic opposition" was only going to get "more orderly and systematic."[2]

It was time for him to leave Germany.

He got on an early train from Munich one morning, along with Ellie Nerac, his colleague and future wife. It went to Lake Constance, a holiday destination near the Swiss border, where they spent the night in an old hotel. Everyone there—the hotel's owner, a friendly waiter, other guests—said that the neighborhood supported democracy and that the Nazis would never take it over. Even so, Franz and Ellie kept their plans to themselves. The next morning, after eating breakfast and settling their bill, they told the staff that they were going hiking, and that they'd spend the night in another hotel wherever they ended up. They took two small bags and some loose change. They left behind the rest of their luggage, hoping that the hotel would agree to send it on when the time came.

A bus brought them closer to the Swiss border. The skies were gray, and the air was slick with rain. Franz had only the vaguest idea of where to go. A friend in Munich had told him about a path near the last stop that led to a ruined castle in the forest. If they could find the castle, his friend said, then they'd know that they'd reached the Swiss side of the border.

It was a struggle just to find the path. They had to ask some local peasant children for directions, and then they had to follow what they hoped was the right route into the forest. Hours had passed when Franz, tired and lost in thought, stumbled on a rock. Was the path blocked? He took a long look at the rock and realized that it was part of an ancient wall. It must once have been part of a magnificent building. It was the castle.

"We were in Switzerland. We had escaped. We were free," he wrote. "We felt as though we were floating through the air, defying the force of gravity." They kept going, each step taking them further into their new home, "trusting our stars while risking the leap in the dark."[3]

*

The Nazi Party was founded in Munich in February 1920. It came out of the German Workers' Party, which was founded the previous year and came out of another workers' organization. The Nazis were one of many far-right political-cum-paramilitary groups that existed in Germany after the First World War.

For their first few years, they were almost completely insignificant. They were still winning less than three percent of the vote in national elections as late as 1928. Their leader, Adolf Hitler, was a drifter and a wannabe artist. He'd already spent years scraping by on the fringes of society by the time he joined the German Workers' Party in 1919, having squandered the benefits of his family's solid middle-class background through a series of personal failures. More than one historian has described him as a "nobody" at this stage of his career.[4]

With all that in mind, it isn't surprising that there was almost no resistance to Nazism for most of the 1920s. Hardly anyone in Germany thought that it posed any real threat. The exceptions were the artists and intellectuals who sounded the alarm on it almost immediately. They included the playwright Ernst Toller, the political commentator and one-time anarchist Paul Kampffmeyer, and journalists and writers like Lion Feuchtwanger, Konrad Heiden, and Carl von Ossietzky. But the most persistent of these early resisters were the cartoonists who worked for satirical magazines.

There was a booming magazine culture in Germany at the start of the twentieth century. Magazines were tied to edgy art movements like Dadaism and Expressionism on the one hand, and to the glitzy world of the cabaret on the other. The Café des Westens in Berlin had a "newspaper waiter" who brought magazines to tables, all stamped with the words, "Stolen from Café des Westens."[5] At this and other cafés, magazines would be passed from table to table, with people swallowing the message of their large, whole-page cartoons in a single glance. They'd spark the conversations and debates for which Europe's coffee houses were famous.

One of these magazines was *Simplicissimus*, or *Simpl* for short. It was founded in 1896 by Albert Langen, a publisher, and Thomas Theodor Heine, an artist. They designed the magazine's logo: a bright red, muscular bulldog bearing its fangs, and with its leash snapped in two. It was a sign that they'd broken free of society's chains and were ready to attack anyone. In an editorial note written that summer, by which time *Simpl* was already printing over 50,000 copies of every issue, Langen promised that *Simpl* would never spectate from the sidelines. Instead, it would support any effort to strip Germany's "hypocritical veneer." (This veneer was a product, perhaps, of becoming ever more modern and urban while holding onto the traditions and social norms of the past.[6]) Although generally liberal, *Simpl* wasn't affiliated with any particular party—and it took no prisoners. It was just as likely to bite the educated middle-class that formed its readership as it was the stuffy aristocrats, wealthy businessmen, and loudmouth politicians who embodied the German establishment.

Franz Schoenberner, a Berlin-born student of literature and art history, and a First World War veteran, became the editor of *Simpl* in 1929. Looking back from exile in 1943, he said that Hitler had been their "Public Enemy Number One" from the moment he came onto the political stage.[7] He was ridiculous as well as loathsome, making him a "God-sent enemy." It was almost too easy to satirize him.[8]

Simpl had run one of the first ever anti-Nazi cartoons on May 28th, 1923: Thomas Theodor Heine's "What Does Hitler Look Like?"

Hitler's image has been iconic for the best part of a century now. His side-parting, toothbrush mustache, and overblown speaking poses remain very familiar to us. But when Heine drew his cartoon, if people knew about Hitler at all, then it was through newspaper articles or hearsay. No one had seen a photo of him because he refused to have his photo taken. Photos could be copied and distributed en masse. He thought it'd damage the mysterious aura he was trying to cultivate if everyone knew what he looked like.

Heine speculates on Hitler's appearance in a set of twelve miniature portraits. He lays them out in three rows of four, like the charts of "racial types" that far-right racists made in the early twentieth century. Each portrait is captioned with a question that sounds like gossip bouncing around a beer hall. "Is it true that he only appears in public with a black face mask?" "Surely his mesmerizing eyes are the characteristic feature of his face?" "Or is his mouth the most important thing?" Another asks, "Does he have a beard,

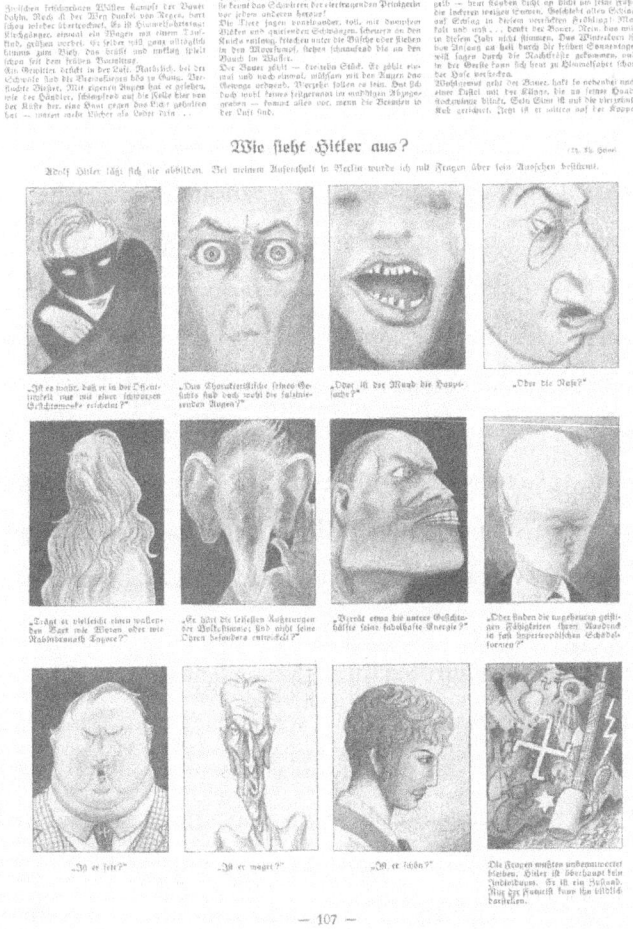

FIGURE 1.1 *Thomas Theodor Heine, "What Does Hitler Look Like?" in Simplicissimus, vol. 28 no. 9 (May 28, 1923), page 107.*

like Wotan or Rabindranath Tagore?" Wotan is chief of the gods in Richard Wagner's epic opera cycle, The Ring of the Nibelung. He's also a scheming and profoundly flawed character. Rabindranath Tagore was an Indian poet who won the 1913 Nobel Prize in Literature, and who toured Europe and the

United States, where he was sometimes regarded as a "spiritual guru." Simpl tended to poke fun at him. Some of their cartoonists even portrayed him as an overrated, manipulative phony. Another caption asks if Hitler has a big nose. The accompanying portrait is an antisemitic caricature that foreshadows Nazi propaganda. Heine was Jewish, though, and here the message is that only someone who's insecure about their own appearance could be so hateful of others. The final caption says that no one can know what Hitler looks like because he isn't a person; he's a *condition*—and you'd have to be an abstract artist to draw this condition. The accompanying portrait is the most sinister of the twelve. A providential eye stares down from the clouds, firing out beams of light. A bolt of lightning rips through the sky. The fasces (an ancient symbol used by twentieth-century European fascists) protrude from a beer mug, a scornful reference to Nazism's birth in the rowdy world of Munich's beer halls. The towers of Munich Cathedral loom in the background like disfigured human silhouettes. A dagger, a gun, and a Star of David hover over swarming crowds. A white swastika cuts through the center of the picture, shadowed by a smaller, black swastika hurtling through the night sky.

Heine's cartoon shows us that Hitler was already known for his mesmeric stare, his public speaking skills, and for his antisemitism, by 1923. Those who looked critically saw a scheming phony manipulating the public. It also shows an early awareness that Hitler's vision was brutal and chaotic, and that his rise was symptomatic of bigger issues in German and European culture after the First World War.

Alois Florath drew a similar cartoon for the front cover of another satirical magazine, *The True Jacob* (*Der Wahre Jacob*), on August 17th, 1923.

It's called "Munich Summer Scene," and it shows a crowd staggering through the street. One man holds a lamppost to stay upright. Another vomits on the sidewalk. There are people in the crowd with warped mouths, lolling heads, and gnarling teeth. Their eyes, which have misshapen pupils, stare in strange directions. They look like they've been drugged or hypnotized, or like they're

FIGURE 1.2 *Alois Florath, "Munich Summer Scene," in* Der Wahre Jacob, *vol. 40 no. 967 (August 17, 1923), p. 141.*

deranged. At the front is a man with one eye that's shrunken and another that's enlarged. The enlarged eye has a swastika for a pupil. His view of the world is (literally) impaired, and the little that he can see is filtered through Nazism. The caption is a question-and-answer joke: "Have they had too much to drink or gotten sunstroke?" "Nah, Hitler-Adolf intoxicated them with his words!" (Hitler's first and last name are inverted, perhaps to make the answer itself sound drunk.) Like Heine, Florath had already clocked Hitler's ability to mesmerize people and the essential phoniness of Nazism.

In April 1924, Hitler was sentenced to five years of "fortress incarceration" after the Nazis tried and failed to seize power in the so-called "Beer Hall Putsch." (Fortress incarceration was a comfortable minimum-security prison, reserved for criminals whose motives were deemed honorable.) The Italian fascist Benito Mussolini had seized power through a mass demonstration in Rome in 1922, and in early 1923, France had occupied the Ruhr, an industrial region in West Germany, after Germany fell behind with its First World War reparations. The Nazis were inspired by Mussolini and outraged by the French occupation. But with hardly any planning, and with no support from the army or any state institutions, their coup (*putsch*) was easily put down. Some leading Nazis fled abroad, while others, including Hitler, were arrested, tried, and sentenced. The Party was outlawed, and Hitler was banned from public speaking in most parts of Germany until at least 1927. Meanwhile, Germany's fledgling democracy and its economy were stabilizing. All this left Hitler more irrelevant than ever. But the cartoonists didn't drop him from their jaws. Partly because, as Franz Schoenberner admitted in his autobiography, it was too easy to satirize him. But it was also because they wanted to keep him contained. Their cartoons were constant reminders to the public that he was a conman whose ideology had no substance.

Simpl ran a cartoon by Erich Schilling on the front cover on August 31st, 1925. It was called "As Recent as Yesterday on Proud Steeds . . . ." (A German saying equivalent to "pride goes before a fall" or "how the mighty have fallen.")

It shows Hitler in a beer hall, hawking copies of his speeches and *My Struggle*, the tedious political manifesto-cum-autobiography that he wrote while in fortress incarceration. Two old men look at him like he's interrupted their conversation. They both have a bulbous nose, which at the time was seen as a sign of alcoholism. He bows to them obsequiously while dogs sniff

FIGURE 1.3 *Erich Schilling, "As Recent As Yesterday On Proud Steeds . . .," in* Simplicissimus, *vol. 25 no. 22 (August 31, 1925), page 313.*

and growl at his legs. His satchel is filled with books, so it must have been a bad night—he hasn't made any sales. The caption is written in the drawl of a Munich boozehound: "The booklet costs twelve Marks? It's a little expensive, pal . . . . Any chance you're selling matches as well??"

A similar cartoon by Willibald Krain was printed in *The True Jacob* on November 24th, 1928, shortly after the last of Hitler's public speaking bans was lifted.

It shows him sad and alone on a park bench. Leaves fall from a tree against cold, gray skies. At his feet is a record player decorated with swastikas. Broken

FIGURE 1.4 *Willibald Krain, "Hitler," in* Der Wahre Jacob, *vol. 49 no. 24 (November 24, 1928), page 8.*

vinyls are scattered all around. The caption says: "Hitler is allowed to speak again. Why? Because he has nothing else to say!" Like many others drawn between 1923 and 1928, these cartoons rub Hitler's failures in his face, making him look as pathetic as possible and mocking Nazism as a movement that was out of steam.

Everything changed in fall 1929 with the Wall Street Crash, which triggered the Great Depression and the collapse of America's economy. American banks recalled the loans given to Germany after the First World War. Germans' taxes went up, their benefits went down, and new tariffs pushed the price of everyday goods skyward, plunging people from all walks of life into deep, sudden poverty. The country's political life destabilized and lurched to the right, producing the so-called "Cabinet of Barons." This clique of upper-class, far-right politicians wanted to get Germany back to the "good old days" of the Kaiser. They believed that the country had become too liberal and that its problems could be fixed by restoring Christian cultural values and replacing democracy with an authoritarian dictatorship. Meanwhile, the public was becoming more receptive to the extremism of both the Communists and the Nazis.

In the September 1930 election, the Nazis took over 18 percent of the vote and 107 seats in the Reichstag. In the next election, in July 1932, they won over 37 percent of the vote and 230 seats—enough to make them the largest party but not enough to win a majority.[9] With the country locked in a stalemate, the "Cabinet of Barons" decided to try and use the Nazis to force their own agenda through. To them, Hitler was just a noisy new kid on the block with no idea of what he was doing. On January 30th, 1933, they made him Chancellor. They put him in charge of the government but surrounded him with politicians they trusted to keep him under control. Their "snobbery and social arrogance" blinded them to the possibility that such an "inferior individual" might outmaneuver them.[10] Franz von Papen, the new Vice-Chancellor, and one of the hapless Barons who paved the way for the Third Reich, famously predicted that "in a few months, we will have pushed Hitler so far into the corner that he'll squeak."[11]

Having only printed two cartoons of Hitler in 1928, *The True Jacob* printed twenty-six in 1930. Likewise, having only printed eight cartoons or articles about him in 1928, *Simplicissimus* printed fifty-one in 1930.[12] Once, these and other magazines had made fun of Hitler. Their cartoonists had drawn him as a clown, a savage, and a snake-oil salesman, and as a knock-off version of Mussolini. As one historian put it, they often saw him "as eccentric rather than dangerous."[13] After the September 1930 election, though, their work became darker and more macabre. On February 27th, 1932, Karl Holtz drew a cartoon for the front cover of *The True Jacob* that cast him as a butcher. His proportions are distorted. He towers over the storefront and sharpens a knife with large arms. Written on his apron in blood is "War with France," "War with Russia," "War against our surrounding states," and "Heads will roll" (a line that Hitler often used in speeches in the 1920s and early 1930s). There's also an ominous smeared handprint and a Star of David. A sarcastic caption says: "... and I warmly recommend myself to the esteemed audience for all possible occasions." It'd be hard to imagine a starker warning. The risks of giving Hitler power were perfectly clear to anyone who listened to what he was saying and who took it at face value.

The day after he became Chancellor, Hitler called an election for March 5th. He was still part of a coalition government—and he wanted to get out of it and establish a Nazi majority as soon as possible. To increase their chances, he unleashed a wave of violence against his rivals. Meetings were broken up, audiences were beaten up, and politicians were attacked in their homes. The situation came to a head at the end of February when the *Reichstag* (the German parliament) was burned down by Marinus van der Lubbe, a Dutch Communist. For Hitler and the Nazis, the "Reichstag Fire" was a convenient excuse to act on their long-held goals of suspending parts of the German Constitution, and of restricting personal freedoms and the freedom of the press.

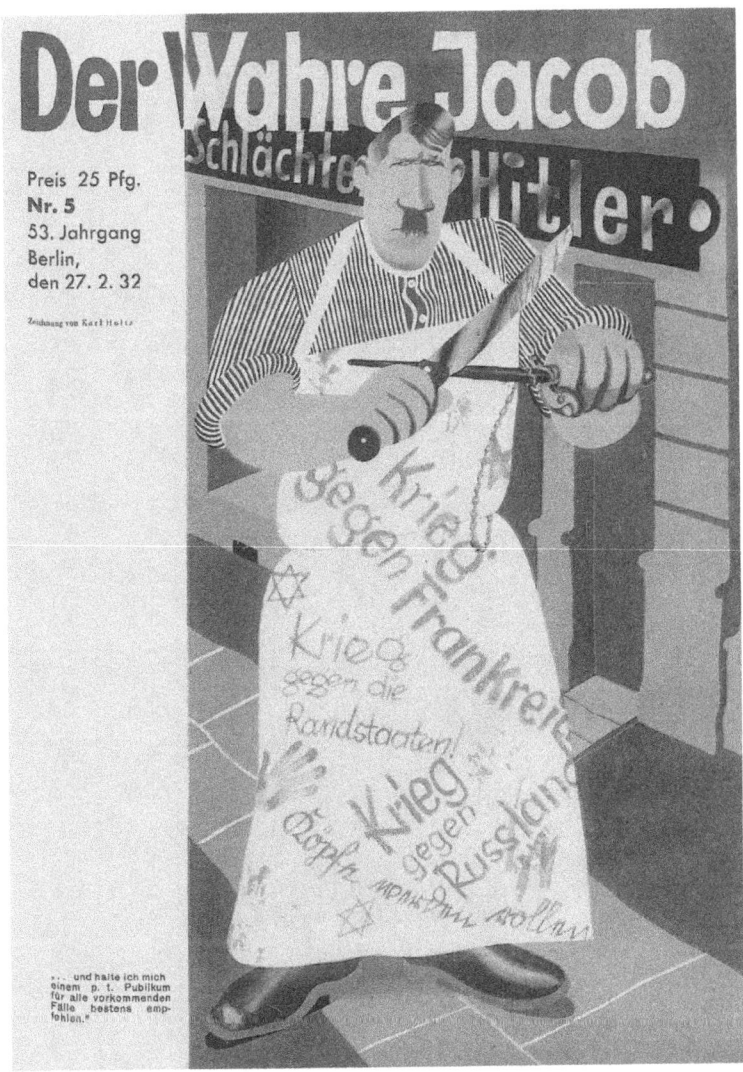

FIGURE 1.5 *Karl Holtz, untitled cartoon in* Der Wahre Jacob, *vol. 53 no. 5 (February 27, 1932), page 1.*

On the day of the election, against the chaotic collapse of German democracy, *Simpl* ran an arresting front-cover cartoon by Thomas Theodor Heine called "The German's Spring Song."

In the foreground, cheerful people wait to cast their votes, singing songs and carrying flowers as if they were going to a spring festival. In the background,

FIGURE 1.6 *Thomas Theodor Heine, "The German's Spring Song," in* Simplicissimus, *vol. 37 no. 49 (March 5, 1933), page 577.*

gray figures beat each other to death with clubs, and the ruined buildings of a ransacked town smolder on the horizon. Beyond criticizing the Nazis' use of violence, it criticizes the German public for acting as if nothing unusual was happening. The cartoon was Heine's last significant contribution to the magazine.

On October 4th, 1933, the Nazis introduced the "Editor's Law" (*Schriftleitergesetz*). It paid lip service to the ideals of the free press with patronizing reminders that editors should report the news accurately and truthfully. At the same time, though, it told them to leave out anything "calculated to weaken the strength of the German Reich abroad or at home, the community will of the German people, German defense, culture, or the economy."[14] It also barred Jewish people from working in journalism. By this time, Germany's professional press association was led by Otto Dietrich, the Nazis' press chief, and membership was compulsory for anyone who worked in journalism. The association had also promised to screen members for "racial and political reliability."[15] These were just some of the developments that gave the Nazi Party a stranglehold on the German press.

The careers of cartoonists at left-wing magazines like *The True Jacob* were destroyed. Karl Holtz and Willibald Krain were both banned from illustrating. They tried to save themselves by applying to join the press association, but their applications were always rejected. One rejection letter to Krain, dated November 5th, 1935, shows how long-lasting the Nazis' grudges could be. "As a press illustrator for *The True Jacob* between 1932 and 1933," it said, "you expressed your attitude and views toward the National Socialists and the leaders of the NSDAP in such a crude manner, that allowing you to stay as a creative force in the press could never be justified. People like you believed that they could combat the National Socialist worldview with the clumsiest means of crude 'caricatures.' There is no longer any place in the German press for such people."[16]

He and Holtz were among the luckier ones, though. Beyond losing their careers, those who'd been active in left-wing politics or who were Jewish were in enough danger to have to leave the country. At one of his last *Simpl* editorial meetings in early 1933, Heine, who was already in his mid-60s, quietly but confidently said that "one must simply go into exile—pauper fashion."[17] He fled Germany, going first to Prague, then Oslo, and then Sweden, where he wrote a superb quasi-autobiographical book, *I Wait for Miracles*.[18] Walter Trier was a Jewish artist who drew for *Simpl* in the 1910s, and for a Berlin-based magazine called *Comic Pages* (*Lustige Blätter*) in the 1920s. He fled to England in 1936, where he drew anti-Nazi cartoons for the Allies. They included a pamphlet called *22 Lessons in Nazi-German* that was air-dropped over Nazi-occupied countries during the War. It satirized the Nazis' fakery and hypocrisy. Lesson 9, for example, defined a criminal as "any person who differs from Hitler," and Lesson 17 defined an Aryan as anyone who was "blonde like Hitler, slim like Göring, tall like Goebbels."[19] Erich Mühsam wrote for *The True Jacob*, and was also Jewish, an anarchist, and a vociferous critic of Nazism. He was arrested and ultimately beaten to death in the Oranienburg concentration camp in 1934.

Cartoonists that the Nazis considered Aryan and who'd drawn for magazines that didn't belong to a left-wing party, like *Simpl*, were generally given a chance to disavow their old work and continue illustrating. Karl Arnold, Olaf Gulbransson, Eduard Thöny, and Erich Schilling were among those who stayed at *Simpl* after 1933 and turned it into a vehicle of Nazi propaganda. They gave up their right to protest in favor of protecting "their fine suburban homes, bank accounts, and social standing."[20] In the 1920s, Erich Schilling had drawn Hitler as an air-headed vandal destroying Munich at the whim of more powerful people, and as a circus clown making a fool of himself in front of a crowd.[21] After twelve years of kowtowing to Hitler's regime and of drawing cartoons with antisemitic and anti-democratic messages, he ended his own life on April 30th, 1945 (the same day as Hitler), when he heard Allied troops near his home.[22]

There was also a small handful of cartoonists who weren't Jewish and who engaged in more active resistance against the Nazis. Alois Florath, for example, was expelled from the press association in 1933. He went into exile, going first to Prague, then Copenhagen. He fell seriously ill in 1936 and had to come back to Germany, where he led an anonymous life in Kagar, a remote village about

70 miles north of Berlin. But, in autumn 1942, when he heard a rumor that the Nazis were murdering Jewish people in gas vans, he convinced Susanne Veit, a Jewish friend, to go into hiding. They pretended that she was his secretary. He plugged into a network of allies to keep her safe until his death from stomach cancer in 1944. At that point, his widow took charge of keeping her hidden. Susanne survived the War and later testified to Alois's actions.[23]

Franz Schoenberner wasn't Jewish either, but his opposition to Nazism, and his concern for his own safety, were both strong enough to make him leave Germany. By the time he wrote the first of his three autobiographical books in 1946, he believed that he'd failed at *Simpl*. Back in the 1920s, he'd thought that if ridicule could kill, then Hitler must have been suicidal. With hindsight, he realized that there was a perverse logic to his behavior. By refusing to acknowledge that satire had exposed him for what he was, he somehow immunized himself against it. Franz was angry at himself and at the *Simpl* cartoonists for their faith that the public's common sense would stop this foolish, unserious man from getting anywhere. He agreed a severance package with his colleagues—or his "friendly enemies," as he came to call them—having told them that he was "perfectly willing to resign rather than make *Simpl* a Nazi newspaper."[24] Forced to watch its transformation from abroad after 1933, he said that *Simpl* became "a living corpse, a phantom of its former self."[25] To him, it felt like the magazine was publishing and republishing its own obituary every week. He wrote, glumly, "We shall never forget this lesson: a man can be irresistibly funny and at the same time extremely dangerous."[26]

*

There's a large replica Dalek from *Dr. Who* standing in the far corner of Professor Richard Scully's office at the University of New England in Armidale, Australia, and the walls are lined with books from floor to ceiling. He's telling me how he got into the history of cartoons. His eyes dance when he says that he loved drawing as a child. He was leafing through one of his parents' old books when he saw *Dropping the Pilot*, a famous cartoon by John Tenniel. It satirized young Kaiser Wilhelm II's decision to fire Otto von Bismarck, who'd been Chancellor of Germany for nearly two decades, in 1890. It shows Bismarck as an upright sea captain, walking off a ship in port and leaving it in Wilhelm's hands. Wilhelm shrugs his shoulders and looks down disinterestedly on the old man from the deck.

"For some reason—I don't know why," Richard says, reflectively, "it has always just spoken to me."

Years later, as a college student, he got into a discussion about *Dropping the Pilot* with a professor at Monash University in Melbourne. She encouraged him to write his thesis on the representation of Germans in the nineteenth-century British satirical magazine, *Punch*. That thesis was the start of his journey to becoming one of the world's foremost experts on satirical cartoons in nineteenth and twentieth-century Europe.

"As I've pointed out in every seminar I've ever taught," he says, "there's *always* a cartoon, from the Reformation through to the present. Whatever the issue, there's always some kind of satirical visual comment on it." He goes through the ways to analyze and understand these visual comments, and the pitfalls to avoid. "You have to talk about everything: who the cartoonist was, the magazine, and the technology involved in creating and publishing it. There's always a danger of writing an attractive visual history without revealing much about cartooning as an industry, or, indeed, about what it achieved. You have to put the cartoons at the center, and then flesh out the details around them."

Our conversation moves to magazine culture in Germany during the 1920s and early 1930s. Richard tells me that it was highly competitive and that it had a huge impact on society.

"There was a war fought between cartoonists," he says. "*Simplicissimus*, *Der Wahre Jacob*, they all read each other's work, they all look at each other's cartoons, and often they respond directly. Some were printing hundreds of thousands of copies each week. And they didn't all go to private homes.

Der Wahre Jacob went to workers' clubs and other kinds of collective working-class spaces, for example. If just a few copies out of every hundred had ten readers, then suddenly you'd be talking about millions. And that's just the readers. What about the people who bought something else from newsstands where satirical magazines were on display, and the cartoons were showing? You're waiting for your newspaper, and Heine's latest cartoon is right in front of you—and you *look* at it, you *see* it," he says, with emphasis. "Maybe it prompts a reaction. Newsstands were important disseminators of political awareness in that sense, just like print-shop windows in the eighteenth century."

There's a rich tradition of studying and writing about these cartoons in Germany. But I tell Richard that I've been struck by how little I've found about them in English, even though they had an important place on the cultural landscape of the 1920s.

"Would it be fair to say that these cartoons are understudied?" I ask.

"Definitely," he says.

"Why do you think that is?"

He sighs heavily before answering.

"There's a widespread inability among historians to take comic images seriously. Even thinking about images generally, it wasn't until Peter Burke wrote *Eyewitnessing* that attitudes toward images and image-making among English-speaking historians started to change." (Peter Burke, a famous cultural historian, has written books about everything from conversations to ignorance. *Eyewitnessing*, which was published in 2001, is about pictures, photos, and other images, and how to use them as historical evidence. It begins with a telling-off: "historians still do not take the evidence of images seriously enough."[27]) "Working with image-based sources did become more important after that," Richard continues, "but cartoons still aren't taken as seriously as other images today. There's been some amazing work in cartoon studies, but the field has always been kind of peripheral."

We begin to get into individual cartoonists and their works. I tell Richard that The Ninth Candle often uses Karl Holtz's 1932 cartoon of Hitler as a butcher in its educational programs. Holtz was imagining the worst-case scenario rather than making a prediction. Still, the cartoon must have shocked people who saw it when it came out—and it may be even more shocking for us today, given how prescient it seems in hindsight. I ask Richard, where does a cartoon like this get its power to shock, and how was Holtz able to draw something that turned out to be so accurate?

"Its power to shock probably has something to do with the mode—with the fact that it's an image, not a newspaper article saying the same thing," he says. "It's an unpalatable argument presented in a way that's so easy to digest. As for how accurate it turned out to be, cartoonists did have their fingers on the pulse. It was their business to keep up with Hitler's speeches and the stuff being printed in Nazi newspapers. They also worked in a hothouse environment in which everyone demonized their enemies. All of that combined to produce the extreme forms of engagement that we see in the cartoons of Holtz and others."

The cartoonists in this chapter are in a different category from almost everyone else in this book: they challenged Nazism before Hitler seized power, and most of them either buckled to his regime or were silenced by it after 1933. As my time with Richard draws to a close, I ask how, if at all, their work could be seen as a form of resistance.

"The comedian Peter Cook is supposed to have said that satire peaked in 1920s Germany—and look how it stopped Hitler from coming to power! It was a dark joke," he says with a chuckle. He rests his chin on his hand, murmurs "The purpose of satire . . . ," more to himself than to me, and drifts into thought for a moment. Then he says, "There was a spectrum of resistance to Nazism. Everything from grumbling occasionally, to deliberate disobedience, all the way up to trying to assassinate Hitler. Satire was resistance in that it tried to raise awareness, it tried to spur people into action. That's where there was a failing. Cartoons don't change the world. People look at them and absorb their message—and then *they* change the world."

*

Dr. Hans Zimmermann responded to my request for an interview by offering to answer questions by email instead. At first, I thought it wouldn't work. It'd take too long, and there'd be none of the spontaneous give-and-go of the conversations that I was having with other interviewees. Over the course of several months, though, the slow-burning pace of our emails immersed me in this topic more deeply than any other.

Hans is a retired literary historian based in Weimar. Through the 2010s, he led a team of academics that digitized nineteenth- and twentieth-century German satirical magazines for the Duchess Anna Amalia Library—including both *Simpl* and *The True Jacob*. Their funding ran out before the database indexing could be completed as fully as Hans had intended, but they did manage to produce a detailed, searchable website that's still live. It provided the invisible backbone for this chapter.

"These caricatures no longer have an immediate effect because their historical context doesn't match the world as it is today," Hans wrote to me. "But it's precisely for this reason that they still have something to say." He explained that because we can't understand them straight away, they spur us to delve into the past. First, we must decipher them, and then we must figure out what they mean for our own time. "That's how I'd describe my motivation to begin the database project," he continued. "I wanted to create something that could be used to illuminate the cartoons' historical backgrounds, uncover allusions, reveal connections, and thereby make access to history easier."

We traded many emails about the lives of individual cartoonists. Hans's knowledge of them and their works is voluminous. He steered me through dozens of examples, helping me to understand their individual styles, and what made one magazine different from the next. When I asked if the cartoonists were famous, and how they'd resisted Nazism, if it all, he told me that he was always surprised by how "normal" they were.

"There were no political rebels among them," he wrote. "None is remembered as having shown heroic or martyr-like behavior. Unfortunately, there are no documents from the editorial meetings of *Der Wahre Jacob*. However, for *Simplicissimus*, there are multiple sources to show that their meetings were marked by intense debate over political content and how close it was to the imaginary 'red lines' of censorship and public opinion. It would be a mistake to see the cartoonists uniformly as upright heroes with unwavering stances. They weren't noble white knights with a steadfast gaze on the devil. In short," he concluded, "they were by no means anonymous, but they were also not public figures. They were simply private individuals."

*

After reaching Switzerland in 1933, Franz Schoenberner and Ellie Nerac went to France, where Franz learned French and tried to start a new magazine. He wanted it to be "a mouthpiece of the free Germany in exile."[28] It failed, but he kept waging his "much-too-private warfare" against Nazism as a freelance writer.[29] He became "a forlorn outpost of the desperately small troop of professional and professing intellectuals who, true to their calling and their cause, never abandoned the losing battle."[30] When the Second World War began in 1939, the French classified him as an "enemy alien," interned him, and put him to work in a brickyard. In June 1941, he and Ellie escaped from France and emigrated to the United States. He was again classified as an "enemy alien." Now in his fifties, and living in his fourth country, he quickly learned his third language, English. He became fluent enough to give lectures about Nazism and to write articles about it.[31] He also worked for the Office of War Information, where he created broadcasts to "counteract the big lie of Nazi propaganda" for German audiences.[32] Today, if he's remembered at all, it's for the three autobiographical books that he wrote after the War, all in English.

The first two came out in the late 1940s: *Confessions of a European Intellectual* and *The Inside Story of an Outsider*. The third didn't come out until 1957. By then, Ellie had died, and so had his best friend (he dedicated it to the two of them), and Franz had been paralyzed in a brutal, random assault. While he was recovering in hospital, a nurse told him, "Well, after all, you still have your head!" He took this unbelievably tactless comment as a "simple statement of fact," and he was enamored by it—so much so that he turned it into the thesis of his third book.[33] He even called it *You Still Have Your Head*. Much of it is dedicated to analyzing the rise and fall of what he called "the Nazi-Beelzebub." He always believed that he was the loser in his struggle against Nazism, but he never gave up. To him, winning was less important than advocating for what he knew to be the truth.

2

Sebastian Haffner

The Lost Book by the German Who Fled the Nazis and Helped the Allies

In 1920s Berlin, "strangers were received with a friendly, curious goodwill and with a conscious determination to understand," Sebastian Haffner wrote. "Our doors were flung open [...] How much more interesting, more beautiful, and richer it made life!"[1] He belonged to a social club, which was one of his favorite things about the city. Some members, like him, were born and raised in Germany. Others had immigrated from around the world. They met to play tennis; to eat and drink; and to dance, debate, and listen to music together.

The club fell apart when the Nazis seized power in 1933.

Looking back on how quickly this had happened, and on the loss of many other things that he'd loved, Sebastian couldn't decide what was more incredible: "That all that could have existed in Germany scarcely ten years ago, or that it has been so thoroughly and completely obliterated in just ten years."[2] By the time he wrote these words in the late 1930s, he'd fled to England, where he was working on an ambitious autobiographical book. It analyzed the failure of German democracy while revealing how that failure had changed his own life. But he never published it. Instead, it stayed hidden in a desk drawer for over sixty years. When it finally came to light in 2000, it caused a global sensation.

*

Throughout the book, Sebastian stressed that "there was nothing particularly interesting or startling to say about my life."[3] He also stressed that he saw himself as neither a hero nor a martyr. He was just an ordinary person who wanted to keep "his integrity, his private life, and his personal honor."[4]

Sebastian was born into a middle-class family in Berlin in 1907. His father was a school principal and a civil servant, and his mother, who was eleven years younger than her husband, came from a long line of teachers. The First World War defined his childhood. No bombs were dropped in Berlin, and no bullets were fired there. This made it easy for him and his friends to imagine that the War was a game. They read army bulletins religiously, fought pretend battles in the schoolyard, and waited for victory as if waiting for Christmas. They followed the War like sports fans follow their clubs. He thought that this left a dangerous mark on them: their illusions would reappear as "a deadly serious political ideology twenty years later."[5]

The end of the War was followed by a succession of dramatic events in Germany. Kaiser Wilhelm II abdicated in 1918, bringing an abrupt end to the country's monarchy; Communists tried and failed to take control in an abortive revolution the same year; and the economy went into hyperinflation in 1923, spiraling out of control until cash was worthless. It was only in the mid- to late 1920s that Sebastian experienced what seemed like lasting peace and stability. As he saw it, Germany had become liberal, orderly, and tranquil. People had been invited to focus on themselves and to find their own paths to happiness. Then, he wrote, something strange happened: "That invitation was declined." He believed that tough times in childhood had made his generation both practical and worldly, which freed them from old prejudices around class, sex, and race. But those tough times had also shaped their lives. When they ended, it felt less like a gift, more like something had been taken away. "They waited eagerly for the first disturbance, the first setback or incident," he explained, "so that they could put this period of peace behind them and set out on some new collective adventure."[6]

Sebastian didn't identify as "left" or "right," and he didn't belong to a political party. But "the Nazis were enemies," he wrote—"my enemies and the enemies of all I held dear."[7] When he saw the headlines about Adolf Hitler becoming Chancellor in the evening papers on January 30th, 1933, he "physically sensed the man's odor of blood and filth, the nauseating approach of a man-eating animal—its foul, sharp claws in my face."[8] While the Nazis tightened their grip on power, Sebastian's life continued. He and his girlfriend still had dinner-and-movie date nights, he still hung out with friends, and his family still celebrated birthdays and other occasions together.

Sebastian's father hoped that he'd follow him into the civil service. He was more interested in writing, but he honored his father's wishes by starting an internship for aspiring judges and other civil servants called a *Referendiat*. For a while, it went like any internship—although there was one Jewish judge whom people started to treat with "a certain tactful delicacy," as if he'd caught a disease.[9] In private, Sebastian sometimes lost control and told his parents that he was going to quit his job, leave Germany, and convert to Judaism. But he didn't follow through on any of these threats. Not at first. Like so many others, he was reluctant to risk derailing his life completely. Looking back, it was precisely that reluctance, he said, that made "immense catastrophes of civilization such as the rule of the Nazis" possible.[10]

At the end of March 1933, he and his girlfriend, Charlie, who was Jewish, went walking in the Grunewald, a wooded area outside Berlin. They found a grassy patch surrounded by fir trees, sat down, and tried to enjoy the arrival of spring. A school happened to be running field trips. Every ten minutes or so, a group of children went past, looked at them, and shouted, "Jews perish!" ("*Juda verrecke!*") "Perhaps it was just a friendly greeting," Sebastian wrote. "Perhaps, though, it was intended for us and was a challenge."[11]

He was reading in the court's library on the last day of the month when the sounds of thudding footsteps and banging doors broke the silence. The SA were throwing Jewish people out of the building ahead of a nationwide boycott of Jewish businesses that Hitler had announced for April 1st. Some people in the library packed up their things and hurried off. A handful broke into laughter. Others sat back and lit cigarettes—a breach of the library's rules, and a sign that normal life was over. Soon the doors were thrown open, and SA men stormed in. They announced that "non-Aryans" must leave immediately. One came to Sebastian and asked him if he was "Aryan." Without thinking, he said that, yes, he was. The man looked briefly at his nose and moved on.

Sebastian felt shame and defeat a moment too late. He hadn't lied—according to Nazi law, he was "Aryan." But his conscience said that he'd done something worse than lie. He'd justified the question by answering it, selling a chance to stand up to the Nazis for the right to work in the library in peace. "I had failed my very first test. I could have slapped myself," he wrote. That night, he and Charlie tried to distract themselves by going to the cabaret. It was full of people "staring at the next day as if into an abyss," and the air was filled with "a strange, morbid ecstasy." [12]

The April boycott was a revolution, Sebastian thought, not against a government or a king, but against "the basis of human society on earth."[13] The Nazis' increasingly rabid antisemitism had raised "the specter of the downfall of humanity."[14] At work, the Jewish judge—a vastly experienced man whose career had begun under Kaiser Wilhelm II—was demoted to an administrative job in a lower court. His seat was filled by a much younger, blonde-haired man, who was rumored to have a senior role in the SS. It soon became clear that he knew nothing about the law he was meant to represent. Sometimes, when his mistakes were pointed out, he backed down. Other times, though, he gave ebullient speeches and declared that the law had to make way or that its "meaning" was more important than its wording. Then he'd quote Hitler before giving a verdict that would have been impossible just a few months earlier.

Whenever this new judge spoke, Sebastian saw the older judges look down at their notes "with an expression of indescribable dejection, while their fingers nervously twisted a paperclip or a piece of blotting paper." Before 1933, they'd have failed him in his legal exams. Now, they were letting him present nonsense "as the pinnacle of wisdom," knowing that he had "the full power of the state" behind him.[15]

Sebastian felt like his world was dissolving. "Every day another piece vanished quietly, without ado. Every day one looked around and something else had gone and left no trace."[16] At first, he figured that he could escape Nazism by retreating into his private life. As 1933 went on, though, he realized it'd never work—because the regime was intruding ever further into people's private lives. The only way to escape Nazism was to escape Germany. But the thought of leaving tore him apart. He was proud "of the better points that one sees here and there in German history and the German character," and he felt that he belonged to Germany like people belong to their families. "To give up this sense of belonging," he wrote dejectedly, "to turn away and learn to look on one's home country as an enemy, is no small matter."[17] He resolved to go to Paris for the final stage of his internship—once his training at the courts was over but before he'd written his thesis.

Sebastian's plan was half-baked, though. He'd never lived away from home, and he had no idea of how he'd cope in France. Still, he presented it to his father. It was pointless, he said, to be a civil servant in Hitler's Germany. He asked to be supported with a monthly allowance, for as long as it remained legal for Germans to send money abroad. His father was a fierce patriot. Just a few months earlier, this conversation would have prompted a quiet but superior smile and some patronizing advice to stay put. Now, Sebastian wrote, it was almost surprising how little opposition he offered. In the short time since Hitler had become

Chancellor, he "had grown very old. He no longer slept at night. The drumming and alarms at the nearby SS barracks kept him awake, but more so, perhaps, his thoughts."[18] The Nazis' restructuring of the civil service had lain waste to his profession. "There had been great pieces of legislation in his administrative area, on which he had worked closely," Sebastian wrote. "Important, daring, thoughtful, intellectual achievements."[19] To see them undone at this stage of his life was worse than a failure. It was a catastrophe. And the situation soon became even worse. The Nazis ordered him and all other retired civil servants to complete a questionnaire about their political beliefs and to sign statements of loyalty or lose their pensions. After several days, during which time he spent hours sitting at his desk, staring into space, he completed and mailed it. When he got home, "he had hardly sat down at his desk again when he jumped up and began to vomit convulsively." It was the start of a long stomach illness that killed him, "cruelly and painfully," two years later.[20]

Sebastian took his exams. It felt like they counted for nothing, though. Why answer questions about the law as it had existed in the 1920s when the Nazis had already destroyed it? His only goal was to finish them and leave for Paris. Then, when he had just one exam left, the Nazis announced that all civil service interns (*Referendars*) now had to attend an ideological training camp to get a passing grade. "I saw red and went berserk," he wrote. Punching the walls, he "screamed and sobbed and cursed God and the world."[21] But he acquiesced. A few weeks later, he was at a training camp in Jüterbog, a military base south of Berlin, along with dozens of other young men from across Germany who wanted to pass the same exams. He wore jackboots, a uniform, and a swastika armband. They went on hours-long marches, sang Nazi songs, and learned to shoot rifles. He wanted to complete his internship, and, by this stage, he was "utterly convinced of the futility of any kind of resistance" to Nazism.[22] Going along with all this didn't turn him or any of the others into Nazis, but he did think that it turned them into "usable Nazi material."[23] "It was so dreadfully shaming," he wrote.[24] His autobiographical book ends with this frank account of his final humiliation.

*

Sebastian did go to Paris after the ideological training camp at Jüterbog, but the anti-immigrant, anti-German atmosphere there made it impossible to settle. He returned to Berlin in 1934 and started working as a journalist. He also began a relationship with a new girlfriend, Erika. Her family had once been Jewish, but they'd converted to Christianity generations ago. This didn't matter to the Nazis. When she became pregnant, it was a violation of the "Nuremberg Laws." These racial laws were introduced on September 15th, 1935, and they were augmented with additional, clarifying decrees in the months that followed. They tried to define who was and wasn't Jewish. (It all hinged on whether someone's grandparents had practiced Judaism—proof of how flimsy the Nazis' so-called "racial science" really was.) Among other things, the Nuremberg Laws forbade extramarital sex between non-Jews and anyone with Jewish ancestry. With them, wrote Richard Evans, antisemitism "became a principle governing private life as well as public," and it began "penetrating larger areas of German society more deeply than ever before."[25]

Sebastian's experiences in France had made him think that immigration was impossible, but now he and Erika had no choice. As a Jew, she was able to get into Britain as a refugee relatively easily. Sebastian had to get creative to join her. He cooked up a proposal to write a few articles about Britain, wrangled a commission from a newspaper editor, and got his hands on a six-week British visa. He arrived there on August 29th, 1938, and married Erika straight away. Their first child, a son named Oliver, was born in October. All the while, Sebastian was going back and forth to London to get short-term renewals on his visa. He was also struggling to find an income. He tried and failed to get a job at the University of Cambridge (where his brother-in-law taught math), and he wrote several short articles about England for the

German press that were rejected. "The money I earn these days is just enough for the bare necessities of life," he wrote to a friend on June 18th, 1939, "and my many small creditors are already putting terrible pressure on me."[26] He also began working on an autobiographical book about his experiences in 1920s and 1930s Germany. Frederic Warburg, a British publisher who'd represented Thomas Mann, among others, was so impressed by a synopsis that Sebastian pitched that he offered him a weekly advance to finish it. He also intervened with the British immigration authorities to get his visa renewed again. Later, he described the synopsis as "the most brilliant synopsis ever put before me."[27]

Within weeks of this personal breakthrough, Germany invaded Poland, starting the Second World War. Sebastian put his autobiographical book to one side and began a practical guide to help the Allies understand how Hitler and the Nazis had seized power instead. It would be called *Germany: Jekyll and Hyde*. Sebastian had already been writing articles and essays under a patchwork of aliases, for fear that the Nazis would punish his relatives who still lived in Germany. These included names like Lambert Martin, "A Student of Europe," and "Liberator."[28] When *Germany: Jekyll and Hyde* came out in June 1940, it was under the name "Sebastian Haffner." Having been born Raimund Pretzel, he used this name for the rest of his life. By 1943, the book had sold 2,500 copies of the 3,000 that were printed, which was enough to make him famous. Thomas Mann described him as "the greatest living German," and the British press praised him for the depth of his insights into Nazism's fatal appeal.[29]

While all this was happening, though, the British government started interrogating the German and Austrian immigrants in their country, believing that enemy spies were among them. Having entered on false pretenses, and then having finagled more than one renewal of his visa, Sebastian was put into the most dangerous category of immigrants. He was detained in squalid conditions in British internment camps for months on end, even missing the birth of his second child—a daughter, Sarah, in April 1940. Warburg petitioned for his release and brought his case to the attention of the British Parliament.

In August 1940, Sebastian's name was mentioned in a debate in the House of Lords. People began to see his detention as proof that the mass internment policy wasn't working. He was released that same month, and he remained forever grateful to Warburg. "Even in 1969," one historian wrote, "Haffner was willing to accept financial disadvantages in contract negotiations" with Warburg because he'd "saved his life."[30] After *Germany: Jekyll and Hyde*, Sebastian went on to become one of his generation's most successful writers. He was a constant presence in the German media, and he wrote several historical and political books that are still popular today. (The best-known, *The Meaning of Hitler*, was published in 1978, and it inspired a Netflix documentary of the same title in 2020.)

Shortly before his death in 1999, Sebastian told his children, Oliver and Sarah, about a novel and some other unpublished works that were hidden in his office. They were only allowed to read them once he was gone. When the time came, Oliver went looking for them. Although he found the novel, he was more struck by a mysterious autobiography—perhaps because his father had never really shared any personal memories with his family. He sat down and read the entire thing in one go. Convinced of its brilliance, he spearheaded an effort to get it published. It came out in German in 2000 as *The History of a German* (*Geschichte Eines Deutschen*), and in English in 2002 as *Defying Hitler*. Some missing chapters were later discovered and restored by Jürgen Peter Schmied, a German historian and one of Sebastian's biographers. Although *Defying Hitler* is technically unfinished—Sebastian planned to add more chapters to cover the years 1933 through 1938—it still gave an unprecedented look into one person's struggle to live in Germany during the rise of Nazism. It was a bestseller celebrated by critics the world over.

But then, in 2001, an article in the upmarket German newspaper *Frankfurter Allgemeine Zeitung* (known as the *FAZ*) made an extraordinary allegation: *Defying Hitler* was too good to be true. It would have been impossible for anyone to write such a clear, cogent analysis of Nazism in the 1930s. It had to be an elaborate hoax, written in secret, long after the War—a desperate attempt on Sebastian's part to wash his hands of any involvement with the Nazis and to cement his postmortem fame.

*

Jürgen Peter Schmied has been telling me excitedly about his research on Sebastian Haffner and how he came to write one of the first biographies of him. Bright eyes shine behind a pair of glasses. He has a broad smile and a speaking voice that's soft but authoritative. "Of course, *Defying Hitler* is one of the most important books that he wrote," he says. "It describes the duel between the state and people in their private lives in a way that's unique. It's really fascinating to see. It shows us how the state—the totalitarian state—takes control of one private life at a time."

Jürgen helped to restore some of the missing chapters of *Defying Hitler*. He realized that Sebastian had transplanted some into other projects. In 1942, he'd used the ones about his time in the Jüterborg ideological training camp for a six-part serial piece in an émigré newspaper that he founded called *Die Zeitung* (*The Times*), for example, which he published under yet another alias, "Joachim Runge."[31] The ones about the boycott of Jewish businesses were used for an article in *Stern*, a German magazine, some fifty years after the event. Jürgen also discovered a handwritten draft of other chapters among Sebastian's papers in the German state archives. During all that research, I wonder, did he ever ask himself if it was all a hoax?

"Well, I was a young academic at the time that the allegations were made, so I had to be careful. My professor said, 'To prove the allegations, one would have to find a point where Haffner gives information that he could not have had in 1938.' There is no such information in this book. So, there was no strong argument—just rumor and speculation. And then the analysis of the paper made it clear."

German criminologists analyzed the manuscript of *Defying Hitler*. They concluded that it'd been written on two kinds of paper and on two typewriters. The paper wasn't commercially available after 1940, and the typewriters were made in the 1920s. The manuscript was also littered with Sebastian's handwritten corrections. Then, in 2002, the film producer and editor Jutta Krug added further proof of the manuscript's authenticity. She interviewed Sebastian in 1989, when she was a student. In the interview, he mentioned an unfinished book that was "very personal" and that was "still lying in a drawer."[32] In the wake of the controversy around *Defying Hitler*, Jutta revisited her recording of the interview, transcribed it, and published it as a short book called *Sebastian Haffner Disguised as an Englishman*.

I want to know if the act of writing *Defying Hitler*—even if it stayed hidden for decades—could be seen as a kind of resistance against Nazism.

"That's a philosophical question," Jürgen says, thoughtfully. "Haffner was, in a way, a humble man. He said that he wasn't made for resistance. He was a lawyer and a special product of what Germans call the *Bildungsbürgertum*." (This word means something like "educated middle-classes.") "He didn't take part in political activism, or smuggle things, or anything like that . . . " His answer trails off into a long pause. "The book describes so superbly how Nazism worked, and how it captured the souls of so many people. But, since it wasn't published in his lifetime, maybe it was a kind of inner resistance, or inner emigration."

The term "inner emigration" has been used since the 1930s to describe people detaching their minds, thoughts, and souls from what was happening in Nazi Germany while staying inside it physically. It's sometimes contentious because it was easily abused after the War by those who wanted to exonerate themselves and because it's so hard to disprove.

"But then, in England," Jürgen continues, "after Haffner had stopped working on the autobiography, he moved to more obvious types of resistance by writing *Germany: Jekyll and Hyde*, founding *Die Zeitung*, and some hopeless attempts to begin a new German army in London."

Unlike many others, Sebastian was also deeply critical of himself after the War. In 1981, for example, he declined an invitation to give a lecture in memory of Hans and Sophie Scholl, siblings who were murdered for their role in the White Rose. He feared that it would be hypocritical, given what he described as his "pragmatic political detachment."[33]

"He was a nonconformist all his life. He was disgusted by Nazism—he was repelled by it," Jürgen says. He picks up a German edition of *Defying Hitler*, which is lying on his desk, and waves it at me, showing the photo on the front cover. It's of Sebastian in a dapper suit with a waistcoat, a pristine white button-down shirt, and a patterned necktie. He's gazing intently, but away from the camera, as if lost deep in thought. "I mean, if you look at him, he was a dandy!" He laughs before picking up and leafing through another book that's on his desk, *The Life of Pedestrians*, which he edited. It's a collection of articles and essays that Sebastian wrote in the 1930s.[34] "There's a piece in here called 'Little Credo,' where he makes an opposition between having a 'worldview' and having 'taste.'"

We talk about the "Little Credo" for a while. The "tasteful" person is conservative and liberal, socialist and religious, patriotic and internationalist. They discuss their opinions but leave them out of serious decisions. People with "worldviews," on the other hand, believe what they're told. They have newspapers instead of eyes and radios instead of ears. Their world is simple: they decide whether something is good or bad based on the slogans that they've seen in the media. Worldviews free people from obligations, and they belong in the same category as instant soup and package holidays.

"Haffner was always on the side of people who had taste," Jürgen says. "And I think that's what we can learn from him today: do not just go with the majority. His legacy for us lies in his nonconformist behavior and thinking."

*

I start my interview with Oliver Pretzel by asking if he can tell me about himself and his own career.

"Well yes," he says, looking away from me slightly, and sounding confused and perhaps a bit nonplussed. "But that has very little to do with either my father or Germany."

Oliver is Sebastian Haffner's son but that's not the only reason I want to speak to him. He also discovered and translated *Defying Hitler*, and he drove it to publication. When we meet, he's 84 years old. Reluctantly, he gives me a brief overview of his life. "I was a reasonably good but not great mathematician. I have a research standing and so on, and I was at Imperial College London, which is perhaps the best mathematics department in Britain, but . . . ." He trails off before saying again, "I don't think that has very much to do with my father, or with the Nazis. Although I am the reason that my parents emigrated."

From here, he unfolds his father's story. I can tell from the smoothness and the clarity of the presentation that it's one he's told many times before. He tells me how painful it was for him to be interned in Britain as a dangerous immigrant and to be separated from his family. Then he adds, "There are echoes with so many people's attitudes toward immigrants and refugees today. I think, you know, that in the current climate, my father would have been branded an 'illegal' and deported immediately." The way that Oliver interweaves *Defying Hitler* with contemporary politics prompts me to dive in with a question that I'd planned to save until the end of our time together. Does he think that the book has more relevance today than when it was published in 2000?

"The world has become a worse place since then, and a more dangerous place. There's the war in Ukraine, there's populism all over the place, with all its dangers. I also think the attitude—the *anti-humanitarian* attitude," he says, now speaking faster and stressing individual words and phrases, "the idea that there's 'us and them,' and there are these *others* that have to be downtrodden—*at least* downtrodden if not extinguished and exterminated—I find that *terrible*, I find that *quite terrible*." He shakes his head and a few cracks sound in his voice. "When I published the book, I thought that it still had some lessons for us: how to deal with difficult situations, and how to try and stay honest when things tempt you to be dishonest. But I didn't think it had such general relevance as it has now."

Our conversation makes its way back to his father's story. Sebastian had already pinpointed antisemitism at the core of Nazism by the early 1930s, and he was deeply offended by it, too. This was unusual. Many Germans thought that antisemitism was just a cheap trick that the Nazis were using to stir up the public and that they'd eventually drop it. Even other writers who left Germany and publicly criticized the regime, like Thomas Mann and Hermann Rauschning, had a comparatively limited understanding of the issue. Where did his father's special insight come from?

"That goes back to my grandfather, my father's father," Oliver says. "He was the headmaster of a school in east Berlin, and he believed in child-centered learning, which wasn't popular under Kaiser Wilhelm II. It was very much an authoritarian regime. Children were told what to do. They had to get up and click their heels when the teacher came into class, things like that. My grandfather got relegated to a school in a working-class suburb, and he didn't have a great career. The children there were working class, or Jewish, or both. So, right from a child, my father grew up with Jews. They weren't all practicing, but they loved Jewish attitudes and customs and jokes. My father grew up with that, and it was very close to his heart. He loved Jewish culture very much. The antisemitism hit him directly. It was his friends who were ostracized and punished, just for being who they were."

This goes some way toward explaining Sebastian's extraordinary analyses of Nazism, but I wonder if it would be enough to satisfy the skeptics who believed that *Defying Hitler* had been written in secret after the War. I ask Oliver about the allegations in the *Frankfurter Allgemeine Zeitung*, and we talk about the manuscript being analyzed by criminologists. Did the results prove that it was genuine?

"Well, it's not an absolute proof that it's not a forgery," Oliver says, with the cool impartiality that you'd expect of a math professor. "But there's one conspiracy theory," he continues, smiling impishly. "The book was hidden, I found it by accident among other papers, and my father never talked about it. In this theory, I'm cast as the dupe. My father has a far-reaching plan to secure his postmortem fame by writing this book, secretly, without me knowing about it, during the 1970s and 1980s. And then he hides it—hides it where I'm *bound* to find it." Now he's almost breaking into laughter. "He removes some chapters so that I can spend some time reconstituting it and believe that it's genuine. And there's all this demonic . . . " He shakes his head in disbelief, the sentence crumbles away, and his tone becomes quietly serious again. "My father wasn't like that at all," he says.

In the story that Oliver told me, his father stopped his autobiographical book to start a new, more relevant project instead. But that doesn't explain why he never came back to it, and it also doesn't explain why he didn't destroy or discard it. Is it possible, I ask, that he just forgot about it?

"He didn't forget it," Oliver says. "It was there in the back of his mind. I think he was quite proud of it, actually. He thought that he'd written well. And he'd published some of the chapters that were missing." He goes on to reflect that his father generally didn't throw papers away—he just stuffed them into drawers.

Many of the people in Sebastian Haffner's generation that I've met have been reluctant to share their stories. They were raised to believe that it was inappropriate to do anything that might seem like they wanted to be the center of attention. Perhaps, I say to Oliver, Sebastian knew that he'd written a brilliant manuscript, but he didn't feel comfortable publishing it when it contained details about his love life, and about his own, private struggles under the Nazi regime.

"I think you have a point there," he says. "People of that generation were reticent about what they experienced. Partly because it went so much against their expectations and their view of themselves. This is the only book that my father wrote that is personal. He'd just emigrated to Britain when he started writing it, and he'd had a very traumatic experience that jolted him. His later books are always written in a very impersonal, cool way. In the family, he was prepared to reminisce if you got him at the right moment, and if you asked him the right questions. But they had to be questions of general interest. Just asking, 'What did you do in 1940?' wouldn't get you anything. You'd have to ask, 'What was your opinion of the British interning German immigrants?' Then, suddenly, things would come out. *Defying Hitler* is all about moral difficulties, the problems that you have when you're trying to live in an evil country run by an evil government, and how you can try and stay clean—and you don't succeed, you *can't* succeed completely. A bit of dirt rubs off just because you're there."

As we wrap up our conversation, I ask Oliver to look back at his father's legacy on the one hand, and to look at the state of the world today on the other. What advice might he have for us about resisting far-right extremism in our own time?

"Oh dear, that's terrible!" he exclaims. "I think that's the most difficult question to answer. He surprised me several times while he was alive, and I'm sure that he would surprise me again if he were alive now. He would come up with ideas—he was a very imaginative thinker about political things. But . . . ," he says, pausing for a moment before chuckling. "He said, 'You should follow your nose—if it stinks, stay away from it!' He said, 'The Nazis stank, and they stank immediately, you could just smell it.'" Then his tone becomes quietly serious again, just as it had earlier. "He didn't think that you needed to be an analyst to know they were evil. It was obvious."

*

Sebastian didn't choose the title *Defying Hitler*, and Oliver told me that he would have hated it. The book begins with the line, "This is the story of a duel." The duel was between him and Hitler's regime, and it was one of hundreds of thousands of such duels being "waged in total isolation and out of public view."³⁵ In his mind, he'd lost that duel, or at least backed out of it. He hadn't done anything to defy Hitler.

Or had he?

Richard Evans said that language shapes the way we interact with the world around us. The words we use set limits on what we can think. As soon as they seized power, the Nazis started changing the German language through propaganda and the mass media. They flipped words like "brutal" and "ruthless," turning them from negatives into positives. They described Hitler with religious words to make him sound like a messiah. They used superlatives all the time, so that everything they did was the "best" and the "greatest." Above all, they infused daily conversation with the terms of war. Everything was a "battle," a "fight," or a "struggle." In this way, they prevented "even the possibility of thinking about dissent and resistance, let alone acting it out in reality."³⁶

Nevertheless, Sebastian Haffner found a way to sharpen his critical thinking skills, and then to turn them on himself. He interrogated his own behavior to figure out how he could be a better citizen. The story of him and the manuscript that he kept hidden for over sixty years shows that, in the face of rising far-right extremism, what each of us thinks and does in private still counts. Resistance must begin with our individual actions, choices, and decisions, and in our own minds. Or, as Sebastian put it, "the political struggle is expressed by the choice of what a person eats and drinks, whom he loves, what he does in his spare time, whose company he seeks, whether he smiles or frowns, what he reads, what pictures he hangs on his walls. It is here that the battles of the next world war are being decided in advance."³⁷

3

The Edelweiss Pirates
The Working-Class German Children Who Resisted Nazism

Imagine that you were born in Germany around 1928. The Nazis overhauled the education system just as you started kindergarten. You learned to read from books about Nazism. These books told stories about Hitler's bravery and about happy Aryan families with lots of children. They also demonized Jewish people. There were antisemitic illustrations that got you used to the idea of Jews being dangerous and somehow not human. Later, you joined an elementary school where the long-time principal had been fired for being "politically unreliable." Perhaps he used to belong to a left-wing party, or perhaps someone heard him tell a joke about Hitler. He'd been replaced with a devout Nazi. Every teacher at the school was now aware that they had a choice between toeing the Party line or losing their job. The more opportunistic ones had joined the National Socialist League of Teachers to improve their career opportunities. One or two had even gone to the League's training camps, where they heard lectures about Nazism and learned how to promote it to children.

Like every school in Germany, your elementary school had been ordered to teach in "the spirit of National Socialism."[1] This meant pushing anti-liberalism, nationalism, and racism, and making you happy to serve and sacrifice yourself for the state. Every class started and ended with the so-called "German greeting." Your teacher extended their right arm and shouted "Heil Hitler!," and you and your classmates responded by doing the same thing. You couldn't afford to seem unenthusiastic about it. There was always a chance that someone in the room would report you to the Gestapo.

Class was suspended whenever Hitler gave a speech on the radio. Everyone went to the gym or the assembly hall to listen together. Other "special treats" included watching the movies that the Nazi propaganda ministry made for children. When you were in class, you were always learning things that complemented Nazism in some way.[2] You learned about "racial science" in biology and about "living space" in geography—and about how badly Germany needed more of it. You solved problems with Nazi themes in math. You might have been asked to calculate what it cost the state to keep patients alive in mental asylums, for example, or to estimate how many Germans had blonde hair. Even in physics, instead of just learning about speed and electricity, you learned about the speed of bullets, and about how electricity powers field equipment. Meanwhile, any books that contradicted Nazism had been removed from the school library.

Your indoctrination didn't just happen at school, either. By 1939, you were one of 8.87 million Germans aged ten to eighteen.[3] By now, almost everyone in your generation was in the Hitler Youth or the League of German Girls. These state-sponsored extracurricular youth organizations prepared children for adult life in the Third Reich. The Nazis modeled them on the constellation of youth organizations that had existed in Germany since the late nineteenth century. They tempted you with fun activities like camping, hiking, singing, and sports, and with spiffy, military-looking uniforms. At the same time, though, the Nazis made sure that you had no choice. Older youth organizations were forcibly absorbed into the Hitler Youth—or, if they had any connection with the Nazis' political or social rivals, banned altogether. Meanwhile, during the mid- to late 1930s, laws were gradually introduced to make Hitler Youth membership compulsory.

Through their overhaul of education, and through the Hitler Youth and the League of German Girls, the Nazis built an indoctrination machine that Richard Evans described as "ceaseless."[4] And yet, somehow, there were children who resisted.

*

In July 1941, a teacher in Oberhausen reported a conversation that took place in his class to the Gestapo. A delinquent student had been taken into the care of the state (which likely meant that he'd been sent to some kind of camp). As his classmates gossiped about him, it came out that he'd been in the Kittelbach Pirates. The teacher asked what the Kittelbach Pirates were. They said, "Every child knows the K.P. There are Pirate groups everywhere, and they have more members than the Hitler Youth. The groups all know each other, and they really stick together." When the teacher asked who else was involved with the Pirates, the students gave him three names, "and many others—not just workers, but also rich kids and even girls." The teacher ended his report by requesting action, for fear that these Pirates were indulging in "Communist activities."[5]

The members of groups like the Kittelbach Pirates were mostly boys who were between fourteen and eighteen years old—so, old enough to have left school, but too young to have been conscripted into the military or compulsory labor service. They came from working-class families. They usually had jobs, either as apprentices or, especially as the War went on, as unskilled laborers. This meant that they had gumption and self-confidence, and modest but solid incomes that gave them some independence. They were friends who knew each other from work, from old schools or sports teams, or just from neighborhood hangouts. Different groups in different cities had different names and characteristics. Their names usually implied an adventurous rogue spirit.

There were "The Navajos" in Cologne, "The Kittlebach Pirates" in Düsseldorf and Oberhausen, "The Roving Dudes" in Essen, and others besides. But they all identified with a larger network called "The Edelweiss Pirates." There was one thing that united this network, according to the historian Detlev Peukert: "all Edelweiss Pirates rejected the Nazis."[6]

The Edelweiss is a white, woolly flower that grows high in The Alps. For generations, it was used as a symbol for German patriotism. (As it grows in beautiful places that are so hard to reach, it made people think of Germany's unspoiled countryside on the one hand, and of brave mountaineers on the other.) Under Hitler, it became a symbol for Nazism. It was used on the uniform of the SS Mountain Rangers (*Gebirgsjäger*), for example. By 1933, the connection between the flower and the ideology was strong enough for a cringey pop song called "Adolf Hitler's Favorite Flower is the Simple Edelweiss" to be a hit.

The Edelweiss Pirates formed in the industrial cities of West Germany in the mid- to late 1930s. There are competing origin stories about their name.[7] Wherever it came from, it implies that they were subversively trying to restore the original symbolic meaning of "Hitler's favorite flower." Children joined for a variety of reasons. The most common was that they hated the Hitler Youth. Their hatred wasn't always about ideology or politics, though. For many, it was more personal. As they came from left-leaning families, the Nazis had often arrested or even murdered their parents. Others hated it because it stopped offering authentic outdoors experiences. (Once its membership was into the millions, and especially once the War started, such experiences were impossible to organize.) Others hated the Hitler Youth's leaders. In the early 1930s, its leaders were experienced youth workers. As time went on, though, they were drafted into the military. Their replacements were children from privileged homes who went to elite schools, despite the Nazis' promise to champion the working class.[8] The fact that these replacements were no older than regular members only made regular members more resentful. For others, the Hitler Youth was just too boring. The ideological training and the military drills could be mind-numbingly repetitive.

The Edelweiss Pirates met after work or school, or after their mandatory Hitler Youth sessions. To stay off-radar, they kept their meetings informal and low-key, holding them in open spaces like parks and street corners. They wore white knee socks and loud checkered shirts, and they had long hairstyles. They also wore Edelweiss pins and attached symbolic objects to their belts. As well as creating a "counter-uniform" that went against the all-brown military look of the Hitler Youth, this made it easier for them to recognize each other.[9]

On weekends and public holidays, they left the city and went hiking in the countryside, despite the Nazis' tight restrictions on freedom of movement. Their hikes could last for days or weeks, even during the War. If their supplies ran low, they'd find casual labor to keep themselves going. They took guitars with them and sang songs together. Group singing was used as a community-building tool in the Hitler Youth, too, but the lyrics always promoted Nazism. The Pirates, on the other hand, preferred to sing about beautiful women and adventures in faraway places.[10] They also reworked the lyrics of popular songs, sometimes

FIGURE 3.1 *A group of Edelweiss Pirates. The photo album of Herbert Hechsel / NS-Dokumentationszentrum der Stadt Köln.*

turning them into celebrations of themselves. A popular song called "When the Sirens Sound in Hamburg" had the line "Hamburg girls are loyal," which the Pirates changed to "Edelweiss Pirates are loyal," for example.[11] (This line became an unofficial motto for them.) Some of their songs had openly anti-Nazi lyrics, like the "Song of the Death's Head Edelweiss Pirates," written by a group from Krefeld around 1942.[12] It was about destroying the swastika, freeing Germany from foreign thieves, and dying a hero's death. Songs like this spread through word-of-mouth, although at least a few Pirates wrote them down and collected them. In one instance, such a collection ended up in the hands of the Gestapo.[13]

There were girls involved in the Edelweiss Pirates, too. Mixed-gender meetings were banned in both the Hitler Youth and the League of German Girls. The Nazis preferred boys to channel their sexual energy into sports and military training, while they promoted chastity as a "feminine virtue" to girls. (Salacious newspaper articles about the Pirates—like one published in Düsseldorf on February 15th, 1936, that spoke of members being found in "an indescribable state" after drinking together—can only have tempted more teenagers to get involved.[14])

Surviving reports from the Gestapo and other authorities show that the Nazis saw the Edelweiss Pirates as an irritant at best and as a real threat to the regime at worst. One from December 10th, 1937, said that a "confederation of youths has been detected in most western regions." It warned that their activity had gone past normal teenage rebellion. For political and moral reasons, the Edelweiss Pirates' movement could "no longer be viewed as a so-called local incident. It is expanding ever more strongly in a direction which demands not only that we observe it, but also that we combat it." The Pirates were becoming "a danger to the youth and thus to the nation [. . .] stricter measures must be undertaken."[15]

Some Pirates engaged in more active resistance against Hitler's regime than others. In Wuppertal, for example, there was a group that distributed flyers denouncing the Hitler Youth. Unlike the old youth organizations, one flyer said, the Nazis only wanted to train children to march and shoot. Their goal was to turn the next generation into "cannon fodder for Hitler's insatiable greed for power!" (This line was underlined for extra emphasis.) The flyer concluded, "German youth, rise up to fight for freedom and right, for your children and your children's children, for if Hitler wins this war, Europe will be in chaos; the world will be subjugated unto the Judgment Day."[16] In Düsseldorf, the regional branch of the Nazi Party sent a report to the Gestapo on July 17th, 1943. The Pirates there were "throwing their weight around" and being "more conspicuous than ever"—"they represent a danger to other young people." They'd also vandalized a pedestrian subway with anti-Nazi slogans: "Down with Hitler," "Medals for Murder," "Down with Nazi Brutality," and "The OKW is Lying" (OKW stood for *Oberkommando der Wehrmacht* or "Military High Command"). "However often these inscriptions are removed," the report said, "new ones appear on the walls again within a few days."[17]

By 1944, the Edelweiss Pirates and similar groups had come to the attention of Heinrich Himmler himself. In a memo sent to Nazi security services and the German police on October 25th that year, he said that "youth gangs" were forming across the country in "ever-increasing numbers."[18] They led a "separate and extraordinary existence based on principles not in accordance with National Socialist ideology." Writing in characteristically minute detail, he divided these gangs into types. One type was called "gangs of oppositional political orientation." They engaged in "generally seditious behavior," including the "rejection of the Hitler Youth and other community obligations," "listening to foreign radio broadcasts," and "maintaining the traditions, song repertoire, and the like of the prohibited federated [youth] groups." They also "frequently attempt to infiltrate [Nazi] Party organizations in order to provide a screen for themselves or in order to have the possibility for subversive actions." He ordered "intensified surveillance," saying that the gangs must be "watched closely." Then he signed off with the ominous words, "appropriate steps must be taken against them as needed."

Some individual Edelweiss Pirates shared their stories after the War. Gertrud Koch was born in Cologne in 1924. Her father was a boilermaker and a member of the Communist Party. The Nazis arrested and detained him on several occasions after 1933. When he wasn't behind bars, he lived underground and tried to create and distribute Communist material. Gertrud's resistance began at elementary school, where she refused to give her teacher the "German greeting." When she was called to the principal's office to explain, she said that she'd never greet Hitler after everything that had happened to her father. The principal must have sympathized. The next day, she was sent to a new class and given a seat at the back of the room. This way, her teacher couldn't see if she was giving the greeting or not.[19] After elementary school, she applied to a competitive, academically rigorous high school called a *Gymnasium*—but her application was rejected. The Gestapo had taken her family's savings, so they couldn't afford the fees. Instead, she became an apprentice at a Montessori kindergarten school. She liked the Montessori ethos, which kindled freedom of thought among the children. Soon, though, the school was absorbed into the Nazi Party's Welfare Organization (*Nationalsozialistische Volkswohlfahrt* or NSV). "I was no longer allowed to work there, nor was I permitted to take my final exam," Gertrud wrote. "The Nazis viewed Montessori education as too individualistic."[20] The kindergarten director offered to take her to Switzerland, where she'd be able to finish her apprenticeship in safety—but her mother wouldn't let her go.

Around the end of the 1930s, Gertrud started getting letters from the League of German Girls, telling her to come and register with them. "Of course, I didn't go," she wrote.[21] Her mother covered for her, saying that she was bedridden with flu. She even got an alibi from a pharmacist. Eventually, though, she and Gertrud were summoned to a meeting of the Nazi Women's League (*NS-Frauenschaft*). They were lectured about Hitler's importance for

German women, and they were reminded that they had a duty to have "Aryan" children, preferably with SS men. "We silently endured these tirades," Gertrud wrote, and "after the lecture, we were allowed to go home. Strangely, I was never again asked to join."[22]

It was around this time that she and some friends formed a small, casual hiking group. Together, they explored the countryside around Cologne. "We wanted to be free," she wrote. "We wanted to hike and sing freely, we wanted to make our own decisions about our clothes and our appearances—all desires that were unthinkable under the Nazi regime. And we were willing to fight for them."[23] According to her, this group was the origin of the Edelweiss Pirates. Soon they were producing anti-Nazi flyers and vandalizing houses with slogans like "Finally put an end to the brown horde!" and "Soldiers, lay down your weapons!"[24]

In 1942, Gertrud's family got a letter from the Börgermoor concentration camp. With a single line, it told them that her father was dead, having been "shot while trying to escape." This was a standard Nazi euphemism for murder, as Gertrud and her mother both knew.[25] The same year, she and a handful of others took their resistance further by scattering flyers with the Pirates' slogans from the dome of Cologne's train station. They got away with it on the day, but the Gestapo was tightening its net around young rebels like them. That November, Gertrud was at a Pirates' meeting in Düsseldorf, one of Cologne's neighboring cities, that got busted by the SS. She and others were taken back to Cologne and handed over to EL-DE Haus, the headquarters of the local Gestapo, where they were abused and tortured. Even so, she gave nothing away and said that she didn't know anything about the Pirates. She was released after three days, on the proviso that she'd go and work in a cardboard box factory. (The Nazis' need to fulfill ideological goals was falling behind their need for war supplies.)

None of this deterred Gertrud. She kept going to Pirate meetings, and before long she was back in EL-DE Haus, and then Brauweiler Abbey, a monastery that the Gestapo had turned into a torture center. After being released from a longer spell in detention there in fall 1943, she and her mother decided not to take any more chances. They fled Cologne for Rulfingen, a village in rural southern Germany, where they hid out on a farm until the War was over.

Fritz Thielen was born in Cologne in 1927. He was legally required to join the Hitler Youth when he turned ten in 1937. He enjoyed it at first, especially the games and field trips—but his parents weren't happy about him going. (His father was involved with youth groups and with the Social Democratic Party before the Nazis seized power.) To try and keep him away, they said that they couldn't afford a Hitler Youth uniform. When the organization intervened and told them to buy one regardless, they complied—but they drew the process out over a year, buying one item at a time. Their misgivings may have rubbed off, because, in 1940, Fritz reached what he called a "breaking point."[26]

"I couldn't understand why I had to obey the most stupid and inhumane orders, just because 'an order is an order,'" he wrote.[27] He especially disliked the Hitler Youth's disciplinary system, which was excessive to the point of being brutal. Once, he was given the *Hordenkeile*, a mob beating where a troop of twenty to thirty boys would attack one individual. In the process, his troop stole parts of his uniform, including his traveling knife—a special item that had to be earned through a series of grueling tests. Fritz managed to fight his way out, but this only made his troop leader angrier. He was ordered to get back to the center so that the beating could continue. Fritz yelled "you can all lick my ass!" turned, and ran home. He was suspended indefinitely, and he ignored several orders to apologize over the following weeks. Eventually his parents were told that he'd been expelled. This was a disgrace that followed him into school, where his teachers bullied him for his supposed lack of discipline and for breaking his oath to Hitler.

His ostracization left him with a world of free time. He began hanging out with older teenagers who'd aged out of the Hitler Youth and were waiting to be drafted into the military. Through them, he learned about youth organizations that had existed before 1933—a world without "absurd combat and terrain games," and that wasn't "controlled, meticulously planned, and organized."[28] The spirit of those organizations continued to exist in a gang called the Navajos, which Fritz joined. They stopped meeting after a confrontation with the SA and the Hitler Youth, but he stayed in touch with some of the friends that he'd made.

Fritz left school in October 1941. He passed the entrance exam to become an apprentice at the Ford factory in Cologne, where his father worked—but he wasn't allowed to start an apprenticeship because of his expulsion from the Hitler Youth. Instead, he accepted a meager job as an errand boy, escorting visitors in and out of the factory. Eventually, with some help from his father, he got into the factory's own division of the Hitler Youth, which meant that he was able to become an apprentice after all. Just as it seemed he was integrating into Nazi society, he veered away from it again. In January 1942, he was hospitalized with a hernia. A boy in the bunk above him hummed a tune that he recognized from his time with the Navajos. He started to hum along. Clearly taken aback, the boy asked him how he knew it. When Fritz said that he'd been in the Navajos, the boy invited him to join his gang—the Edelweiss Pirates. Fritz in turn invited the friends that he'd made in the Navajos. "Unlike my old group," he wrote, "the Edelweiss Pirates were more aggressive toward the Nazis. They openly defended themselves and refused to be intimidated."[29]

Word soon got around at the Ford factory that Fritz was hanging out with the Pirates. The foreman and other senior members of staff rarely let him out of their sights. His parents received a letter telling them that his apprenticeship was in jeopardy. Rather than leaving the Pirates, though, Fritz simply started going to different groups in different parts of town. He also took ever more risks, sometimes joining meetings of more than a hundred teenagers who set out to provoke Hitler Youth patrols. Then, one day in October 1943, without warning, he was summoned to EL-DE Haus. Somehow, the Gestapo knew that he was a Pirate—but they weren't really interested in him. They wanted him to tell them about the Pirates' leadership structure and its political affiliations. (Ironically, the Pirates didn't have any leaders or political affiliations.) His interrogation was brutal: he was "repeatedly slammed to the ground, beaten, and thrown against the wall." His interrogators purposefully avoided his face and focused on his ribs and abdomen so that he wouldn't leave with visible bruises. "I don't know how long it went on," Fritz wrote, "but it felt like an eternity."[30] Weeks passed. He was only released when he finally relented and agreed to sign papers saying that he'd been well-treated by the Gestapo, and agreeing that he'd never attend a Pirates' trip or meeting again. When he went back to work at the Ford factory, he found himself reassigned to a group of Russian and Ukrainian prisoners of war who'd been brought into the country as forced laborers.

Seeing how badly these men were treated only strengthened his anti-Nazi resolve. With another Ford apprentice who was also in the Pirates, Fritz began sabotaging military equipment in the factory. They would prize open cases, remove essential parts, and throw them in the River Rhine. They also cracked the heads off glass milk bottles and buried them, which burst the tires of new trucks just as they hit the open road.[31] Outside work, Fritz became more involved than ever with the Pirates, distributing flyers, vandalizing houses with anti-Nazi slogans, and listening to foreign radio broadcasts, all while continuing the hiking trips with which the movement had begun. Further arrests and interrogations followed. His final stay in EL-DE Haus was fleeting. The Gestapo sent him almost immediately to a young person's "probation camp" (*Behwährungslager*) for "reeducation." Roll call was at 5:00 a.m. Ten hours of heavy labor began soon after, in places like sawmills and timber yards. There was little food and no medical care, and most of the inmates quickly became visibly malnourished.[32] He eventually managed to escape. Although he had other spells in Nazi detention, a series of fortunate coincidences and lucky breaks meant that he survived the War.

Today, Gertrud and Fritz are two of the best-known of the Edelweiss Pirates. In their later years, they wrote autobiographies, gave interviews, and worked

FIGURE 3.2 *Gertrud Koch.*

tirelessly to build up the Pirates' memory in German society. Peter Schäfer is less well-known. He joined the Pirates around 1943, when he was thirteen, because he couldn't stand the militant world of the Hitler Youth. His rebellious clothes soon got him arrested. He was interrogated in EL-DE Haus before being sent to Klingelpütz, a notoriously overcrowded prison in Cologne, and finally to a youth detention camp nearly a hundred miles away. He escaped from a death march at the end of the War and managed to make his way home. It was only as an old man that he spoke about what had happened to him. He was on a hike during the Edelweiss Pirates Festival, an annual commemorative event that began in Cologne in 2005. Another former Pirate was meant to be leading this hike, and to be giving eyewitness testimony as it went. When this person dropped out unexpectedly, Peter was left to lead it by himself—"which visibly unsettled him," wrote Jan Krauthäuser, the Festival's director and founder. "He waved to me to tell me that he'd never spoken publicly about his traumatic youth experiences," and "he asked me to step in, and, if necessary, to stop him: 'I don't want to start crying in front of all these people.'" Deep in the forest,

Peter propped himself up against a tree and "finally gathered the courage and told his sad story." Occasionally he interrupted himself by exclaiming, "I was only thirteen, I was still a child!" At the end, spontaneously, he started singing a satirical song, *In the Can*, which he'd learned in Klingelpütz. "Music as resistance and as medicine," Krauthäuser wrote.[33]

In a sense, Peter may be more emblematic of the Edelweiss Pirates than the individuals who are well-known today. It's likely that several thousand children were in the Pirates.[34] There were other teenage resistance groups in Nazi Germany too, like the Swing Youth in Hamburg, who listened to outlawed jazz music, and the Meuten in Leipzig, who had roots in the Communist and Social Democratic Parties. Most of the children involved in such groups remain unknown.

*

"There were gaps in the research on Nazism. Compared to other German states, Saxony hadn't done much work on it," Francesca Weil tells me, with a quiet, steady gaze. She's a historian at the Hannah Arendt Institute for Totalitarianism Studies, a research center at the Dresden University of Technology. At the start of her career, she specialized in the history of East Germany. (Germany was divided into four zones of occupation after the Second World War, which later became two states, West and East Germany. The East was a Soviet satellite state and a Communist dictatorship, along with countries like Hungary, Poland, and Romania. It began to collapse in 1989, paving the way for the country's reunification in 1990.) She's since become an expert on the history of the Nazi era, too.

"In 2009," Francesca continues, "a new director came to the Institute and asked me to move to a position that involved working on the Nazi era, and specifically on Nazism in Saxony. I'd always been interested in the subject, but I hadn't ever actively worked on it." This marked the beginning of a new research department on Nazism at the Institute. "There were political reasons for the director's request. Until then, the authorities in Saxony only cast spotlights on the positive aspects of their history, such as the peaceful revolution of 1989."

"Why were they only interested in investigating the positive aspects of their history?" I ask.

"It was partly about promotion and tourism. They wanted to encourage people to visit sites related to the 1989 revolution," she says. Then she sighs, and adds, "But Saxony's first Prime Minister, a West German, also claimed that Saxons were 'immune' to right-wing extremism, which implied that there wasn't any *need* to investigate it. The Institute pushed forward despite that sort of political resistance, and that was when I started working on the topic. Since then, we've published many books about it. My latest one," she says, cradling a copy of *We Seem to be in the Same Situation as the Führer*..., "is about Saxony's society during the 'total war' years of 1943–1945.[35] It interweaves thirty-one personal stories from people in the region. But my work on childhoods had a different origin."

She begins telling me about an international conference that she organized with two colleagues in 2015.

"In Germany, the debate about 'war children' had been one-sided for a long time. It focused principally on the suffering of German children who lived through the war. The discussion was valid," she says, in a measured tone, "but we argued that it couldn't be limited to German children. A book came out of the conference, *Childhoods in World War Two*, and it was built from stories of children across Europe and Asia.[36] We aimed to showcase a diversity of experiences and not just focus on Germans. The book includes accounts from Polish-Jewish children, and Jewish children who emigrated to England. It was important to show that children from different backgrounds suffered during the War. For example, there was a case in Saxony in which a young Jewish girl escaped a death march and hid in a village. Two local boys found her and took her to the mayor, and he told them that they could do whatever they wanted with her. More children joined them, and together they killed her. This shows," she concludes, "how Nazi indoctrination could turn children into perpetrators."

We begin to discuss nonconformity, indirect resistance, and passive resistance among children in Nazi Germany. The topic soon leads us toward the rise of the populist far right in the twenty-first century and its impact on young people. Francesca talks about Alternative for Germany, a far-right party founded in 2013 that was the first of its kind to win seats in the German parliament since 1945. (Our interview was held just a few weeks after the 2024 Saxony state election, in which Alternative for Germany won over 30 percent of the overall vote.)

"I had a voluntary position with the association at Riebeckstraße 63 in Leipzig," she says. Riebeckstraße 63 is an imposing building that opened in 1892 as a hybrid homeless shelter and forced labor institution. Under the Nazis, it became a detention site for Jewish people, and for Roma and Sinti people. Many of its prisoners were either murdered in the T4 euthanasia program or deported to concentration and extermination camps. Francesca describes it as "a place where, essentially, all the traumas of twentieth-century German history are concentrated. Many young people get involved there, and they're deeply invested in making its history known. Some of them work on it academically, others work on it by developing and expanding the memorial site. So, a lot is happening there. On the other hand, though," she says, her voice darkening a little, "when you look at the statistics from recent elections, particularly the state elections, where a third of 18-to-24-year-olds voted for Alternative for Germany—" She stops midsentence and pauses for a moment. "That's a warning signal, that's something that worries me, that so many young voters—*a third of them*—could choose Alternative for Germany. And it makes me wonder: What do they actually know about the Nazi era? Alternative for Germany isn't the largest party in Saxony, but it is the second largest in the state parliament. Even when it wasn't as large, it was demanding that funding for the Hannah Arendt Institute should be cut. We don't know what's ahead for us, and the same goes for the Saxon Memorial Foundation." (The Saxon Memorial Foundation is a public organization that manages the memorials to victims of Nazism and Communism in the region.) "But I continue to believe in the independence of research and in academic freedom," she says, resolutely. "So, I don't let myself be pressured. We'll have to see how things develop going forward. We just don't know."

*

"The National Socialist Documentation Center of Cologne asked me to organize a project about the music of the Edelweiss Pirates," Jan Krauthäuser tells me. He has dark eyes framed by silver glasses, and suspenders rest on the shoulders of his open-collar shirt in a way that's quietly charming. "In their research, they noticed that in nearly every photo of the Pirates, the children had guitars or violins. They also tracked down former Pirates who were still alive, who said how important music and songs had been for them. I liked the idea, and it turned into a fine project. There was a book, an album, and even a documentary film. We decided to do it again the following year, and to popularize the Edelweiss Pirates. It's kept going ever since."

"Did the Edelweiss Pirates need to be popularized?" I ask.

"They were branded 'asocial' in the Nazi era, and that idea persisted long after the War," he says. "The problem, as you can imagine, is that most people in Germany were involved with the Nazi dictatorship, whether actively or passively. Only a tiny handful of people acted against it. The fact that working-class children were among that handful—the fact that they realized how cruel and criminal the regime was—increased the sense of shame for everyone else. It didn't help that the Edelweiss Pirates weren't from fine families, like Claus von Stauffenberg." Stauffenberg was a disaffected Nazi Colonel whose personal opposition to Hitler was rooted in a weird cocktail of aristocratic ideals and utopian beliefs about medieval Germany. He was part of a large conspiracy to assassinate Hitler, and it fell to him to plant a bomb underneath his conference table in the "Wolf's Lair," his Eastern Front military headquarters, on July 20th, 1944. It detonated but failed to kill the dictator.

"It's a bit ridiculous," Jan continues, veering into what feels like a pet peeve, "that Stauffenberg became a hero for having changed his mind. These children in Cologne and other cities didn't comply with Nazism from the beginning."

I raise a smile and tell Jan it's funny he should mention Stauffenberg, because he often comes up in Holocaust education in the United States. (I'm thinking particularly of classes that revolve around *Operation Valkyrie*, Bryan Singer's 2008 movie starring Tom Cruise as Stauffenberg.) The Edelweiss Pirates, on the other hand, come up rarely, if at all.

"Same in Germany," Jan says.

"Why is that?" I ask, surprised. "Why are they less well-known in Germany than someone like Stauffenberg?"

"It has something to do with the Pirates' societal status," he says, his voice sounding heavier than before. "A status that isn't so well-respected. After the War, it was easy for people to say, 'Oh, these youngsters weren't very educated, they were petty criminals, there's no reason to make heroes out of them.'"

I comment on how much the world has changed since the first Edelweiss Pirates Festival was held in 2004. Back then, the global rise of far-right extremism would have been unthinkable. I ask how, if at all, our shifting political landscape has impacted the Festival.

"It's not the Festival's job to react to politics," Jan says, firmly. "Our job is to give people a different way into history, into a movement that can be a source of inspiration in the present. I spoke with a journalist from a newspaper here in Cologne at a recent Festival. She said, 'You've attracted a really diverse public—is there anybody that you're missing?' Spontaneously I replied, 'Yes, Nazis! We're missing Nazis.' She was a bit shocked," he says, chuckling at the memory. "I explained, 'I'd love to show them what a wonderful culture we're celebrating.' That's a great motivation for me, you know—to celebrate culture. Nowadays, so much education hinges on giving people warnings, and it just doesn't work. We get too used to them, and then we stop reflecting on them. I think it's better if you can trust in art, trust in the stories that you want to tell, and trust in the energy that you bring to your work."

We get on to the Edelweiss Pirates and how they resisted the Nazis. Jan says that they refused to be part of something that the Nazis called the *Gleichschaltung*. (This word literally means "coordination," and the Nazis used it to describe the way that they brought every corner of German society under their control.) They refused to accept that the Hitler Youth was politically legitimate or morally right just because it had millions of members. They continued to believe that everyone could choose to obey the Nazis or not. What's more, they exercised their right to choose, and they dissented from the rest of the country in the process. But Jan is keen to underline that they didn't see themselves as heroes—and that they didn't aspire to be seen as heroes, either.

"Most of them said, 'We were just doing what young people do. We didn't want to be re-educated by Hitler and the Nazis. We didn't intend to offer resistance. We just wanted to live our lives in our own way.'" He pauses for a moment, takes off his glasses, and stares into space. Over the last two decades, he's worked with dozens of former Edelweiss Pirates at the Festival, including those mentioned in this chapter, Gertrud Koch, Fritz Theilen, and Peter Schäfer. He was there on that hike when Peter broke down and told his story for the first time. Perhaps, in this quiet moment, he's remembering them and others. He puts his glasses back on and looks at me intently. Then he says, "Every real hero thinks that they're not a hero. Real heroes make history. It's up to the next generation to make them heroes."

4

Kurt Gerstein

The SS Man Who Tried to Blow the Whistle on the Nazis' Extermination Camps

August 21st, 1942

Goran von Otter was on an overnight train from Warsaw to Berlin. He couldn't find a seat, so he sat on his suitcase in a corridor. A young man in an SS uniform was in that corridor, too. His face was pale and tense, as if he were chewing on words that he wanted to spit out. Later, long after the lights of Warsaw had faded into the distance, the train stopped unexpectedly in dark, open countryside. Passengers were allowed to get off for some fresh air. The man in the SS uniform left. Goran followed, lighting a cigarette. He offered one to the man, who refused. Then, quietly, the man said,

"There is something terrible I have to report." He asked if he could come and visit Goran in Sweden at the country's diplomatic offices. Goran tried to hide his surprise. Somehow, this SS man had found out who he was.

"Of course," Goran said. "But why not now, on the train?"

The passengers were called back—the train was ready to move again. But the SS man kept talking.

"I saw something dreadful . . . " he said.

"The Jews?" Goran asked, instinctively.

The man nodded. "More than ten thousand died yesterday."[1]

*

Kurt Gerstein was a talented scientist, a medic, and a mining engineer. He was born in Münster, Germany, in 1905, to a well-off, middle-class family—the sixth of seven children. The family wasn't religious, but he joined the Evangelical Church when he was a teenager. (A branch of Protestantism, Evangelism in 1920s and 1930s Germany had almost nothing in common with Evangelism as it exists in the United States today.[2]) He also joined the Nazi Party in 1933. At that time, he was a right-wing German nationalist, as were his parents and siblings. But he soon realized that his religious beliefs and Nazi ideology couldn't go together. In 1934, he wrote to a friend, "Bearing witness is becoming for me a necessity from which I am less and less able to escape." Unlike the famous Jewish diarist Viktor Klemperer, Kurt didn't mean "bearing witness" as in recording the Nazis' crimes. He meant bearing witness to Christ—sharing his faith publicly. He also disliked what he called "the progression of trickery" in Hitler's Germany.[3] Lies, opportunism, and selfishness, it seemed to him, were running riot.

That year, he protested an anti-Christian play staged by the Hitler Youth. A group of Catholics had already protested it once, and the local mayor had warned people against further disturbances. But Kurt got a seat in the front row, stood up midway through, and shouted, "We shall not allow our faith to be publicly mocked!" Nazi Party heavies dragged him out of the theater and beat him up, knocking out several teeth.[4] It didn't deter him. While organizing a miners' conference in 1936, he made invitation packs complete with posters for people to hang in train windows. One said, "compartment for travelers accompanied by mad dogs," and another said, "compartment for travelers with contagious diseases."[5] The Nazis didn't tolerate this kind of wisecrack. Someone reported him to the Party, his home was searched, and several thousand anti-Nazi letters and pamphlets were found. Many featured church materials that had already been banned. On September 26th, 1936, he was arrested and expelled from the Party, which cost him his job. (Like a dishonorable discharge from the US military, expulsion from the Party was a rare measure and a mark of shame that followed the person concerned for the rest of their life.)

His family, and especially his father, who worked as a judge, leaned on him to apologize to the Party and to ask for his membership back. Kurt sent groveling letters to local courts and even to the Nazis' Supreme Court in Munich. They didn't work. In 1937, newly married and broke, he considered moving abroad. All the while, he continued to resist the regime in small ways. He was sent to the Welzheim concentration camp in 1938, having been arrested again—this time on suspicion of plotting to restore the German monarchy. He was held there for nearly seven weeks. During that time, the letters that he wrote started to show signs of suicidal feelings that never really left him.

Once Kurt was out of Welzheim, his father doubled down on getting him back into the Party, making personal appeals to judges and courts on his son's behalf. He never succeeded, but in 1939, he did manage to get Kurt's expulsion downgraded to a dismissal. This enabled Kurt to find a new job in the mining industry. By the following summer, the Second World War was underway, and Germany had already conquered Belgium, Denmark, France, Luxembourg, the Netherlands, and Norway, as well as Poland. He seemed to have accepted Hitler's regime and to be willing to live with it. (War successes led many German Protestants to tone down their objections to Hitler and the Nazis.) He made new efforts to rejoin the Party, claiming that he supported Hitler, which may have been true, and that he now opposed the church, which certainly wasn't true.

It was also during that summer that disturbing rumors began to swirl across Germany. They were about disabled people being euthanized in special, secret facilities. And they were true. As early as July 1933, the Nazis had passed a "Law for the Prevention of Hereditarily Diseased Offspring." It made sterilization compulsory for people with hereditary diseases. The Nazis' definition of hereditary diseases, and especially of what they called "feeble-mindedness," had no basis in science. On a doctor's whim, everything from prostitution to shoplifting could be diagnosed as "feeble-mindedness." The law was less about eliminating disease, wrote Richard Evans, and more about crushing "those areas of society that did not conform to the Nazi ideal."[6] There was no more enthusiastic supporter of the Law than Hitler himself. By 1935, he was telling confidants in private that he'd legalize euthanasia when a new war began.[7] The Nazis prepared for this next step during the mid- to late 1930s by putting more and more SS doctors in charge of the country's psychiatric and medical institutions. Then, in 1938, the father of a child born with physical disabilities wrote to the Chancellery of the Führer, Hitler's personal office, asking for the child to be euthanized. Hitler seized the opportunity. Chancellery staff murdered the child and built a nationwide program of child euthanasia on the back of the murder. Then, in October 1939, Hitler signed an authorization for the program to expand and include adults. He backdated it to September 1st—the day the War began. Soon, the program was too large to be handled within his Chancellery. It needed a dedicated team. This team was given their own office in Berlin, in No. 4 Tiergarten Street—a villa once owned by a Jewish family. The euthanasia program became known as "T4," after this street address. By the end of 1941, more than 70,000 German civilians had been branded as "life unworthy of life" and murdered in one of six T4 facilities across the country, most of them in purpose-built gas chambers.[8]

Kurt's sister-in-law, Bertha Ebeling, was murdered in one of the T4 facilities at the turn of 1941. The family was told that she'd been moved to a new hospital where she'd fallen victim to an epidemic and that she'd been cremated immediately to help contain it. Testimonies about Kurt's reaction paint a confusing picture. According to Karl Gerstein, one of his brothers, and to Otto Wehr, the pastor who ran Bertha Ebeling's funeral, Kurt decided to join the SS, follow the trail of the crime, and find out the truth. Others said that he resolved to find a way to suppress the Nazis' murderous orders from within. Still others said that he thought that the Gestapo were tracking him and that joining the SS was the only way to shake his tail. These testimonies were all made long after the War, though, in light of Germany's defeat. Documents show that Kurt applied to join the SS, the Nazis' elite paramilitary organization, as early as fall 1940, months before Bertha had died. No one can know for certain why he did it—but perhaps he began his application for one reason and finished it for another.

He was accepted and quickly rose through the ranks to become the SS Head of Technical Disinfection Services. In this role, he was responsible for providing clean drinking water, sewage treatment, and pest control across the Nazi empire. He was also responsible for shipping dangerous chemicals like prussic acid—or hydrogen cyanide, better known by the brand name Zyklon B. In 1942, he was ordered to collect over 200 pounds of Zyklon B in Prague and to take it to a secret location in the east, along with Wilhelm Pfannenstiel, a professor and a bigwig SS hygiene inspector. After the war, Kurt said that he was "roughly aware" that this order would have something to do with the murder of Jewish people.[9] He said that he accepted it because it was the break he'd been waiting for—finally, he would see the darkest parts of the Nazi regime for himself. He also said that he took the order to subvert it. (He claimed to have interfered with shipments of Zyklon B to camps including Auschwitz by flagging them with all sorts of false or misleading information. But Auschwitz alone used several tons of Zyklon B every year. Even if Kurt's claims were true, there was no way for him to know what impact his interference was making, if any.)

The secret location was Lublin, a city in the southeast of occupied Poland. On August 17th, 1942, SS officials there told Kurt about three new, purpose-built extermination camps in the region: Belzec, Sobibor, and Treblinka. Each of them had stationary gas chambers that were being used to murder hundreds of thousands of Jewish people with carbon monoxide from tank and tractor engines. The 200 pounds of Zyklon B was meant to disinfect the clothes being stolen from the victims. It was also meant to be used experimentally in the gas chambers, as some in the SS thought that it would work faster than the engines. Kurt was given tours of Belzec and Treblinka—and, in Belzec, he saw the process of Jewish people being gassed from start to finish.

He left determined to tell the world about what the Nazi regime was doing. By chance, he met Baron Goran von Otter, the Secretary to the Swedish Legation, on his way back to Berlin. The encounter haunted Goran for the rest of his life. Minor details in his testimony shifted over time, like who spoke first, or who offered a cigarette to whom. But the most important details never changed: Kurt found out from someone on the train that Goran was a foreign diplomat; their conversation lasted the whole journey, with Kurt getting upset and struggling to keep his voice down; and he told Goran that tens of thousands of Jewish people were being murdered every day in extermination camps in occupied Poland. To prove that he wasn't a spy trying to plant fake news, he showed Goran his identity card and a written order for Zyklon B, and he drew a sketch of Belzec. At first, even though Goran had already heard rumors that the Nazis were systematically murdering Jewish people, Kurt's story was just too incredible to believe. But, by the time they got to Berlin, the level of detail, and the authenticity of Kurt's distress, had convinced him that he was telling the truth.

Kurt suggested that Goran liaise with the British and ask them to make leaflets about the extermination camps to be air-dropped over Germany. He thought that Germans wouldn't stand for them if only they knew about them. Goran met a Swedish envoy in Berlin, who arranged for him to visit the Foreign Ministry in Stockholm. There he met Staffan Söderblom, a high-ranking diplomat, who heard him out before suggesting that he take a break and go on vacation. Months later, Goran returned to work and found that nothing had been done. Meanwhile, Kurt tried and failed to arrange a meeting with Cesare Orsenigo, the Vatican's chief ambassador in Germany. He also told friends, acquaintances, and professionals—hundreds of people, he claimed—about the extermination camps in a scattershot way. Apparently, his only aim was to raise awareness among Germans through word-of-mouth.

Increasingly convinced that he'd be arrested at any moment, Kurt became both paranoid and reckless. He grew distant from his family, and he sent them strange letters that they couldn't understand. ("It is the fate of all those with a spark of daring in them to risk all that they possess, even their substance, for the sake of an uncertain gain," he wrote to his father in 1944.[10]) He listened to Allied radio broadcasts, which was illegal. He told people that he wanted Germany to lose the War, which was treason. But he survived. In April 1945, unlike so many SS men who either fled or went into hiding, he turned himself over to the Allies. He believed that he might be the only witness to the extermination camps who wasn't a devout Nazi, and he told the Allies that he wanted the people responsible to face justice. At first, they treated him as an ally and kept him in a local hotel for his own safety. In the space of a few weeks, he wrote three copies of a report about Belzec, one in French and two in German.

The report gave detailed accounts of everything that he'd seen. Among the stand-out parts are those that challenge common misconceptions about the Holocaust today. He describes a torturous scene in which the engine for the gas chambers wouldn't start, for example. The camp's commandant, Christian Wirth, embarrassed by this mishap in front of distinguished guests, whipped his Ukrainian assistant in the face and beat him to a pulp. It took nearly three hours to fix the engine, with Jewish people stuck in the chambers all the while. This hardly makes Belzec sound like our ubiquitous term for the Nazis' extermination camps, a "death factory"—which wrongly implies that they were clean, efficient, and impersonal. Then there are the heartbreaking moments that animate the Jewish victims. One person who stood out for him was a woman "of about forty, her eyes flaming torches, [who] cursed the murderers" as her group was driven toward the gas chambers.[11] In an additional paper, he also recorded seeing "a little girl of five—completely nude—who dropped a little coral chain, which was picked up a few minutes later (a yard away from the gas chambers) by a little boy of three. He examined it with delight—and, a moment later, was thrown into the gas chamber."[12] Lines like these grate against our habit of thinking of the Jewish victims of the Holocaust as a faceless mass.

But Kurt's report isn't without problems. There are inconsistencies between the versions, and in some places, they're just inaccurate. He said, for example, that 25 million people had been murdered at Belzec, Poles and Czechs as well as Jews. Today, most historians estimate that about half a million people were murdered there, almost all of them Jews. This inaccuracy may say something about the mass grave pits in Belzec and what they looked like, though: oceans of corpses so deep that the number was incalculable. It may also say something about the bragging that went on among the perpetrators. Kurt could have been given that number by someone who was trying to impress him.

We don't know why, but the Allies didn't pay much attention to Kurt's report. At the end of May 1945, he was transferred from Rottweil to Constance, and then, a couple of weeks later, to Cherche-Midi, a grim military prison in Paris. There, he was treated as a war criminal, along with other former Nazis and SS men. Driven to despair by this—and probably by his failure to save any Jewish people, too—he ended his life in his cell on July 25th.

*

"The story of Belzec is covered in rust," Tomasz Hanejko, the director of the Belzec Memorial and Museum, tells me. "And it's a very short story. It was development for the first few months, then they paused to rebuild the camp's interior, then there were massive deportations from Galicia, and then—" he takes a sharp breath and claps his hands together so loudly that it makes me jump. "The end. From the start of 1943, they were just dismantling buildings, erasing mass graves, and burning bodies. A simple, tragic history."

On the evening of October 13th, 1941, Heinrich Himmler met with Odilo Globocnik and Friedrich Wilhelm Krüger, two high-ranking SS men stationed in occupied Poland.[13] At this meeting, Globocnik pitched an idea to build a camp with stationary gas chambers to murder thousands of Jews incapable of labor, particularly in the Lublin district.[14] Himmler loved it. The next day, he unfolded it further over lunch with Hitler, and then in a five-hour meeting with Reinhard Heydrich, his deputy.[15] Construction on Globocnik's camp began in Belzec, a remote village on the southeast side of occupied Poland, on November 1st, 1941. In December, a select group of the T4 staff who'd been euthanizing German citizens was transferred there to assist and to prepare the camp for operation. Two similar camps were built in 1942 in other remote villages on the east of occupied Poland, Sobibor and Treblinka. Together, these three camps were known as the "Operation Reinhard" camps—Operation Reinhard being the Nazis' attempt to murder every Jewish person in the "General Government," an occupied area that included most of modern-day Poland and parts of modern-day Ukraine. (The Operation was named after Reinhard Heydrich, who was assassinated by Czech rebels in June 1942.)

The Nazis began to murder Jewish people in Belzec in March 1942, and they demolished the camp in July the following year. Dozens of Germans worked at Belzec, but only eight were ever brought to trial, seven of whom were acquitted. The camp had fewer than ten known survivors, and only two, Rudolf Reder and Chaim Hirszman, gave testimony after the War. (Hirszman was murdered in Lublin by men from Narodowe Siły Zbrojne, a right-wing militia group, on the same day that he gave testimony to the Jewish Historical District Commission—March 19th, 1946.[16])

Tomasz tells me that the destruction of Jewish communities at Belzec was so total that fewer than 40,000 of the victims' names are known today—not even ten percent of them.

"It's a shock for people when they hear that statistic for the first time. In many cases, the Nazis reached their goal, which was to erase the memory of the people who died," he says. This is why the camp's story is "covered in rust."

Tomasz has worked at the Belzec Memorial and Museum since it opened in 2004. Before then, there was a small, nondescript monument, installed by the Communist government in the 1960s, plus a handful of footpaths crisscrossing the site, which the local elementary school had been left to manage. There was almost nothing to indicate its terrible past. In a 2003 interview with *The Washington Post*, Miles Lerman, the third chair of the United States Holocaust Memorial Council, spoke about finding beer bottles and condoms on a visit there.[17]

"We had to do everything from the beginning," Tomasz says. "All the museal activities. We focused especially on education—contacting schools and pupils to give lessons, free tours, and so on. We collected testimonies, and we contacted members of the families of people who probably—*probably*," he stresses, "died in Belzec."

I ask where those testimonies came from, given that there were only two known Jewish survivors who spoke about their experiences.

"The inhabitants of Belzec and the region. They're small parts of the collective memory of the people—about the activity at Belzec, and about the activity of the German camp staff, who had some contact with local inhabitants. It's the background to the main story, but it still helps us to understand. Other important elements that we've collected from the beginning are the personal items of the Jewish people who were murdered. We discovered them during the excavations that were necessary to build the Museum. Today, we have more than three thousand items. Armbands, keys, toothbrushes, empty perfume bottles." He pauses before adding, "Bullets. Every element that we discovered was trash for the Germans—something that they threw out, something that had no monetary value."

"And how have you coped with being at Belzec, and with being around all these items, day in, day out, for nearly twenty years?" I ask.

"It's not easy to touch this history every day," he says, with a tired smile. He describes Belzec's history as something that can be touched more than once—like it's an object that he's handling in the dark, something that he can feel but not fully see or understand. "It's especially hard if you're just teaching lessons or giving guided tours for visitors. Every day, back to that story."

"What drives you, then—and the guides, and the teachers—to keep going back?"

"The Museum's main aim," he says. "Which is to rebuild some kind of memory."

The weight of Belzec's history isn't the only thing that makes it a challenging place to work. Like any other museum, it has to attract footfall.

"We aren't huge. Each year, we get around 30,000 visitors. Compare that with Auschwitz, where they have no less than a million a year. Or Majdanek, a quarter-million." He lets out a small, subdued laugh. "Think about the knowledge of people around the world. Everyone's heard about Auschwitz. Who's heard about Belzec, where nearly half-a-million people died? Maybe it's not good, or not moral, to compare the number of victims. But the scale of annihilation here was huge."

I ask Tomasz to reflect on this for a moment. Why aren't we more familiar with Belzec, the platform for one of the biggest crimes in human history?

"Well, the victims here were mainly Jews from occupied Polish territory," he says, pointing a finger at the antisemitic and anti-Slavic beliefs that lingered in the West after 1945. "And the War destroyed the Polish economy. Poland wasn't thinking about memorials right afterward. The Communist government erected museums in Auschwitz and Majdanek, which was enough for them. At Belzec they decided, 'Okay, we don't have barracks, we don't have any other remnants, the monument will suffice.' So, it's a complicated history," he says.

When I try to shift our conversation toward Kurt Gerstein, Tomasz gives a dismissive wave of the hand.

"He was a member of the SS and part of the Nazi machine, we know his story," he says. He's less interested in Kurt's biography than in his report and how it can be used to scrape the "rust" off Belzec. "He gave us something from the interior, something about the activity of the camp, the process. So, we compare his testimony with others. In Tomaszów Lubelski—it's a town, ten kilometers from Belzec—there's a hospital. During the occupation, that hospital's director was Dr. Janusz Peter. He was a medic in the Austro-Hungarian army in the First World War, so he could speak German, and members of staff from Belzec were treated in his hospital. We have interesting testimony from him. One day in August 1942, he was on his way to work, and he met a medic from the German Army on the street, very agitated. He asked what was wrong. The German said, 'Just minutes ago, I saw Professor Pfannenstiel driving to Belzec.' We know from Gerstein's testimony that he was with Pfannenstiel. Dr. Peter also said that later, a guard came to the hospital with facial injuries. He asked, 'How did this happen?' It was a problem with the engine for the gas chamber. Do you remember that fragment from Gerstein's testimony? It's the same!" Tomasz leans forward, becoming increasingly animated as he pulls these bits and pieces of history together. "What else did Gerstein testify about? A shipment of Zyklon B that he'd buried. In 1962, Zyklon B cannisters were discovered in Belzec. Probably—*probably*," he stresses, in just the same way as earlier, "they're the same cylinders."

(In his report, Kurt says that he falsely marked the 200 pounds of Zyklon B as having decomposed, and that he supervised its burial somewhere near the camp. But he also says that Christian Wirth begged him not to recommend any changes to Belzec's gas chambers. In one of the most grotesque twists of Holocaust history, different methods of gassing became a source of rivalry between the camps. Zyklon B was used at Auschwitz and Majdanek, carbon monoxide at Belzec, Sobibor, and Treblinka. Staff prided themselves on their camp's method being the best. So, did Kurt make a plan to get rid of the Zyklon B and exploit Wirth's hubris to see it through? Or did Wirth ask Kurt to get rid of it, not realizing that he was giving him a chance to act on his true feelings? The report is ambiguous, and there's no way of knowing for certain.)

"And when did Gerstein visit Belzec?" Tomasz continues. "Mid-August 1942. Rudolf Reder was sent to the camp during the huge action in the Lvov Ghetto, which was also in mid-August. Maybe Reder even arrived on the day of Gerstein's visit. We can compare their information about the gas chamber. Reder said that it consisted of six rooms, three on the left, and three on the right. Gerstein said the same. What's especially interesting for me, is that Reder said that the capacity of one room was 750 people. Six rooms, each with 750 people. It's hard to imagine. But Gerstein's report gives the same number, 750 people in each room," he says. He falls quiet and holds my gaze for a long moment. "Very important. Two witnesses, both from the interior." He picks up a pencil from his desk and starts fiddling with it, making little gestures with his fingers. "Small puzzles," he says.

"And was it a form of resistance to Nazism for Kurt to provide that kind of information in his report?" I ask.

Tomasz shakes his head and sighs heavily.

"That's a good question. 'I've seen everything here,'" he says, as if he were Kurt speaking, "'and I must give testimony.' That's the essence of his resistance. He was the witness. But he couldn't stop or do anything."

"What if we found out for certain that it *was* his idea to bury the Zyklon B? Isn't it at least possible that he might have slowed one transport to Belzec, or saved one life?"

"No," Tomasz says, decisively. "The camp was a machine. A very effective machine. Exhaust gas, Zyklon B—what's the difference? The scale would have been the same."

So, Kurt didn't save anyone, I say, and he didn't stop or change anything.

"But he touched the core," Tomasz says. "He went *inside* the Holocaust. He touched evil, and he talked about his experience. He told the truth, he broke the silence. 'I gave information to diplomats and embassies,'" he says, again as if he were Kurt speaking, "'I tried to do something. A little—but *something*.'"

*

After the War, Kurt's widow, Elfriede, and a handful of archivists created Kurt Gerstein House, an educational institution for children in Germany. They also built a collection of Kurt's personal documents and papers, including his report on Belzec. Kurt's descendants and future generations of archivists kept adding to the collection, collaborating with organizations around the world to unearth ever more documents and to frame Kurt's story in a wider context. Kurt Gerstein House shut down in the early 2000s, though, having run out of money. When that happened, the collection was donated to the Evangelical Church of Westphalia. Today, the collection is managed by the archivists Ingrun Osterfinke and Martin Kamp in Bielefeld, a small city in northeast Germany.

Ingrun and Martin are a dynamic pair, jumping between German and English to fine-tune individual words, ensuring that no meaning in our conversation gets lost. Their offices are meticulously organized. They sit in front of large bookshelves, each shelf holding hundreds of binders, each binder holding an unknown number of documents.

I ask them if Kurt is better known in Germany than he is in the United States.

"I can't think of any situation where Germans nowadays are really familiar with the fate or the figure of Kurt Gerstein," Martin says. "It's very obvious, when we're doing a tour through our archives, and we talk about the Gerstein collections, that not many people know anything about him."

This surprises me. Why isn't he famous, like Oskar Schindler or Anne Frank?

"The popularity of Oskar Schindler and Anne Frank is based on the successful media processing of their stories," Martin says, dryly. "I'm pretty sure that before *Schindler's List*, comparatively few people knew the name and story of Oskar Schindler. Plus, Anne Frank's Diary is an unusually dense and well-written source that documents the persecution of the Jews in Europe on a personal level, and through the eyes of the victim. I have to say . . . " He leans back in his chair, as if to let his thoughts settle. "I have to say that I find the comparison with Kurt Gerstein a bit difficult. He's a much more ambivalent figure than Schindler. Schindler saved the lives of hundreds of Jews, which was personally dangerous for him. Whether Kurt Gerstein really joined the SS only to gain insight into the murder machinery and to inform the outside world is open to doubt. To this day, there's no hard evidence that he actually tried to sabotage Zyklon B deliveries. And it doesn't make it easier that there are quite some contradictions and exaggerations in his report."

"And figures like Anne Frank or Oskar Schindler are easy to understand," Ingrun adds. "Anne Frank's Diary is a real, singular document, and Oskar Schindler's success is measurable. He saved a measurable number of people. Kurt Gerstein didn't succeed measurably. We don't know if and how many people could have been saved from the gas chamber when he declared that the Zyklon B was unfit for use. His efforts to inform the Allied nations didn't succeed. His actions and his motivations are all complex, and not easy to comprehend," she says with a resigned laugh.

With all these thoughts in mind, I ask, how did they think Kurt resisted Nazism, if at all?

"That's a very difficult question to answer," Martin says. "It basically depends on whether you believe Gerstein's statements to be true. And maybe that's what we can learn from his story: that categories like perpetrators, bystanders, and resisters, and even victims, can be extremely difficult to define."

We discuss this point for a moment. As someone who was almost certainly sympathetic to the Nazis at the start, and who then turned on them, and who then tried to join the SS for uncertain reasons, and who then gathered information on the Nazis' murderous activities, and who then failed to achieve anything with that information, and who finally ended his own life after going into Allied captivity voluntarily, you could argue that Kurt was a perpetrator *and* a bystander *and* a resister *and* a victim.

Ingrun takes a slightly warmer view. "If we believe everything in Gerstein's report," she says—and from the way that she's been talking about him, I think that she does—"then he resisted Nazism in not giving up his beliefs, his convictions, and his conscience. Resistance can develop with a situation, but it's always based on one's own beliefs."

Her point pulls our conversation toward the dangers facing democracy today. She and Martin both speak with grave concern about the growing popularity of Alternative for Germany. They fear that the far-right party and similar others would dismantle democracy, given the chance.

"Many people like simple answers to difficult questions," Martin says. "This explains why Alternative for Germany is so successful. Our world is complex, and it's only getting more complex. Extremist movements exploit people's fears and insecurities to offer seemingly simple solutions to these complex and global problems."

Ingrun is drawn back to Kurt's story and its relevance for today.

"We must stand up and talk, as Gerstein did. Not only in totalitarian regimes, but in everyday situations. It's called 'civil courage,'" she says. Then she concludes, decisively, "The smallest action is always worthwhile."

*

Kurt Gerstein never looked away from Nazism or its crimes. He committed himself to telling the truth because it was the truth, he constantly interrogated his convictions, and he set out to gain knowledge however he could—all to cultivate his own conscience. The ripples of these simple acts spread through the generations in ways that he could never have predicted. His brief report, written in captivity, has been used as evidence in trials against Holocaust deniers, for example, and by historians trying to understand what the Holocaust was and how it happened. Kurt may not have been able to save any lives or to stop any part of the Holocaust, but he did successfully resist the possibility of it being forgotten.

5

Alexander Pechersky

The Jewish Soldier Who Led an Uprising in a Nazi Extermination Camp

"You find that it's usually in that time after the winter, but before the spring. The snow is melting and there's a lot of water," Łukasz Kukawski tells me. "The ground, it sort of washes up the items." He talks about the site of the Sobibor extermination camp in Poland as if it were a dark ocean, reluctantly giving up its secrets.

*

September 22nd, 1943

Late at night, and five days after its journey began, a train arrived in a remote camp in the southeast of occupied Poland, near the Ukrainian border and the Bug River.[1] It had traveled almost 300 miles from the ghetto in Minsk. (Minsk is the capital of Belarus, which was then part of the Soviet Union.) Some 2,000 Jewish people were on board. About a hundred of them were also Soviet prisoners of war.

They'd been told that they were going to work in Germany. Perhaps, when the train's doors were finally opened in the morning, some of them still believed it. They were in a camp so small it almost looked quaint. There was only a cluster of small wooden buildings with rickety roofs. It could easily have been a country farm.

SS guards walked down the platform and called for single men who knew how to do carpentry and woodwork. A young Soviet officer named Alexander Pechersky, or Sasha for short, was the first to step forward. He knew that it was always wise to volunteer for work if the Nazis presented the chance. Seeing his army jacket, which marked him out as an officer, other men decided to follow his lead. He and about eighty others were chosen and hurried into a fenced area inside the camp. Later, a curious prisoner came to introduce himself to these new arrivals. As they spoke, a tower of smoke rose over the northwest end of the camp, and the air filled with a foul, unnatural smell. Sasha asked what was being burned. The prisoner said, bluntly, "The bodies of your friends who arrived with you."[2]

FIGURE 5.1 *The Sobibor extermination camp. US Holocaust Memorial Museum (In the "Sobibor Perpetrator Collection," Series 1: Photographic Materials, File 9, no. 5).*

"We had all fought in the War and had suffered in labor camps," Sasha wrote. "But we were so horrified about Sobibor that we could not sleep that night."[3] Perhaps what they'd been told about the camp was too monstrous to be believed. Within days, though, they'd seen, heard, and smelled the murder process for themselves. Sasha remembered huge flames in the gray autumn skies, lighting the camp with strange colors, and seeing "the bodies of our brothers and sisters" being burned.[4]

A couple of days later, Karl Frenzel, one of the more senior SS guards in Sobibor, took Sasha and about forty others into the forest that surrounded the camp to chop down trees. Axes were impossibly heavy for prisoners who were starving and exhausted. It wasn't long before Frenzel snuck up behind a flailing Dutch man who was missing his tree with every swing and began to pulverize him with a whip. Seeing this, Sasha lowered his ax from the tree that he was chopping and glared. Frenzel stopped and called him over.

"You don't like the way I punish this fool?" he asked. He pointed to a nearby tree stump and said, "I give you exactly five minutes to split this stump. If you make it, you get a pack of cigarettes. If you miss by as much as one second, you get twenty-five lashes."

Frenzel sat down to enjoy the spectacle, feeling certain that Sasha would fail. Sasha tightened his grip on his ax and started hitting the stump as hard as he could. He smashed it into pieces with about 30 seconds to spare. Without saying a word, Frenzel pulled a pack of cigarettes from his pocket and offered it to him.

"No thanks," Sasha said, nonchalantly. "I don't smoke." (Cigarettes were like currency in the Second World War. Across Europe and beyond, people swapped them for food and favors—so, even if he didn't smoke, Sasha was effectively refusing free money.) Frenzel turned from him and walked away. About twenty minutes later, he came back with some bread and margarine as alternative prizes for Sasha's achievement.

"Russian soldier, take it," he said, offering Sasha the food.

"Thank you," Sasha said. "The rations we are getting satisfy me fully." [5]

Sobibor's prisoners were kept on the most meager rations. If Sasha's unspoken message had been unclear before, there was no doubt now. He wouldn't accept help from a Nazi. Frenzel clenched his whip, and Sasha braced himself for a beating. But, once again, Frenzel turned and walked away. (Later, some of the women who worked in the camp's storerooms told Sasha that he'd hurled the bread and margarine on the floor, screaming about a Russian soldier who said he had enough to eat.[6]) Word about this incident spread quickly among the other prisoners. Speaking back to an SS guard was rare. Stunning one into silence was unheard of.

On September 27th, less than a week after they'd arrived, two of the soldiers from Minsk told Sasha that they'd planned an escape. They'd attack some of the SS guards who patrolled the camp's perimeter fence. We'd only need to kill one or two, they said, to leave part of the fence exposed. Then we'd have a chance to break for the forest. Sasha didn't doubt that this plan would work. But he asked them to think about the hundreds of prisoners who'd be left behind. What would happen to them? "If the plan is to run away," he said, "then we must all run together."[7] Over the coming days, other soldiers came to Sasha with similar plans. He pulled rank and shut down every one of them.

At this stage, he was unaware that a resistance group already existed in Sobibor.

In spring 1943, the number of trains coming to the camp started to drop. This made the prisoners fear that they were the only Jews left in Europe, and that the Nazis would soon kill them, too. Then, one day when a train did come, SS guards shot the people on board in small groups on the platform, rather than killing them in the gas chambers. This was unusual to the point of being suspicious. Only when the prisoners were forced to strip the bodies did they discover what the SS guards were trying to hide. The people had left some secret notes in their clothes. These notes said things like, "We worked for a year in Belzec. I don't know where they are taking us now. They say to Germany [. . .] If all this is a lie, then know that death awaits you, too."[8] The prisoners saw this as confirmation of their fears: the Nazis' extermination program was all but complete, they were closing their death camps, and their final act was to murder the handful of Jews who remained.

Seven men in Sobibor resolved to escape and formed a resistance group. Their leader was Leon Feldhendler, a Pole and the son of a rabbi. The others included heads of Sobibor's workshops, among them a tailor, a cobbler, and a carpenter. Unlike the Nazis' concentration camps, some of which had tens of thousands of slave laborers working in factories, the Operation Reinhard camps had no workforces to speak of—they didn't produce anything. Their sole purpose was murder. However, they did each retain roughly 500–1,000 slave laborers to sort through victims' possessions, to serve the whims of the Germans who ran them, and to do the most appalling jobs that the Germans didn't want to do themselves. (These included removing corpses from the gas chambers and pulling gold teeth from their mouths.)

Leon and his group knew that the only truly successful escape from Sobibor would include every prisoner. But the prisoners were a random assortment of hundreds of people from across Europe. They'd been chosen for their work skills or their physical health, not because they had anything in common with each other. The group's composition changed constantly as people were murdered and replaced with new arrivals. On any given day, some prisoners had been in the camp for over a year, others for just a few hours. Some were religious, others were secular. Some only spoke Yiddish, others didn't speak it at all. They divided naturally into cliques based on experience, language, and nationality, and there was never much trust between them.

Leon and his men didn't know how they'd unite everyone. And even if they found a way, there was still the question of how to escape from the camp. The only ideas that they could come up with felt outlandish and unrealistic. They spoke about using the kitchens to poison the Nazis, or about breaking into their barracks and killing them in their sleep, or about destroying the camp by lighting fires around it. What's more, the camp was surrounded by minefields that would be impossible to navigate. By fall 1943, Leon had accepted that they needed help from someone with a military background—someone with the training and the experience to create and execute a realistic plan.

He could see that the soldiers from Minsk looked to Sasha as their leader, and he knew that they'd been talking about escape. He sent an invitation to Sasha to meet. On September 29th, under the cover of nightfall, they came face-to-face in the women's barracks—which was relatively quiet and secluded.

Leon began by telling Sasha that he'd made a deep impression on the other prisoners. Then he said, "I understand you are up to something, but did you stop to consider what might happen to all of us if you should escape? The Germans cannot afford to have the secret of this extermination camp broadcast."

He kept talking with Sasha looking at him intently. For all that Sasha knew, this was a trap. It didn't do anything to convince him otherwise when Leon said that he'd been in the camp for a year. Surely no one could have been there for so long without trying to escape already. Meanwhile, Leon became suspicious of Sasha the moment he realized that he couldn't speak Yiddish—a language that he assumed all Jews knew. (The two men had to speak Russian instead.) When Leon stopped talking, Sasha said that he wasn't planning anything and turned to leave.

Instinctively, Leon reached out and grabbed his arm.

"Wait a minute," he said. "You wonder why we haven't escaped till now. So I'll tell you. We had thought about it more than once, but we didn't know how. You are a Soviet man, a military man. Take over. Tell us what to do and we'll do it."

They stared at each other for a quiet, lingering moment.

"Would you perhaps know how the field behind the fence is mined?" Sasha asked. "How thick and in what order?" The prisoners had been forced to plant the minefields, so Leon had a good idea of how they were laid out.⁹ He gave Sasha the information, which was enough to persuade him to keep the lines of communication open. Over the coming days, they exchanged more information and gradually built up some trust. Within a couple of weeks, they'd agreed to join forces. Their military and civilian resistance groups combined into a bigger group that they called the "Underground Committee." Together, they would attempt a mass escape from Sobibor.

Their first plan was to dig a tunnel out of the camp. They began work around October 6th. They went through the night in teams of four—two men digging, two getting rid of the dirt. They made quick progress, but then autumn rains flooded the fledgling tunnel and destroyed it. Sasha was only so disappointed, though. Doubts had nagged at him before the first spade had even hit the earth. To get far enough from the camp, the tunnel would have to extend at least 115 feet—nearly the width of a football field. How long would it take for over 600 prisoners to crawl that far, one by one, and what would happen if someone panicked or got stuck?

According to one account, the day after the tunnel flooded, Sasha saw some SS guards chasing a flock of geese around the camp. Another transport had arrived, and thousands of Jewish people were being herded into the gas chambers. For a while, the flock's loud honking was enough to drown out the noises of murder and death. Then, the scream of a child crying for its mother cut through. It was a terrible, high-pitched sound that pierced Sasha, filling him with memories of his own daughter. In that moment, he decided that every SS guard in Sobibor would be killed.¹⁰ Once they were gone, the prisoners would simply walk out of the camp's main entrance and head for the forest.

Sasha fleshed out a plan and presented it to Leon in the carpenter's workshops on October 12th.¹¹ It hinged on turning the Nazis' corruption and greed against them. The belongings of the Jewish people being murdered in Sobibor were meant to go to Germany for distribution among the German people—in theory, at least.¹² But SS guards routinely looted cash, clothes, jewelry, and other valuables for themselves. In Sasha's plan, the prisoners would lure them to the camp's workshops, one at a time, with news that something particularly fancy had been found. Then they'd kill them with the tools in those workshops, like axes, hammers, and screwdrivers. Once a guard was dead, the prisoners would take his pistol. While this was happening, other prisoners would cut the camp's electrical and telephone wires, to stop the Nazis from calling the outside world for help, and others would sabotage vehicles in the camp's garage to stop any survivors from chasing them. Still others would raid the camp's armory, to give the prisoners heavier weapons, like rifles, to take into the forest. The plan would begin at 4:00 p.m. and finish within an hour. That way, Sasha could just announce to the mass of prisoners at the daily 5:00 p.m. roll call that there'd been a revolt and that they were going to escape together under the cover of dusk. Sasha wanted to act immediately, because he'd learned that the camp's commandant, Franz Reichleitner, along with four other senior SS guards, Kurt Bolender, Hubert Gomerski, Johann Klier, and Gustav Wagner, were all about to be on leave at the same time. Their combined absence would give the Underground Committee a rare advantage that couldn't be squandered.

The revolt was launched two days later, on October 14th, 1943. That morning, members of the Underground Committee handed out money and valuables to other prisoners, to give them a chance of surviving in the outside world. Some members got dressed up. One SS guard, who clearly had no idea of what was about to happen, sarcastically asked a member named Yanek if he was going to a wedding.¹³

When 4:00 p.m. struck, a prisoner assigned as a messenger went to Johann Niemann, the highest-ranking SS guard in the camp that day, and told him that a fine leather coat had arrived in the tailor's workshop. It would be perfect for him. Niemann was at the workshop within fifteen minutes, and the prisoners there invited him inside for a fitting. While he was busy admiring himself in front of a mirror, another prisoner leaped out from a hiding spot and split his head open with an ax. He died almost instantly. The prisoners hurriedly hid his body under a pile of clothes.

From here, there was no going back.

Siegfried Graetschus, the SS guard who was effectively Sobibor's chief of staff, was lured to the tailor, also with the promise of a fine coat, and killed in the same way. In the cobblers' workshop, and the carpenters' workshop, and the camp's offices, more and more SS guards were killed, along with their Ukrainian assistants. As the revolt neared completion, a Committee member got carried away and spontaneously murdered an SS guard, Walter Ryba, in the camp's garage. The garage was exposed, so it was impossible to hide a body there. The rebels could be rumbled at any moment. It was 4:45 p.m. Sasha quickly decided that their only choice was to start roll call early. This deviation from the normal timetable was enough to cause unrest. When a Committee member stabbed a Ukrainian guard to death in full view of everyone in the roll call area, the situation boiled over. Prisoners ran for the main entrance. By now, twelve SS guards and two of their Ukrainian assistants were dead.

In Sasha's postwar memories of this moment, the prisoners cheered as they made a break for it. "The slogans reverberated like thunder in the death camp, and united Jews from Russia, Poland, Holland, France, Czechoslovakia, and Germany," he wrote. "Six hundred pain-wracked, tormented people, surged forward with a wild 'hurrah' to life and freedom."[14]

The reality was surely more chaotic. Some prisoners thought that it was safest to avoid the melee and went back to their barracks. Others panicked and climbed over the fences or cut holes through the barbed wire, which led them straight into the minefields. Meanwhile, at the main entrance, the gates collapsed under pressure from the crowd. When the handful of surviving SS guards finally pulled themselves together, they began shooting at prisoners indiscriminately, some with automatic weapons. The Underground Committee's plan had fallen apart.

By the Nazis' own estimates, 365 prisoners tried to escape from Sobibor on October 14th, 1943. A little under 165 were killed in the process, being either shot or caught on landmines. The rest made it to the forest. The Nazis began a search for them that was both ruthless and meticulous. Local people were offered rewards for any information or sightings. Reinforcements came to comb vast areas of land with sniffer dogs, while airplanes were deployed to look from the skies. Some escapees were caught and killed. Others died at the hands of Polish partisans in the forest, many of whom were as antisemitic as they were anti-German.

The Sobibor Uprising, as the event is called today, was a shock and an embarrassment for the Nazis. Hans Frank, the Governor General of occupied Poland, told a meeting in Krakow that it proved that camps with Jews were "a great danger."[15] Soon after, an unprecedented mass execution named "Operation Harvest Festival" was launched. Beginning on November 3rd, thousands of regular German soldiers and policemen, as well as SS men, shot around 42,000 Jewish prisoners in camps across occupied Poland, all in the space of forty-eight hours. Heinrich Himmler had already decided to end Operation Reinhard before the Uprising, but it prompted him to change the plans that he'd made for Sobibor. Instead of being repurposed as a concentration camp, it would now be completely dismantled.[16] The Uprising also changed his relationship with Odilo Globocnik, the SS man that he'd trusted to manage Operation Reinhard. He now saw him as an irredeemable failure. Along with several high-ranking members of his staff, Globocnik was posted to Italy with an order to fight partisans in Trieste. One of the men concerned described the posting as a death sentence. None of them had any combat training, so it felt like they were "an embarrassment to the brass: they wanted to find ways and means to 'incinerate' us."[17] (He may have been right. Globocnik's second-in-command, Christian Wirth, was killed in action shortly after he arrived in Trieste.)

The Sobibor Uprising didn't go as planned. Hundreds of Jewish people died, and the Nazis flew into a vindictive, spiteful rage in the aftermath, shooting tens of thousands more. It also didn't stop their extermination program, which they simply shifted to another camp on the other side of occupied Poland: Auschwitz-Birkenau.

Nevertheless, about fifty of those who escaped survived the War, including Sasha Pechersky.[18] After the Uprising, he found his way back to the Soviet Army and rejoined the fight against the Nazis, along with other prisoners of war from Minsk who'd also been in the camp. One of them, Simjon Rosenfeld, eventually reached Berlin, where he carved the word "Sobibor" into the wall of Hitler's Reich Chancellery. Many of the other escapees told their stories in the years after the War. Some gave interviews that can be seen freely online today. Others testified at the trials of Nazi war criminals in Germany and Israel. Thomas "Toivi" Blatt, Philip Bialowitz, Dov Freiberg, Stanislaw Szmajzner, and others all wrote books about Sobibor—books that I used to write this chapter.

As the end of the War neared, Odilo Globocnik grew sick with fear that the Allies would discover his crimes. On January 5th, 1944, he begged Himmler to erase Belzec, Sobibor, and Treblinka from history by destroying all evidence relating to Operation Reinhard.[19] Sasha Pechersky and the other members of the Underground Committee may not have achieved all of their goals—but without them, we wouldn't know nearly as much about Sobibor as we do.

*

"You've got to find a way to love it," Łukasz Kukawski says. We've been talking about his work at the Sobibor Memorial Museum in Poland. He's been the Museum's deputy head, and the head of its Education and Visitor Center, since 2020. He has a warm, friendly smile, and he stops to nod at colleagues who bustle past his desk while we speak. "It would be quite difficult without that," he continues. "You have to love history, and you have to love working with people."

"Does it ever get overwhelming?" I ask.

"Actually, when you're giving guided tours, you can easily end up behaving like a record on repeat. But, even so, there are times when I read the survivor testimonies—and especially when the testimonies talk about small children . . . " he stops and looks away for a moment. "My heart still breaks. I'm just a normal person, you know?"

Throughout our conversation, Łukasz comes back to the children of Sobibor time and again—both the camp's child victims, and the children of the perpetrators who worked there. He tells me that he has young children, and he often begins his answers by saying, "To me, as a father."

"I can talk to you," he says, "and I can smile, but what happened here . . . " Then he says, resolutely, "We are the caretakers of this place. We are the guardians. Without that sense of purpose, it would be impossible to work here."

When the Nazis dismantled Sobibor, they intended to leave no trace of their crimes. "They tried to make the world forget about it completely," Łukasz says. "Us, as museum workers—we help visitors to find out what happened, through artifacts, and by showing them peoples' faces." Artifacts are still being discovered today. They're sent to the state museum of Majdanek—another former extermination camp—to be cleaned, cataloged, and preserved. He shows me a small green bottle that's sitting on his desk. It was recently churned up by the wet earth in Sobibor. Most likely, he says, it was used in the camp's pharmacy. It's one of nearly 60,000 small objects that have been discovered and cataloged so far.

"The main part of our exhibition is a display case that's 25 meters long. It contains 700 objects. Some belonged to the victims, some belonged to the perpetrators. They're all important because they all tell a story. And whenever I guide people through the exhibition, I'll always stop to tell the story of the ID tags."

When I hear "ID tags," I think of army gear, and so I guess that they belonged to the perpetrators. This confuses me. Why would the Nazis issue ID tags to people working on Operation Reinhard, which was shrouded in secrecy?

"Actually," Łukasz says, "they're tags with children's names. Parents probably gave them to their kids in case they got lost, so that someone could help them. There's one that belongs"—he stops to correct himself—"*belonged* to a six-year-old girl from The Netherlands. Her name was Lea Judith de la Penha. Her name is on the tag, and her town, Amsterdam, and her date of birth. We've got the artifact, and we've got a picture of her, too. We can use these things to bring her identity into the present. We're breaking down what the Nazis tried to do. They were trying to wipe out any kind of identification completely."

I ask Łukasz if there's any object in the exhibition that's especially important to him.

"Yes, there is one small object—it's a pin that a kid would attach to their clothes. It has Mickey Mouse on it. My kids watch cartoons, and they love watching Mickey Mouse. The kids who were taken to Sobibor watched the same films."

It sounds, I say, like this pin fits into a bigger project at the Sobibor Memorial Museum—which is to humanize the people who died there.

"Yes, definitely," he says. "At least, we try to do that as much as possible. When visitors enter the exhibition, they see photos of Jews from Włodawa—the town where I live, along with most of my colleagues. There was a ghetto there during the Nazi occupation. Almost the entire Jewish population—over 6,000 people—was murdered at Sobibor. But there were no transport lists, they weren't registered in the camp, and their personal documents were burned. They just completely disappeared. However, we do have some photos of them. An album was hidden in Włodawa and found after the War. So at least we can memorialize them in some sense."

Our conversation shifts to the Sobibor Uprising. Łukasz smiles deeply when I mention Sasha's name. "Alexander 'Sasha' Pechersky," he says, slowly and solemnly, accenting every syllable. "When the Uprising started, before the other guards realized that SS men had already been killed, on the roll call square, Pechersky is supposed to have said to the other prisoners, 'Those of you who survive, should bear witness to this. Let the world know what happened here.' His words are important for the Museum. They're our motto. They're carved into the wall at the end of the exhibition." He says them again, in the same solemn way that he said Pechersky's name a moment earlier. "'Let the world know what happened here.' And this is what we do." Then he says that Sasha was a hero of the twentieth century.

I ask him to describe his heroism.

"He fought against his fate. He found enough courage in himself to keep moving forward even once he found out that Sobibor was a death camp." He goes on to recount the story of Sasha chopping the tree stump, and of him refusing cigarettes and food from Karl Frenzel. I ask him what he thinks the moral of that story is. He considers the question for a long moment, before saying, "Pechersky knew that the Nazis were heavily armed, but he still found a way to tell them, 'I'm more powerful than you.'"

Sasha is well-known to historians, museologists, and Holocaust educators. But while there are a couple of movies about the Uprising—*Escape From Sobibor* (1987), which has aged poorly, and the more recent Russian-made *Sobibor* (2018), which is littered with historical inaccuracies—the wider public remains unfamiliar with him. If he really was a hero of the twentieth century, I ask, then how come his story is in the shadows?

"Well, there were only about fifty survivors from Sobibor," Łukasz says. "There were so few people to spread information after the War. And then the Communist government said that it was only Soviet soldiers who were killed here, so they didn't tell the history in the right way. They tried to hide it. Only over the last ten or fifteen years have things begun to change. And that's why we're here now—to remember Pechersky and all the other survivors and victims in the right way."

*

"There aren't many Holocaust movies about Jewish resistance," Yaron Tzur says, thoughtfully. He wears a white button-down shirt that's open at the collar. He has strong features, but his speaking voice is soft and considered. "And that's because Hollywood narratives about the Holocaust victimize Jews. Audiences don't want to see Jewish fighters. They want to see Jewish victims. Ask yourself: would a film about the Warsaw Ghetto Uprising win an Oscar? Would it be popular, would people be interested? Or would they say, 'Well, it may have happened, but it has no historical significance'—that's the question."

Yaron is the Pedagogical Director at Ghetto Fighters' House Museum in Israel. Founded in 1949 and known as "GFH" for short, it was one of the world's first Holocaust museums. It was also founded by Holocaust survivors, many of whom participated in uprisings during the Nazi era—including the one in Sobibor. (For years, GFH exhibited the shirt that Sasha wore during the Uprising.) Yaron tells me that, in its early days, the Museum's guides would recount their own stories of resisting Nazism as part of their tours.

"The uprisers were very young people," Yaron says. Sasha was thirty-four years old when he was sent to Sobibor, and others who fought, escaped, and survived with him were even younger. Thomas Blatt was only sixteen, for example, and Stanislav Szmajzner was fifteen. Many of the Jewish people who fought in the ghetto uprisings were teenagers, too. "They give us an educational example for our young visitors," Yaron continues. "It can inspire them to think about their strength and their ability to create change. Many young people today don't seem to believe that they can create change. I sense that they feel a bit lost."

"Why do you say that?" I ask.

"It's like they're drowning in social media," he says, with a heavy sigh. "Sometimes it really narrows their world and their worldviews, and it can make them feel so small. They want to be social media *influencers*, but they don't think about how they can be *influential*. So, this is the message that we want to give them: 'Look at these people. You are them, and they are you.' The next time they ask themselves, 'Can I create change? Can I do something, can I do anything?', we want them to believe that they can."

I tell Yaron that I've seen two words used repeatedly in Holocaust museums around the world: "upstander" and "ally." Whether the museums are talking about uprisings or Kristallnacht or Auschwitz, the lesson always seems to follow the same pattern. A story of horror in the past is followed by an invitation to become an ally or upstander in the present. I tell him that I'm not convinced it's effective.

"Ah, well, there's a paradox in most Holocaust museums," he says with a knowing smile. "We do have a model of the Treblinka extermination camp at GFH. But you can't tell a visitor, 'See this model of Treblinka? Do the opposite!' You can't educate through examples of evil. You need to show that moral choices were made during the Holocaust. Human beings aren't good, human beings aren't evil. Human beings make choices. That's who we are. It's what defines us. We want our visitors to ask themselves, 'What choices am I making in my life today?'"

"And what can they learn from the choices that Sasha Pechersky made, when they were such extreme choices made in such extreme circumstances?"

Given the name of the Ghetto Fighters' House Museum, and that this conversation took place shortly after October 7th, 2023, and the invasion of Gaza that followed, I admit that I was anticipating an answer about fighting. But Yaron went in a completely different direction.

"There's something so inspiring about Pechersky and those Soviet soldiers being imprisoned in Sobibor and actively planning an escape with civilians. It's so amazing, and so shocking, and it happened only once during the Holocaust. But," he continues, "our Museum tries not to see their choices from a militaristic point of view. It was more a matter of spiritual resistance, you know."

I ask him what he means by "spiritual resistance."

"Resistance isn't only about fighting. There were many instances of resistance—Jewish and non-Jewish—against the Nazis that didn't involve any weapons." He stares into the distance for a moment, before turning back to me with new light in his eyes. "In one of our exhibitions, we have an artifact: some wooden scales. Three female inmates made them in a subcamp of Auschwitz. They used them to divide food equally between them. This was spiritual resistance. The Nazis were trying to dehumanize them. For them to say, 'We want to be fair with each other, and to divide everything equally'—that's resistance. Antek Zuckerman, one of the founders of our kibbutz and the Ghetto Fighters' House Museum, and one of the leaders of the Warsaw Ghetto Uprising, said, 'I don't think there's any need to analyze the Uprising in military terms, but if there's a school to study the human spirit, there it should be a major subject'.[20] That's how I think we should see Sasha's story, too."

6

Field Security Sections

Finding and Arresting War Criminals in the Ruins of Nazi Germany

Flensburg, May 3rd, 1945

Rudolf Höss was waiting for the order to end his own life. And he was ready to do it. At least, he thought he was.

Rudolf was one of dozens who'd arrived at the Naval Academy in Flensburg over the last few days. It was a magnificent building—a living reminder of the days of the German Empire, perched on the country's northernmost tip, where it overlooked a harbor that yawned into fjords and the Baltic Sea. Here, it almost felt like the War had never happened. As moonlight glowed through a Prussian eagle in the stained-glass window above the main entrance, Rudolf glared at Richard Glücks and Gerhard Maurer, the colleagues who'd come with him. Bitter thoughts filled his mind. Glücks had never taken him seriously, and Maurer had deliberately made his job harder.[1]

Behind closed doors, their boss, Heinrich Himmler, was groveling to the heads of the so-called Flensburg Government. This government had formed three days ago to run what was left of Nazi Germany. It was led by Karl Dönitz, the admiral that Hitler nominated as his successor shortly before he killed himself. Himmler was trying to win over the government's leaders. He was "absolutely indispensable," he said. He would be a "suitable conversation partner" for General Eisenhower, and Eisenhower would need the SS because a new war between the Allies and the Soviet Union was sure to start at any moment.² Dönitz wasn't convinced. To him, this all seemed like a desperate fantasy. Besides, he knew that Himmler had already tried to make peace deals with people overseas without permission, which was treason.

Himmler was unceremoniously dismissed. But he forced himself to smile as he left Dönitz's office in the Academy's sports hall and to leap up to his subordinates enthusiastically. Rudolf couldn't believe how chipper he seemed. For a flickering moment, he wondered if his boss had achieved the impossible. But then Himmler said that they had to vanish. They could dress up in other uniforms and take the identities of Germans who'd died in the War. That way, they'd be able to hide among regular servicemen. He assured them that they'd only need to stay hidden like this for a few weeks. Soon, the world would come to its senses. He reached out to shake Rudolf's hand. It was a calm gesture that said, "well done and goodbye-for-now," and nothing more.

Rudolf's disappointment was still palpable when he wrote about this handshake in his memoir two years later. "This was the goodbye from the man I respected so highly," he said, "whose orders and sayings were gospel."³ He had good reason to be disappointed. He was effectively being ordered to desert, which hardly aligned with the SS virtues that Himmler had preached since becoming its head in 1929. The desertion plans also seemed unrealistic—and indeed, the Allies captured and arrested Himmler just a few weeks later.⁴

Still, whether out of blind obedience, a deluded belief that he might go back to his old life, or simply being too afraid to kill himself—or perhaps a mix of all three—Rudolf did as he was told. He took the identity of Franz Lang, a dead rank-and-file German sailor, before fleeing to another naval base. This one was on Sylt, an island about 50 miles from Flensburg. The British soon overran it, but Rudolf was freed thanks to his fake identity. He ended up on a disused farm back in Flensburg, where he lived like a peasant, sleeping in a barn that doubled as a slaughterhouse.

*

Intelligence-gathering had always been part of wars, but it took on new significance in the twentieth century. For the first time in history, battles were fought in the skies as well as on the seas and the land. Radar detected enemy aircraft from over a hundred miles away, while sonar detected submarines, mines, and other obstacles deep underwater. Wireless technology allowed encoded communications to cross countries instantly. Battlefield machinery and weaponry became both heavier and more accurate than ever before. Winston Churchill famously used the term "Wizard War" to describe the Second World War. "Only with difficulty is it comprehended, even now, by those outside the small high scientific circles concerned," he wrote in his memoirs. "No such warfare had ever been waged by mortal men."[5]

These changes in the nature of warfare were the backdrop to the British Army's decision to establish an Intelligence Corps on July 19th, 1940. Field Security Sections, or "FSS" for short, were the building blocks of this Corps. Around 1,000 FSS were operative at different moments in the Second World War and across every corner of the conflict.[6] Each FSS was attached to an infantry or armored division or to a specific geographic area. They consisted of around fifteen people of varying ranks. These people usually spoke at least two languages, and they had deep knowledge of cultures beyond their own. Their work included everything from collecting intelligence for the battlefield, to interrogating prisoners of war, to advising on security for their partner division. In spring 1945, as the Allies went into Germany and the War came to an end, one of their biggest jobs was to track down and arrest Nazi war criminals.

The rest of the military was suspicious of the FSS. According to one historian, this was because of the nature of military work: military personnel must be willing to obey and conform, but FSS members had to question everything. Also, in Britain in the 1930s and 1940s, it was commonly believed that there was something "ungentlemanly" about covert work, and that those who did it were "unreliable" and "mercenary."[7] Glimpses of these attitudes can be seen in FSS members' descriptions of themselves and in the way that they downplayed their experiences. According to one former member, for example, they were just "schoolmasters, journalists, encyclopedia salesmen, unfrocked clergymen and other displaced *New Statesmen* readers." He added that the rest of the military treated them "with ill-concealed distaste and disdain."[8] Another said that FSS members were "unique among the odd million chaps who went to France," because they passed their time on the boats taking them to the D-Day landings by playing cards.[9] Whether this is true or not, it shows that the FSS saw themselves as misfits—as part of the military, but also outside it. They liked to think that they'd joined less because of their careers or qualifications, more because of their character, which mixed bravery and fatalism, and a gallows sense of humor.

The role that the FSS played in bringing Nazi war criminals to justice has been all but forgotten. This is partly because the history of intelligence itself is so murky. Professor Christopher Andrew wrote a sweeping book about it in 2018, called *The Secret World*. He begins by saying that intelligence is "the only profession without a serious literature," thanks to there being "so little record of most of its past experience."[10] For FSS members, the Official Secrets Act 1939 obligated them—along with everyone else who worked in the Intelligence Corps—to keep their stories untold, under threat of prosecution. In practice, the Secrets Act could be hard to enforce. In 1987, for example, Peter Wright, a former British intelligence officer, revealed intelligence practices during the Cold War in his scandalous autobiography, *Spycatcher*. The government tried and failed to suppress it with the Secrets Act, but they inadvertently turned it into a bestseller in the process. In most cases, though, the average FSS member's sense of duty to the Secrets Act lasted the rest of their lives. Even their own families had no idea what they'd done during the War.[11] But today, thanks to a handful of memoirs, interviews, and declassified documents, it's possible to get a sense of their work, and of how they helped to extinguish Nazism in Europe.

Germany was in ruins when the Nazis surrendered. Entire towns and cities had been destroyed, and much of the country was on the brink of famine. Displaced people had to find their way home through this devastated landscape. They included millions of decommissioned German soldiers and hundreds of thousands of civilians who'd been detained in concentration camps. For war criminals, these masses were camouflage. Former members of the SS, the SA, the SD, and the Gestapo, as well as members of far-right organizations in Nazi-allied nations, tried to hide among them by using fake identities, disguising themselves as victims, and fleeing to towns, cities, or countries that weren't their own. Uncovering and arresting them wasn't easy.

In winter 1946, Derek South, a member of 8 FSS working in northwest Germany, got a tip-off from the network of contacts that he'd built in the region: a wanted SS man was planning to have a night out at a local dance hall. Derek didn't reveal the SS man's name, but he did say that he was an *Obersturmbannführer*—a senior SS rank equivalent to lieutenant colonel, held by Adolf Eichmann among others. Derek went to the hall with a partner from 8 FSS. He manned the only exit to make sure that no one could escape while his partner jumped onstage, stopped the music, and, speaking in German, announced that everyone's identity cards (*Ausweiskarte*) had to be checked. The dancers begrudgingly formed into a line. The air grew heavy with whispers and the smell of sweat. Derek and his partner got about halfway down the line before they found the man they were after. They took him outside and bundled him into a waiting car. As they drove, the man tugged on Derek's sleeve and begged to be released. He said that his arrest would devastate his mother. He became more desperate, started sobbing, and leaned on Derek's shoulder. "The journey was completed with our detainee huddled miserably in the corner of the car," Derek wrote.[12]

96 FSS entered the Austrian towns of Radkersburg and Mureck at midday on July 27th, 1945. The local SS had embraced Hitler's "scorched earth" policy and left them in ruins.[13] Looting, rape, and venereal disease were rife, the police force was non-existent, and there was no jail. The men of 96 FSS were tasked with restoring order and with dissolving whatever was left of the Nazi Party. To do this, they began to track everyone who went through the towns and everyone who crossed the nearby border with Yugoslavia (as it was then). They monitored the formation of new political organizations; the public's mood, which was hit by everything from the Nuremberg Trials to the weather; as well as all the rumors that they heard. (These were about everything from the Nazi regime being on the brink of a comeback to Hitler "cruising the Mediterranean in a submarine."[14]) They built lines of communication with FSS in other towns, keeping them informed about SS members from Radkersburg and Mureck who'd fled elsewhere. They also recovered and analyzed Nazi documents, which was life-threatening work. The Nazis had mined their Radkersburg headquarters, and at least one person died in explosions there.[15]

The men of 96 FSS approached all this calmly and quietly. They spent their first few weeks in Radkersburg and Mureck securing the former Nazi headquarters and creating a long-term policy for the towns' renewal. Meanwhile, they deliberately avoided "a hurried plunge into an orgy of arrests."[16] Their approach paid off. One by one, they captured every former local Nazi leader.

Franz Hartl, a former SS *Obersturmführer*, was one of their first scalps. He tried to defend himself by telling them that he'd been sickened by "Nazi terror," and that he'd quit the SS to fight with anti-Nazi partisans in April 1945. 96 FSS didn't buy it. "One month before the capitulation," their captain wrote, incredulously, "and after he had been a policeman since 1928 and had served with an SS police regiment on the Russian front...."[17] Other important arrests included Arnulf Lill, a District Leader (*Kreisleiter*), and Ernst Huallenz and Anton Oswald, two Local Group Leaders (*Ortsgruppenleiter*). Huallenz was supervising forced Hungarian-Jewish laborers in early 1945 when Lill ordered dozens who'd caught typhus to be shot. Oswald led the shooting.

Lill was "truculent" after his arrest, and initially, he denied being involved in the shooting. He confessed before long, though, and "freely" turned in his former colleagues, too.[18] Huallenz was "a slippery customer" who admitted that he'd been in the SD but who claimed not to know his own job title.[19] Oswald had already fled by the time 96 FSS arrived. He returned after just a few weeks on the run, evidently satisfied that he was in the clear. He was "the least to expect arrest," and 96 FSS found him "reclining in a deck chair enjoying the literature of Grimm." Their report also added—in a classic example of FSS gallows humor—that "his future took on a Grimmer outlook, if the remark may be permitted." It took three days of interrogation before he admitted his role in the shooting. His deposition dripped with self-pity: "I protested and said I wished to have nothing to do with that [...] I told him [Arnulf Lill] it was not my duty [...] I said that I didn't want it on my conscience." But he was also remarkably cool and detached about what he'd done: "I was present when they were shot. I took part in the shooting myself, with a machine pistol."[20] Once these three had been arrested, 96 FSS reported with quiet satisfaction that "some of the hard kernel" of the Nazi regime had "begun to crumble away."[21] (In November 1947, Lill and Oswald were both sentenced to death, although their sentences were later commuted to a fifteen-year imprisonment.[22]) The last surviving report of 96 FSS is dated May 8th, 1946. By then, they'd arrested dozens of former Nazis, and "all possible work from our records has now been accomplished on the liquidation of the NSDAP [...] practically no office holders are left in this district."[23]

John C. Clark was a member of 64 FSS and 30 FSS. He was born in France to British parents, and he was fluent in French and English. He also had a strong command of German. He was unusual for keeping a diary in the field and for writing some short pieces about his activities in fall 1945, including a memoir. (None of them was ever published, though, and as late as 1997, he added a handwritten note to the front page of his memoir to explain the lack of names in it: "Official Secrets Act oblige[s].")

John crossed the English Channel ten days after D-Day, working first in France and the Netherlands before going into Germany. In Germany, villages were ruined and deserted, and fields, trees, and bushes somehow didn't look the same as in other countries. The only signs of life were occasional white flags fluttering from windows. "We were coming into the unknown," he wrote. "We were coming into a country which, for more than five years had been closed to the rest of the world."[24]

John and his FSS were responsible for arresting Nazi war criminals in Soltau, a town south of Hamburg, and then in Hamburg itself. "When we came to pick them up, it was always the great tear scene, with the wife starting the show followed by the children and very often the man himself," he wrote.[25] In Hamburg, his FSS simply ordered all former District and Local Group Leaders to be at the town hall at 9:00 a.m. the next morning—and 243 out of 250 did as they were told. "All we had to do was take down their names and addresses and place them in the police car to be arrested," John wrote, matter-of-factly.[26] Their highest-profile arrest was Friedrich Suhr, a senior figure in Adolf Eichmann's office of "Jewish Affairs" who'd managed the deportation of Jewish people from across Europe to concentration and extermination camps. He also led an *Einsatzkommando*, which meant that he was responsible for shooting thousands of Jewish men, women, and children.[27] There wasn't a search for him. One day, out of the blue, an informant just turned in his name and address. John and his team went to pick him up in the dead of night. "When he came out, he looked very much afraid," John wrote. "He more or less had a fit, but when he recovered, he was quite calm and denied any connection with the SS." He was taken to prison, where his shoelaces, tie, and belt were confiscated, along with anything else that he might use to hang himself. The next morning, though, he was found with injured wrists. He'd tried to slit them with a broken teacup. After a nurse stitched up the wounds, he confessed to his role in the mass murder of Europe's Jews.[28] Such incidents weren't uncommon. John saw another former Nazi try, unsuccessfully, to slit his wrists while in custody, having hidden some razor blades inside his wooden leg. (And Suhr eventually succeeded in ending his own life in prison in 1946.)

John Clark didn't think that there was anything extraordinary about chasing down Nazi war criminals and mass murderers in postwar Germany. In fact, he was modest to the point of being self-deprecating. "Our job, although it was not altogether tranquil, was safe and small compared to the fighting men who made history during the greatest campaign ever fought," he wrote.[29] He even included a disclaimer of sorts at the start of his memoir. It sounds like it was meant to be a joke (FSS gallows humor again), but it also suggests that he doubted whether his experiences were worth recording at all: "This story will not contain anything to elevate the mind, or any grand theories; and apart from personal satisfaction, it has no purpose whatsoever."[30]

Perhaps the most significant Nazi war criminal arrested by any FSS was Rudolf Höss, the former Commandant of the Auschwitz-Birkenau concentration and extermination camp. 92 FSS began pursuing him in 1945, through "continuous investigations, interrogations and extensive searches."[31] They arrested his wife, Hedwig, in November that year. She claimed not to have seen Rudolf since April 30th—the day that Hitler killed himself. "By assessing various psychological aspects of her story," wrote Captain Victor Cross, "members of this Section gained the firm impression that she was lying."[32]

92 FSS spent the next five months gathering more information on the Höss family before arresting Hedwig again on March 5th, 1946. For the first six days in custody, she insisted that Rudolf was dead and repeatedly threatened to go on a hunger strike. Eventually, though, she was tricked into revealing the truth. There was a railway near the prison. 92 FSS arranged for an old steam train

that was noisy enough to be heard from Hedwig's cell to be driven outside. She was told that it was going to Siberia, and that her eldest son, Klaus, would be put on board. She'd never see him again. Then, after a long, quiet moment, she was told that he'd be spared if she revealed where her husband was. She was given a pencil and a blank piece of paper before being left alone in her cell to think about it, with the train huffing and puffing in the background. Within ten minutes, she'd written down Rudolf's fake identity, Franz Lang; his location, Gottrupel, a village near Flensburg; and the man who owned the farm where he was hiding, Hans Peter Hansen.[33] Mind-games like this were standard for the FSS. "Any and every ruse is permissible in order to extract information," said one pamphlet for new recruits. Such ruses may go as far as "frightening PW [prisoner-of-war] by threats that they will be shot, or even staging a mock firing squad."[34]

Within a matter of hours, a team of nearly thirty men was on its way to Hansen's farm. These men included personnel from 92 FSS, the men of another nearby FSS, Captain Hanns Alexander, a German who'd fled to England and joined the War Crimes Investigation Team, and a doctor. Some of them—including Captain Alexander, and Bernard Clarke and Karl "Blitz" Abrahams of 92 FSS—were Jewish. It was nearly midnight when they showed up, heavily armed, in a fleet of military vehicles. Rudolf's arrest report says that he was "forced down immediately and his mouth prized open," and that he was subject to a medical exam. This exam probably extended to a search of his anus.[35] By this time, it was common knowledge that men of his rank used cyanide capsules to take their own lives, as Himmler had while in custody in May 1945—and that they often hid these capsules inside their own bodies. After the exam, Rudolf gave the men his fake identity papers. Under fierce questioning, he insisted that he was Franz Lang. Wondering if it might provide them with a clue, Captain Alexander ordered him to remove his wedding ring. Rudolf refused, saying that it was stuck on his finger. He quickly changed his mind when Captain Alexander threatened to cut off the finger in question. Rudolf relented and gave the ring to Captain Alexander, who saw the names "Rudolf" and "Hedwig" engraved inside.[36] The Commandant of Auschwitz, where over one million men, women, and children were murdered, had been found.

*

"The Memorial Museum's employees are confronted with grave ethical problems every day," Wojciech Soczewica says. He's telling me about one of the most precious, and one of the most terrible, objects on display at the Auschwitz-Birkenau Memorial Museum in Poland: a mass of human hair. The Nazis shaved prisoners' heads in their concentration and extermination camps. This practice began as a way to dehumanize and humiliate. It also made it easier to spot anyone who escaped. But it was later discovered that human hair could be made into felt, which in turn could be used for submarine insulation, among other things. This discovery was the Nazis' ultimate debasement of their victims. It turned them from humans into sources of raw materials to be harvested. "Approximately two tons of human hair can be seen by everyone who visits," Wojciech continues. "It's a remnant of human life. For many years, there was a debate about its adequate treatment—for example, whether it should be buried. This debate was only settled when Auschwitz survivors said their hair may be among the mass on display—and they wouldn't want it to be buried, at least not while they were still alive."

On July 2nd, 1947, the Polish government made the ruins of Auschwitz I and Auschwitz-Birkenau into a Memorial Museum. It became a UNESCO World Heritage Site in 1979. Under the twin pressures of growing visitor numbers and the passage of time, the entire site began to erode. It also became a lightning rod for social and political disputes, from the Carmelites who opened a convent next door to it in 1984, to the team of Iranian "researchers" who tried to visit it in 2006. In 2009, driven by Władysław Bartoszewski, the Polish politician and activist, and by Piotr Cywiński, the Polish historian, the Auschwitz-Birkenau Foundation was created. It was meant to catalyze an apolitical, multinational discussion about the Memorial Museum and its future, and to open an endowment that would finance its preservation. Wojciech is an expert in international relations and a career diplomat who worked in Bartoszewski's office at the time the Foundation was created. Today he serves as its director general. His work provides insight into the crimes that the FSS had to investigate.

"Bartoszewski and Cywiński believed that we needed an international, expert consultancy, one that would foster a dialogue about the Memorial, the authentic camp remains, and its priorities," Wojciech explains. "They also wanted to draw attention to the fact that the place was falling apart. Our biggest enemy is time. There are forty-five brick barracks left in Birkenau. They were built by prisoners without any particular construction skills, in conditions of absolute terror. These buildings are just one brick thick—less than five inches. Between the muddy ground, the thin walls, and their heavy roofs, they kept collapsing. The Foundation leads an international coalition to raise funds to finance the Memorial, so that we can protect them and everything else in Auschwitz-Birkenau—to preserve it all for future generations. We've reached out to countries, cities, corporations, and private philanthropists around the world to say, 'We've been taking care of this place for decades, but the responsibility should be global.' Today, there are more than forty professional conservators on site—experts in protecting wood, paper, plastic, brick, stone, you name it. And they're skilled, dedicated, and aware of the unprecedented nature of their mission. This mission drives them every day, and they work in a monstrous place that overflows with evidence of crimes beyond imagination," he says. Then he raises an index finger and emphasizes, "Crimes that are *completely* beyond imagination. When you have thousands of eyeglasses that need to be preserved, and you realize that behind *every* pair there was a human being whose story you don't know . . . " He stops speaking and pauses for a long moment. "It was Adolf Hitler's mission to destroy *every* trace of Jewish life. I am proud that the Foundation can support the conservators' mission. Together, we're doing everything possible to save *every* single item."

"Are you ever able to link any of the items to the people who owned them?" I ask.

"Sometimes," Wojciech says. "The conservators discovered a signet ring by chance while they were working on a barrack in Birkenau. Maybe it was smuggled in and hidden by a prisoner—we don't know. But we can assume that it was important to someone. An emblem was found on it during the preservation process. Historians identified this emblem as one that jewelers in the Litzmannstadt Ghetto used. We don't know the prisoner's name, but, most likely, we can assume that they lived in the Litzmannstadt Ghetto before being deported to Auschwitz. So, the owner is no longer totally anonymous. There are other stories like that. They're puzzles that we put together over time. They help us to build the memory of those who were murdered by the Nazis," he says, reflectively. Then, just as Łukasz Kukawski said to me about Sobibor, he adds, "The whole place is really a guardian of memory."

Our conversation turns to the life and crimes of Rudolf Höss, the most infamous Nazi war criminal captured by any FSS.

"After he testified at the Nuremberg Trials, Höss was brought to Poland where he was tried, found guilty of war crimes, and sentenced to death," Wojciech says. "The sentence was carried out in his former place of work. He was hanged in Auschwitz I, on purpose-built gallows between the gas chamber there and his private villa. Today, those gallows are part of the Memorial's guided tours. Everyone who visits Auschwitz-Birkenau is taken past it. But," he says, lugubriously, "while Höss was one of Nazi Germany's worst criminals, he was also just one person. Thousands of people worked in Auschwitz every day to make the extermination program happen. Meanwhile, the Höss family lived here in relative peace, in a villa with a beautiful garden. Sometimes I'm asked if the family knew about the extermination program, and I'm always reluctant to get into that question. They knew, of course," he says, "but for me, there's an additional layer there, another more important question that we must ask: how are people able to turn off their conscience, and their consciousness, in the face of criminal acts that are so self-evidently criminal? Nowadays—without wanting to draw any direct comparisons—so many of us seal ourselves off in beautiful gardens, metaphorically speaking." Now he holds my gaze with an intense stare. "We know about crimes and injustices happening on our doorstep and all around the world. How can it be that we find it so easy to do nothing?"

*

The story of the FSS and Rudolf Höss's arrest led me from the Auschwitz Memorial-Museum, one of the largest museums in the world, to the Military Intelligence Museum in the village of Chicksands, England, nearly a thousand miles away. The Military Intelligence Museum only has about 2,000 visitors each year—fewer than Auschwitz has on a single morning. Of all the museums mentioned in this book, it's the smallest by some distance.

"But considering our format," Owen Fullarton, the Museum's archivist says, "2,000 is quite a lot. The Museum is on an active military base, so we have to follow the rules set out by the Ministry of Defense. People can't just show up here. Every visit must be booked in advance."

Owen helps researchers with their inquiries and gives tours of the Museum, but his principal role is to care for its collections. These include several items and documents relating to 92 FSS and their arrest of Rudolf Höss.

"Victor Cross himself donated these," he says, shuffling through an archival file sitting on his desk before pulling out a single, yellowed piece of paper. "He says in this letter, sent to Colonel Felix Robson on March 27th, 1985, 'I enclose the following, if they are of any interest for your Museum: one pair of handcuffs with the name of Rudolf E. Höss, and of two others of that type; Höss's signed statement; a signed photo of Höss; a photo of Höss with his details; and photos of 92 Field Security Section.' That is from Victor Cross himself," he says, with a note of pride in his voice. "So, that's how that material found its way into the Museum."

I repeat part of the letter, hardly believing that Victor Cross could have written something so demurring: *if they are of any interest for your Museum.* We talk about the handcuffs that were used to arrest the Commandant of Auschwitz sitting in a residential home in England for nearly four decades. Beyond keeping the handcuffs, he also had them engraved with Rudolf's name and with the names of two other major war criminals whom the 92 FSS had arrested. (They were Hans Bothmann, the commandant of the Chelmno prototype extermination camp, and Rudolf Renner, the chief of the Gestapo in Aarhus, Denmark.) The engravings suggest that Victor knew he'd done something historic. But he never told his family about his wartime activities. His children only found out about them as adults, long after he'd died.[37] His story encapsulates the way in which so many FSS members kept their extraordinary work secret for many years, if not their whole lives.

"Why do you think it took Cross so long to tell anyone about all this?" I ask.

"It's a really, really interesting question," Owen says thoughtfully. "We get a lot of genealogical inquiries from people who say that their father or grandfather never spoke about their work, and I can only offer an educated guess to explain it. Army culture was to be as secretive as possible—although that has started to change recently, especially with institutions like ours. But intelligence groups like 92 FSS felt an unusual sense of duty to keep their work forever under wraps, to keep it quiet. And," he adds, after a deep breath, "we have hindsight. We look at them and think, 'These are amazing moments in history!' But for them, they just felt, 'I was doing a job.' They were humble about it."

I tell Owen about a handful of books and articles that I've read, all of which single out different members of 92 FSS as "*the* man" who arrested Rudolf Höss (almost all of which were written by descendants of the individual concerned). What does he think of these competing claims?

"Personally, I think that claims like that can be quite dangerous." Then he stops and reshapes his answer. "Maybe 'dangerous' isn't the right word, but everyone in the Section deserves credit. When you eulogize a particular person, you risk diminishing the collective—and capturing Höss and bringing him to justice *was* a collective effort. It involved a lot of different people," he stresses. "Each should be honored for the part that they played."

Owen's answer makes me think of the first line in Victor Cross's arrest report: "This Section has succeeded in arresting SS *Obersturmbannführer* Höss."[38] He doesn't say that *he* arrested Höss, and he doesn't name any other individuals, either. He says that his whole Section did it.

Toward the end of our time together, we discuss the tangled legacy of the Field Security Sections and the Nazi war criminals that they arrested—whether they were notorious men like Rudolf Höss or forgotten men like Anton Oswald. As Owen thinks aloud, he keeps returning to the word "cooperation" and the phrase "collective effort."

"Cooperation—working with other people—is an instrumental part of the human experience, and military intelligence wouldn't survive without it. When people think of military intelligence, they tend to think of lone spies going out and doing something heroic. But no," he says, almost languidly. "It was the collective efforts of groups like 92 FSS that got results. We can take inspiration from stories of people who were brave, but it's important to understand that they had a variety of roles. There's an important lesson for today there: sometimes we may think that what we're doing isn't making a difference, but there are many ways to contribute to the improvement of society, and there are many ways to make it fairer, kinder, and more respectful. Cooperation is the key. Understanding each other and working *with* each other."

*

In the weeks after I spoke with Wojciech and Owen, I often found myself thinking back to John Clark's memoir. Apart from "a feeling of relief in the air," the Allies' declaration of victory on May 8th, 1945, didn't make much difference to him or his FSS—"as we had a lot to do." They listened to Churchill's speech and then had a quiet celebration before getting back to work.[39] "Now that the War has ended, the only thing that interests us is demobilization," he wrote. "Back to civvy-street, home, and above all, freedom from khaki [. . .] let us all get back into civilian clothes, to a decent and useful life, in a world of peace."[40] These aspirations for the future may seem breathtakingly modest. But it was precisely the absence of the simple human qualities that he describes—decency, and the wish to live a useful life in a peaceful world—that made Auschwitz possible. It was also these qualities that defined the bravery of the Field Security Sections and that enabled them to track down as many Nazi war criminals as they did.

7

Leon Bass

The Black American Soldier Who Told the World about Buchenwald

Benjamin Franklin High School, PA, around 1975

The principal was wandering the school corridors when a commotion pricked his ears.[1] He knew the sound well. The school had been a chaotic place ever since he joined in 1968. Still, something about this commotion felt unusual. Trusting his educator's instinct, he followed it until it led him to a classroom. He pushed the door open and found a group of students running riot. At the front of the class was a guest speaker—a woman, about the same age as him, who was desperately trying to restore order. Above the noise, the principal heard the color of an eastern European accent in her voice.

"Cool it," he bellowed.

Quiet fell on the classroom and the students scurried back to their seats. The principal decided to stay a while, standing guard and listening to the guest speaker as she resumed her talk. She told them about the Grodno Ghetto, where she, her sister, and her parents had shared a single room. Her parents had been deported to an unknown destination in November 1942, and she never saw them again. The following January, she and her sister were deported to Auschwitz, where her sister died of typhus within a few months. She only avoided death herself thanks to a prisoner who worked as a nurse and who took her under her wing, saving her from the gas chambers on four separate occasions.[2]

The speaker's vivid account of her experiences in Auschwitz forced the principal's mind back to that day nearly three decades ago and to the sights that he'd tried so hard to forget. Those skeletal faces with their sunken eyes. The body parts in jars of formaldehyde. The lampshade made from human skin. He'd barely spoken about it to anyone. Now it felt like his three decades-long silence was about to crack.

"Listen to what she is saying," he told his students. "I was there, and I saw it. You need to hear about it."

*

Leon Bass was born in Philadelphia in 1925. His parents were from South Carolina, but they left after the First World War. His father had fought in that War, and he'd been told that he was helping "to make the world safe for democracy."[3] But, when he got home to the United States, he found that the Jim Crow laws—which segregated white and Black people—were intact and as robust as ever. This convinced him that he and his family had no future in South Carolina. Like many Black Americans in the early twentieth century, they went north in search of a better life.

Leon went to an all-Black elementary school in Philadelphia and then to a mixed junior high. He didn't experience what he called "overt racism" as a young adult. It was always there, though, like a background hum. Whenever he wanted to buy something, he had to go to Black-only stores. When he went to the movies, he had to go to a Black-only theater or take a balcony seat in a mixed theater. He did have a friend at school who was white. Their friendship lasted three years—but they never visited each other's homes, so it didn't exist outside of school. "Without being told," Leon wrote, "we both knew that racism had put limits on our relationship."[4]

In 1943, at the age of eighteen and having graduated with only average grades, Leon decided to join the United States Army, hoping that it would help to further his education. He went to the Philadelphia induction center with a group of white boys who'd also just graduated high school. When they arrived, a sergeant at the door sent him to the right and the others to the left. It was his first taste of what he called the "institutionalized racism" of the Army.[5] He was assigned to an all-Black unit with around 600 other young men. In three months of infantry training, they learned to assemble and disassemble firearms until they could do it blindfolded, and they endured 25-mile training hikes with heavy equipment on their backs. Leon was later assigned to a smaller Intelligence Reconnaissance Section, where he was trained in core surveillance and engineering skills. In August 1943, this section was named the 183rd Engineer Combat Battalion. Like most Black American servicemen and women, they would provide what one historian described as the "behind-the-scenes support and supply work that helped the Allies win the War"—opening paths through European battlefields for Allied infantry to march to Berlin.[6]

Leon's mom broke down when he enlisted. Partly at the thought of her son going to war, partly because he'd have to train in the south. He'd never been allowed to visit South Carolina—she'd tell him, "You don't know enough not to get yourself killed."[7] In the end, his training took him not just to South Carolina, but across the south to Arkansas, Georgia, Louisiana, Mississippi, and Texas. He felt the full impact of segregation for the first time on this tour. It was there in second-rate training facilities that were falling apart; in movie nights in which scenes with Black actors had been removed; and in "motivation sessions," in which white officers danced around the fact that they were asking their Black charges to fight for freedoms they didn't have. One day in Mississippi, Leon decided to visit Tougaloo College, a historically Black college north of Jackson that was only a bus ride away from his base.

The front of the bus station was beautiful, but he already knew Mississippi well enough to know that he wouldn't be allowed in that way. As he got closer, he saw other Black people going down a dingey alley at the side of the station. He followed them. It smelled of urine, and it was lined with trash. Prostitutes loitered in the shadows. Near the end of the alley, there was a line for a hidden ticket window. It was barely moving—Black customers were only served when there were no white customers inside the station. Leon patiently waited for his chance to buy a ticket. A long time passed before he got to the window. As he handed over his money, a white man snuck up behind him. "Mary," the man said to the ticket agent, "You got any n*****s that need to be cut?" He said it as if it were a joke, but Leon knew that it was a threat. He saw this man again later: he was driving the bus that he took to Tougaloo College.

Leon recorded that the buses in Mississippi all had signs that said things like, "Colored must sit at the rear."[8] This kind of signage was used to enforce segregation across the south and elsewhere in the United States. Leon found that the rear was often full, which meant that he had to stand, even if the seats at the front were empty. There were times, he remembered, when he stood for over a hundred miles, staring at empty seats that he couldn't use—"I kid you not," he wrote.[9] One day he resolved to take a seat in the white-only section. The bus driver yelled at him and called him "Boy." Leon didn't respond, which only incensed the driver further. He stopped the bus, got up from the wheel, and strode toward him. With hatred flashing in his eyes, he pointed at the sign and asked if Leon could see it. Leon lied and said that he couldn't read. The driver turned and strode back toward the wheel. At that moment, an elderly Black woman leaned over and hissed at Leon to move or be killed. He'd heard rumors about bus drivers with guns, and so he did as she said.

"I can't begin to describe how I felt," he wrote with palpable anger. "I was dressed in the uniform of an American soldier. I had taken an oath to defend these people with my life if that became necessary. What a damnable experience to have when you are 18 years of age and you have volunteered to serve your country."[10]

Leon completed his training and was sent to England in 1944. It was nearly Christmas by the time he and the 183rd Combat Engineers crossed the English Channel and went into France and then Belgium. One of their first jobs in Belgium was to rebuild a bridge in a town called Martelange. The Nazis had destroyed it in the "Battle of the Bulge"—a final, failed counteroffensive against

FIGURE 7.1 *Leon Bass. United States Holocaust Memorial Museum (Photograph Number: 08577).*

the Allied invasion of occupied Europe. It was needed to rescue American personnel from the 101st Airborne Division, who were encircled by the Nazis in another town, Bastogne. Leon and the 183rd Engineers worked on the bridge day and night in sub-zero temperatures. The Nazis had also peppered the area around it with landmines, and they were running nonstop shelling and aerial bombardments against it to try and stop the Allies' progress. Nevertheless, the 183rd Engineers reopened it in just five days. The Allies went on to rescue their soldiers and to send more troops toward Germany. In contributing to the Battle of the Bulge, Leon had contributed to what Winston Churchill described as "the greatest American battle of the War."[11] He and the rest of the 183rd Engineers progressed through Belgium and into Luxembourg, rebuilding and reopening more roads and bridges as they went. They were in a convoy of trucks headed for the German border when they drove past a unit of white American infantry soldiers. "One of the soldiers looked at me," Leon wrote, "and yelled, 'Fellas, look! We are winning the war because the n*****s are here!'"[12]

Even before this moment, Leon had been at war with himself. Surrounded by death and destruction and haunted by the possibility that he too could fall at any moment, he kept thinking back to the public water fountains in the United States that he couldn't use, and to the restaurants where he couldn't eat, and to the bus seats where he couldn't sit. Rage was beginning to surge inside him. "My country was placing me in harm's way to fight and perhaps to die to preserve all those rights and privileges every American should enjoy," he wrote. "But at the same time, my country was letting me know, in so many different ways, that it thought I was not good enough to enjoy what I was fighting for."[13]

Then, on April 12th, 1945, in Weimar, a small town in central Germany, a lieutenant approached Leon and two other men.

"Take your gear and rifles and come with me," he said. They were used to doing what they were told without question, and so they followed him onto a truck. Only once they were sitting did Leon ask where they were going.

"We're going to a concentration camp," the lieutenant said. Leon knew nothing about concentration camps—they hadn't been mentioned in training, and the lieutenant never explained why he needed to take other men with him.

The camp was Buchenwald.

By this time, the Allies had already discovered several Nazi camps, including Natzweiler in France, and Majdanek and Auschwitz in Poland. These camps were all concrete evidence of Nazi atrocities, but they were also abandoned and partially destroyed. Buchenwald, on the other hand, still held 21,000 starving prisoners, and it had crematoria, execution rooms, and a hospital used for medical experiments that were still intact. As one historian wrote, Buchenwald gave the world a chilling new glimpse into "the brutality and inhumanity inherent in the Nazi system."[14]

Buchenwald took its first prisoners on July 15th, 1937. Before then, the Nazis' camps were comparatively small, often visible to the public, and improvisatory, popping up in places like disused factories and city workhouses. They held about 5,000 prisoners in total, almost all of whom were political rivals of the Nazi Party. Together with Sachsenhausen, Buchenwald was a milestone in the evolution of the Nazi penal system. From the beginning, as one historian put it, these camps were designed to be "small cities of terror."[15] They'd have their own infrastructure, be massive but concealed, and be surrounded with barbed wire and watch towers. Buchenwald alone was on more than a hundred hectares of land and was intended to hold an initial 6,000 prisoners. In 1944, it took 100,000 prisoners from more than thirty countries. Thanks to this catastrophic overcrowding, wrote Richard Evans, "death and disease, aided by the brutality of the camp guards, became more common even than before."[16] Today, Buchenwald is perhaps most infamous for a macabre object that the Allies discovered there at liberation: a lampshade made of human skin. (For decades, it was believed that Ilse Koch, the wife of camp commandant Karl-Otto Koch, had made it. Most likely, the culprit was Erich Wagner, an SS doctor whose "research" involved skinning prisoners for their tattoos, which he believed were connected to criminality.[17])

A mass of people staggered toward Leon as he stepped through Buchenwald's entrance gate. They held onto each other to keep from falling. Some wore prisoner uniforms, others were naked. "They were just skin and bone," Leon wrote. It was obvious that they'd been "tortured, beaten, starved, and denied everything."[18] One man held up his hands to show Leon his fingers, which had webbed together with scabs and sores from malnutrition. Prisoners surrounded Leon, reaching out to touch him and trying to talk to him. He heard many languages but couldn't understand any of them. Eventually, a young Polish man who spoke English came forward. He told Leon about Buchenwald, and about the prisoner communities there: Jews, Roma and Sinti people, Jehovah's Witnesses, trade unionists, Communists, homosexuals. The list went on. Leon called it a "litany," and it seemed to be endless. "As a soldier, I had seen death and dying," he wrote, "but nothing like this."[19]

He wanted to see the rest of the camp, though. As he explained, "I needed to know more." The young man agreed to show him around. He took him to a barracks where prisoners slept. Even holding his breath, Leon could barely make it through the door. "The odor and the stench that comes from death and human waste was overwhelming," he wrote.[20] In another part of the camp, he was shown human body parts in jars. Eyes, ears, fingers, hearts, livers, kidneys, and genitalia. The Nazis had removed them from their victims in sham medical experiments. He also saw pieces of human skin and the infamous lampshade. Then he was taken to a building where prisoners had been tortured and interrogated. Torture instruments still hung on the walls, and the cement floor was still stained with blood. Finally, Leon was taken to the crematorium. Outside, a massive pile of bodies was stacked against one of its walls, four feet high and five feet wide. Inside, there were six ovens. Leon walked up to one and peered into it. Blackened remains of human skulls and rib cages were among the ashes. His stomach began to churn, and he felt himself gasping for air. He turned and hurried out of the camp. As he passed through the gates of Buchenwald, he wrote, "I realized that I was not the same anymore. Something had happened to me."[21]

*

Leon Bass was honorably discharged on his twenty-first birthday in January 1946. He decided to become a teacher, having left Germany determined to "do something to help change things" when he got home to the United States.[22] That year, he was one of a handful of Black candidates accepted into West Chester State Teachers College in Pennsylvania (now West Chester University). Here, once again, he was touched by racism. He wasn't allowed to live in the college's dormitories, and he was barred from many other areas of the campus, too. He couldn't do his student teaching at the local high school—while it had admitted a small number of Black children, the faculty was still all-white. Instead, he had to find an all-Black school where he could train separately. "At this point in my young life," he wrote, "I understood what James Baldwin meant when he said, 'To be Black and in America is to be in a constant state of rage.'"[23] Despite all these challenges, Leon graduated in 1949 and got a job at George G. Meade Elementary School, an all-Black school in Philadelphia. He would stay there for more than a decade, during which time he got married, had a family, and earned a master's degree from Temple University.

In 1968, Leon became the principal of Benjamin Franklin High School. It served deprived areas in Philadelphia, and it was home to a violent gang culture. But, over several years, and through many initiatives and careful negotiations with students, teachers, and the Board of Education, Leon transformed it. One of his initiatives, which began in the early 1970s, was for community guests to visit and meet the students. This is how Nina Kaleska, a Holocaust survivor, ended up speaking there.

Once Leon had got the class under control, Nina resumed her story. "I saw them begin to sit quietly and really listen and absorb her pain," he wrote.[24] At the end, after a thoughtful question-and-answer session, they left the classroom in silence. He could tell that she'd touched them. He stayed and talked with her, and, for the first time, he found himself opening up to someone about Buchenwald. Neither of them ever publicly shared the details of what must have been an intensely personal conversation; but Leon did write that Nina told him, "Young man, you have something to say."[25] Her encouragement was enough to convince him. "I thought to myself, 'If she can communicate with these boys and get through to them, what about me?,'" he wrote. "I wanted to let my students know where I stood. That I didn't believe that coming out and attacking your problems with a baseball bat was the right way. I wanted to be an agent of nonviolent change."[26]

Tentatively, Leon volunteered to give a 15-minute talk at Temple University, one of his alma maters. Most people in the audience were Jewish, and he was the only Black person there. His talk threaded his experiences in Buchenwald with his reflections on being asked to fight and die for a country that wouldn't let him use the same water fountains as white people. "The hate that bus driver felt in Mississippi when he told me to stand at the back of the bus was the exact same hate, just taken to another level, that had allowed Hitler to kill twelve million people. It was all about saying, 'You are not good enough.'"[27] The talk got a lot of attention, and Leon continued to share his story. Before long, he was a sought-after speaker at Holocaust memorial events. In 1981, he addressed the International Liberators' Conference in Washington, DC, an event that brought together soldiers from Allied nations who'd liberated Nazi concentration camps.[28] He gave testimony to USC Shoah, and he worked with the organization Facing History and Ourselves. The way that he melded Black and Jewish experiences wasn't always well received, and some people told him that his criticisms of the United States were unpatriotic. But he was always resolute that "it was the same hate, and it had to be exposed."[29]

Soon after the International Liberators' Conference, he got a phone call from Vancouver, Canada, inviting him to speak at a symposium on the

Holocaust there. The caller also said that someone in their community knew him.

"I do not know anyone who lives in Vancouver," Leon said.

"Well," the caller responded, "he says he knows you."

*

I tell Matthew Delmont that his book, *Half American*, had challenged everything that I was taught about the Second World War. Matthew holds multiple positions at Dartmouth College: Associate Dean of International Studies and Interdisciplinary Studies, Sherman Fairchild Distinguished Professor of History, and Chair of the Department of African American Studies. He went to St. Thomas Academy, a military school in Minnesota, before winning a Reserve Officers' Training Corps (ROTC) scholarship to go to Harvard. With his upright posture, broad shoulders, and calm but authoritative voice, he still has a military bearing.

Like most children who grew up in Europe or the United States in the late twentieth century, I was raised to see the Second World War as "the good war." The Allies' victory over the Axis was a victory for democracy over tyranny, and for freedom over racial and religious persecution. *Half American* debunks those ideas, using the "Double Victory Campaign" as the starting point for its argument. This campaign was launched by the *Pittsburgh Courier*, an African American newspaper, in 1942. The "double victory" would be victory over fascism abroad, and victory over racism at home. The latter was never achieved. Through archival records, *Half American* also shows that Black troops played a decisive but unsung part in Nazi Germany's defeat, and that "nearly everything about the War—its start and end dates, its geography, its vital military roles, its home fronts, and its international implications—looks different when seen from an African American perspective."[30] I ask Matthew, where did the idea of "the good war" come from, and why are Black soldiers like Leon Bass so poorly represented in our collective memory?

"Very few Black troops were in combat roles, and traditionally, when Americans think about the Second World War, they think about stories in which combat is foregrounded—like troops storming the beaches at Normandy. Many Black troops were in supply and logistical roles, so there are fewer Black stories like that to tell," Matthew says. Then he adds, decisively, "Another reason is just straight-out racism. Certainly, in the years immediately after the War, there were concerted efforts to cast aside or ignore Black contributions to it, and it's really a credit to Black veterans that they took it upon themselves to ensure that their stories weren't completely forgotten." (This makes me think about Leon's autobiography, which was self-published.)

One of the most striking parts of Leon's book, and of his speeches, was that he framed anti-Black racism in the United States and antisemitism in Germany as intertwined struggles. I ask Matthew, did other Black Americans look at Nazi ideology and see the reflection of Jim Crow too?

"Absolutely, absolutely," he says. "That's one thing you see so clearly when you look at Black newspapers from the 1930s. They covered the rise of Nazism so extensively, and they just—" he pauses for a moment, and then says, with emphasis, "they just *got it*, in a way that most white Americans didn't: the tenor, the violence, and where it might lead. The language they kept using was, 'This is two sides of the same coin.' Nazism in Germany is the other side of racism and Jim Crow segregation—sometimes they even called that fascism— here in the United States. Their domestic experience enabled them to analyze the European situation earlier, more clearly, and with a larger sense of urgency than a lot of other Americans."

We begin talking about Leon Bass and his story.

"One of the things that's particularly inspiring about Leon Bass's story is that he worked to build bridges with different peoples and groups," Matthew says. "That kind of collaboration takes work. In post-1960s America, different groups were moving to different places, meaning that there were fewer opportunities for cross-racial, cross-class, or cross-religious points of encounter. You didn't see a lot in the workplace or in schools, or in housing patterns. Leon Bass invested so much time in it, which was important and unique. It helped to build trust. It helped to show people that they could recognize a shared sense of humanity and a shared sense of struggle, despite having very different experiences—and without erasing their differences."

"In his autobiography, Leon writes about a person criticizing him after a Holocaust memorial event and saying that it was unpatriotic to talk about racism in the United States. So—was he unpatriotic?" I ask.

"No," Matthew says. "Patriotism and dissent have often been intertwined, particularly in the Black American experience. I'm inspired by the stories of the Black soldiers and veterans from the Second World War era—because not only did they fight for the United States, they came home and kept fighting. They wanted to make America truly a democracy, a place where anyone, regardless of their background, could be free. That meant that they had to dissent from majority opinion. Today, some people think that patriotism exists only among some people and dissent exists only among other people. But it's important to understand that someone can love their country, and sometimes that love can lead them to demand that it improve itself—that it challenge itself to be a more inclusive, and equitable, and better place."

*

Vanessa Molden is telling me the story behind the logo of The African American Military History Museum in Mississippi. It's a silhouette of a woman standing upright with her hands behind her back.

"Ruth Bailey Earl was the first African American woman to enlist from Hattiesburg, Mississippi, to serve in the Second World War," Vanessa says. She wears large eyeglasses with a thick frame, and she speaks with a flowing southern accent. "She was a nurse. But her white counterpart soldiers did not feel it was appropriate for a Black woman to give care to them. So, when she arrived in Europe, she was sent to prison-of-war camps, where she cared for

German POWs. During that time, a picture was taken of her standing with her hands behind her back—the parade rest poise—and that picture was circulated around the United States. It was used to recruit women and African Americans, and it was put on posters, because it was felt that her posture exemplified the unbreakable spirit of the African American service member. So, she's the soldier that you see in our logo," she says, before repeating her name. "Ruth Bailey Earl of Hattiesburg, Mississippi."

Vanessa has worked as The African American Military History Museum's Operations and Education Supervisor for nearly a decade. The Museum opened in 2009, and it remains the only one of its kind in the United States.

"There are museums of African American history that may focus on a particular service unit or conflict," Vanessa explains. "But none focus on the African American military experience in its totality. That's why we take our work very seriously, and why we take great pride in it. We know that we have a unique role to play in shedding light on a significant part of history that's usually not told, or that gets told inaccurately. We tell the stories, we honor the stories," she says. Then she adds, speaking louder than before, "And we tell people: *it's American history*. Whether it's good or bad, it must be told. It happened. It's the truth. In addition, the Museum is one of the only Second World War USOs of its type built for African Americans that's still in public use."

Our conversation moves to the people who visit the Museum. Vanessa says that many of them are currently servicemen and women—although it's not always easy to spot them.

"Camp Shelby is one of the largest training mobilization posts in the United States, and it's about twenty miles south of us. A lot of service members who are stationed there will come and see what we have to offer. But the people that visit the museum are diverse."

"Diverse in what sense?" I ask.

"We have historians, educators, pre-K to high school students, college students, church groups—the list goes on. Sometimes families will include a tour of the museum as part of their family reunions. We have veterans from across the country, of all branches, races, and ethnic backgrounds. And whoever they are, before we start telling our guests the story of African Americans who've served in our armed forces, we try to engage them, and to find out what their story is. That way, we can tailor their visit. Sometimes it's difficult for us even to identify that they are service members, though, because they don't want to share that part of their lives, whether it's because of trauma—or just, for whatever reason, they don't want to tell. And we honor and respect that."

These comments lead me to Leon Bass, who kept his story to himself for decades.

"Do you think that the public has understood the contribution of Black Americans like Leon to the Second World War and other conflicts?" I ask.

"No," she says. "No, the public generally does not understand or know their stories."

"Do you have a sense of why that is? A sense of why so many of them have been forgotten?"

"Well," she says, with a wry smile, "you use the word 'forgotten,' but I don't think the public ever knew that they existed. Even for those that were told, they were usually told in part, and not in full. The service that African Americans gave was simply not regarded in the same way as the service of their white counterparts."

I ask Vanessa what lessons people can learn from visiting the African American Military History Museum, beyond its stories of military history.

"That we're going to always have differences," she says, "but that our differences do not necessarily make us different." Then, just as Matthew Delmont said to me about Leon Bass, she adds, "We must focus on our shared humanity. When you come through our doors, and you hear these stories, if you take away the racial element, they were just humans who served in the military because they wanted freedom, civil rights, and political liberty."

I've reached the end of my questions. For a time, we chat about our organizations and the points of overlap between them. We get onto inquiry-based learning, and then onto the research requests that the African American Military History Museum gets from people across the United States and the world.

"We were recently contacted by a lady in the Netherlands," Vanessa says. "There are some graves there—graves of Black soldiers who fought in Second World War. She's been upkeeping them, and she stumbled upon our Museum. Now we've got a project going to try and identify the soldiers, and to learn more about their stories." She shares this matter-of-factly, as if it's an everyday request for the Museum. Maybe it is. But the thought of American soldiers serving their country only to be buried in anonymity on foreign soil has haunted me since.

*

"When you were born, Robbie?" I ask.

"I was born in 1931."

"And where were you born?"

"In Poland."

It's thanks to the Vancouver Holocaust Education Center that I'm speaking with Robbie Waisman, who was one of their founding members. When I first contacted them, they offered to put me in touch with his daughter, Arlaina. She said that she was happy to set up and facilitate a meeting, and that Robbie was determined to speak—but she also said that he had dementia. "One never knows in advance how he will be on any given day," she wrote in an email. "His long-term memory is still good. His short-term memory, not so much."

Robbie begins our conversation by telling me his story in outline. I recognize it from the interviews and the extensive video testimony that he gave to USC Shoah earlier in his life, and from his autobiography, *Boy from Buchenwald*.[31] He speaks haltingly but with purpose, and with a pronounced eastern European accent. He grew up in Skarżysko, a town between Warsaw and Krakow. The Nazis built a ghetto there in 1941, where he and his family were imprisoned. Along with his father and brothers, he was used for slave labor in a munitions factory, while his mother was murdered in the gas chambers of Treblinka. Late in 1944, with the Soviet Army approaching from the east, the surviving Jews of Skarżysko were sent to camps deeper in the Third Reich. Robbie was separated from his father and brothers and ended up in Buchenwald. The Nazis there mistook him for a political prisoner. He was also given protection by a handful of camp elders who took a shine to him. These favorable circumstances enabled him to survive until liberation—at which point he was fourteen years old. He later discovered that his father and brothers had all been murdered. Only his sister, Leah, had survived.

By early April 1945, rumors were circulating among Buchenwald's prisoners that the War would soon be over, and that the Nazis would blow up the entire camp before letting the Allies find it. One afternoon, Robbie and a friend were hiding in their barracks, debating whether they should make a run for it, or even try to get transferred to another camp, when a hush fell over Buchenwald. Robbie poked his head outside to see what was going on. A convoy of jeeps and soldiers in uniforms that he didn't recognize began to pour in through the main gate. He and his friend went to take a closer look. When Robbie saw two Black soldiers, he told his friend that they must be American. Having been born in a rural part of eastern Europe, he'd never seen a person of color before.

Robbie emigrated to Canada after the War. Despite everything he'd been through as a child, he mastered English, became an active member of his local Jewish community, and built a successful business career. Just like Leon Bass, though, he didn't discuss his story publicly. That only changed in the early

1980s, after the so-called "Keegstra Affair." James Keegstra, a social sciences teacher in Alberta, was fired and charged with hate crimes for telling his students that the world was controlled by Jewish "Illuminati," that Jewish people planned and orchestrated the Second World War, and that there was no Holocaust, among other things.[32]

"Keegstra said that the Holocaust never happened. That it was a lie," Robbie says. "And that woke me up."

Robbie began working with other survivors in Vancouver to start a Holocaust memorial organization. (In 1994, this organization became the Vancouver Holocaust Education Center, which today stands as the largest Holocaust museum in Western Canada.) Around the same time, he spotted a Second World War era photo of Leon Bass in a news article about the 1981 Liberators' Conference. More than 35 years had passed since he saw him coming into Buchenwald, but he recognized him instantly. The survivors' group decided to invite Leon to speak in Canada. For whatever reason, Robbie didn't make the call himself, but he was there, listening. The phone was passed to him when Leon said that he didn't know anyone in Vancouver. As Leon remembered this moment, "The stranger got on the telephone and in a very loud voice said, 'I know you; you were my messiah! You were my liberator!'"[33]

Robbie was waiting in Vancouver airport when Leon landed. "It was an emotional meeting for both of us, the liberated and the liberator," Leon wrote. "We hugged and kissed while the Canadian Broadcasting Company televised our meeting."[34] When it came to the event itself, Robbie gave an introduction for Leon. It was the first time that he spoke publicly about the loss of his family in the Holocaust, and "tears came down his cheeks, and his pain touched all the listeners."[35] From that day on, Leon and Robbie were partners, giving joint presentations on the Holocaust and anti-Black racism across the United States and Canada.

"We became very good friends," Robbie tells me. "And audiences were always wonderful about it. After we finished speaking, they didn't leave. They wanted to talk to us. We traveled all over the place together. We did our share."

Arlaina speaks about her memories of Leon and his wife visiting their home, and about the friendship that blossomed between Leon and her father. "They were tight," she says, raising her hand and crossing one finger over another. "For me personally," she adds, "listening to Leon—I heard him speak with my Dad many times—what really came across was that misunderstandings of difference can breed hatred and intolerance. It was quite a powerful balance."

I want to know what Robbie would like people to learn from the wealth of material about the War and the Holocaust that he and Leon created, and from their remarkable friendship.

"For all human beings, different colors shouldn't matter," he says. "And I want them to appreciate other people, and what they have at home—their families. I want them to have something meaningful in their lives. And . . ." He stops talking for a moment. I wonder if his train of thought has come to an end. Just as I'm about to jump in with a new question, he adds, stridently, "Do something good in life."

8

Emmi Bonhoeffer

The German Activist Who Helped Holocaust Survivors in the Frankfurt Auschwitz Trial

Frankfurt, 1964

Josef Piwko, a seventy-year-old former officer in the Polish Army, was testifying to the court when a prosecutor interrupted him.

"This is probably the most horrifying thing that has been said here. It is almost beyond belief. Did you really see it?" he asked.[1]

"I do not retract my testimony," Josef said firmly.

The judges pressed him. Did he realize what his testimony meant for the defendant? Was he certain that he'd told the court nothing but the truth? Once again, Josef refused to retract his testimony.

He'd been a prisoner in Auschwitz. He was hiding in some bushes near the so-called "Gypsy Camp," the camp for Roma and Sinti people, when the Nazis liquidated it. Prisoners were herded onto trucks and driven to the gas chambers. Some children, whom Josef supposed were between four and seven years old, tried to hide in their barracks. But SS men found them and dragged them outside to the defendant—Second Lieutenant Wilhelm Boger.

"Boger first trampled on them," Josef said, "then grabbed their little legs and smashed their heads against the wall."

The judges continued pressing him. No one else has told us this. Did you see it with your own eyes? Are you certain that you aren't confusing Boger with someone else? Josef became tearful as he tried to keep up with their questions. He asked for a moment to compose himself. Meanwhile, Wilhelm Boger, who was sitting on the other side of the court, angrily complained about everything that had just been said. Among the members of the public watching this trial from the gallery, a small group—most of them women—was becoming increasingly appalled by the treatment of survivors like Josef. One of those women was Emmi Bonhoeffer.

*

Emmi Delbrück was born in Berlin in 1905. She and her future husband, Klaus Bonhoeffer, were childhood sweethearts who grew up just a few minutes apart from each other. (Klaus often joked that they were already engaged as children.)

Emmi rejected nationalism, racism, and far-right politics from an early age. The Delbrück home was a cradle of critical thought, and she and her

FIGURE 8.1 *Emmi and Klaus Bonhoeffer.* Bildbiografie Dietrich Bonhoeffer. Bilder aus seinem Leben, *edited by Eberhard Bethge, Renate Bethge, and Christian Gremmels (Gütersloh: Gütersloher Verlagshaus GmbH, 2005).*

siblings were raised to think of themselves as Europeans, not Germans.² One of her favorite school teachers, a Jewish woman, was fired when a rich parent complained about a Jew working there. As late as 1989, Emmi still remembered this and said that she'd never forgiven it.³

Emmi and Klaus married in September 1929, just as the Nazis were edging toward power. While some Germans felt that Hitler should be given a chance, Klaus always said that he was "the devil himself" and that he would draw "not only Germany but all Europe into the ground."⁴ He and Emmi spent their nights talking about the rise of Nazism. What could they do about it, and who could they convince to help them? In 1935, Klaus became a corporate attorney for the aviation company Lufthansa, and in 1937, he was appointed as their General Counsel.⁵ He traveled a lot for his job, which enabled him to connect with networks of people who opposed Nazism across Germany. They included intellectuals, religious leaders, and politicians from Communists to conservatives, as well as several high-ranking military personnel.

By 1941, the Allies' bombing of German cities had intensified. Klaus and Emmi decided that she and their three children would leave Berlin for the countryside, while Klaus would stay behind and work on an ambitious plot to assassinate Hitler and overthrow the Nazi Party.⁶ This plot culminated in a dramatic attack at a conference in "The Wolf's Lair," a Nazi military headquarters in occupied Poland, on July 20th, 1944. Claus von Stauffenberg planted a bomb that detonated and killed four people, but Hitler wasn't one of them. He survived with just minor burns and burst eardrums. In the following months, the Nazis retaliated against anyone suspected of having any connection to the plot. Around 5,000 people were arrested, many of whom were executed. The most brutal executions were certainly filmed on Hitler's orders. Whether he watched the footage or not is uncertain.⁷

On September 30th, Klaus came home from work and saw a strange car parked outside his front gate. People that he didn't know were inside. Fearing the worst, he turned and went to his sister's house. He must have been seen, because the Nazis came and arrested them both the next day. His brother

Dietrich, his brothers-in-law, Rüdiger Schleicher and Justus Delbrück, and his friend Eberhard Bethge were all arrested, too. At this time, Emmi and the children were in Stawedder, a small village in northern Germany, around 200 miles from Berlin. She didn't know what to do. She wanted Klaus to know that she was trying to help, even if it wouldn't make a difference. But she also knew that he'd tell her to save herself and stay with the children. Eventually, she made a decision based on some advice that she remembered from a late uncle: "If you don't know what to do, then do what you want to do the least."[8] She told the children that their father was ill and that he needed her to take care of him. Then she went to Berlin alone.

Her first stop was the Offices of the Gestapo, where she found the man who'd arrested Klaus. He refused to tell her anything and tried to get rid of her. After a long back and forth, and determined to have the last word, she said that she felt sorry for him. When he asked why, she said, "It can't be fun to destroy happy marriages and to take fathers away from their children." Something in his demeanor changed. He stood up from his desk and offered to walk her out, and, before they parted, he shook her hand for so long that she had to pull away. Looking back on this years later, Emmi said, "When I trusted this brutal man with a human emotion, it suddenly appeared."[9]

Klaus was detained in the Moabit, a notorious prison on Lehrter Street in Berlin. In his first interrogation, he was beaten up before having his hands shackled behind his back. Except for eating and going to the bathroom, they stayed shackled like this for two weeks before his second interrogation. But he didn't speak. It was only in his third interrogation, when the Nazis said that they'd shoot Emmi and send their children to a Nazi training school, that Klaus finally broke. According to Emmi, he signed a bogus confession without even reading it. On February 2nd, 1945, the so-called "People's Court"—a kangaroo court that the Nazis used for show trials—sentenced him to death. His sentence was the last one that the People's Court passed. The next day, an Allied bombing raid destroyed it, killing the judge who presided over it. Even the People's Court had procedures, and its destruction stopped them in their tracks. Klaus had been given an unexpected reprieve. By this time, the Allies were closing on Berlin, and everyone knew that the War would soon be over. Klaus and Emmi both allowed themselves to hope. There was a chance that he'd get out alive. On April 22nd, one of her cousins—a shrewd and resourceful man who'd already used bribery to get several people out of prison—said that he'd bring Klaus home the next day. Overjoyed, she prepared their house for a party, decorating it with flowers and using the last of her rations to bake a cake.

Then, she waited.

Others who'd been arrested began trickling home, but there was no sign of Klaus. More days passed. Hitler killed himself, Nazi Germany collapsed, and, like many Berliners, Emmi began to starve. She scavenged scraps from abandoned homes and fields and cut the flesh off dead horses to survive. All the while, she chased every rumor that she heard about Klaus. She searched for him in Berlin's prisons, and she watched mass graves being exhumed around the city. Eventually, a friend of a friend who'd been detained with him told her the terrible truth. On the night of April 22nd–23rd, just before his rescuer was meant to arrive, he was taken from his cell and shot on Hitler's personal orders, along with around fifteen others. Their bodies were thrown into a bomb crater in a nearby cemetery.

After a memorial for Klaus on June 11th, Emmi wrote, "I had nothing more to do except get back to the children. My husband was dead, my house was wrecked—what could I do in Berlin?"[10]

But the children were hundreds of miles away, and Germany was in ruins. To make the journey, Emmi teamed up with Charlotte Dieck and Lotti Diem, two other women who were also trying to reunite with their loved ones. They took a train as far northeast as it went. At the end of the line, they hopped onto bikes and rode through the countryside. On June 20th, after nine days on the road, they arrived in Neu Kaliss, a village about halfway between Berlin and Stawedder. The Elde, a river that separated the British and Soviet zones of occupation, cut through it. The Soviets had already placed tight restrictions on who and what could cross from one side of the river to the other.

Emmi knew that Viktor Bausch, a businessman who'd operated in the same resistance circles as Klaus, lived in Neu Kaliss. The three women showed up on his doorstep at 6:30 am. In war-torn Germany, unexpected knocks at strange times of day were always cause for alarm. But Viktor trusted his instincts and answered regardless. When he heard the name "Bonhoeffer," his face lit up, and he and his wife agreed to house them. The next morning, Viktor's secretary took them on a long walk down the Elde. It was about 65 feet wide, 15 feet wider than an NBA court. It was also heavily patrolled by Soviet soldiers. Even so, Emmi wrote in her diary, "I just can't get my head around the idea that this ridiculous obstacle"—a large river being used by opposing military powers to divide occupied territory—"should be insurmountable."[11] At first, she tried to make the crossing legally. On June 22nd, she found the Soviet commander in charge of the area and asked permission to go to the other side. Even though he recognized her maiden name—he'd studied her father's work on military history—he refused to let her go.

On June 23rd, Emmi, Charlotte, and Lotti left their bicycles at Viktor's house and walked about half an hour out of the village, taking the bare minimum of belongings with them. They found a quieter area of the Elde and spread out to reduce their chances of getting caught. But no sooner than Emmi set foot on the riverbank, Soviet soldiers emerged from their hiding places and stopped her from getting in the water. She tried to act innocent and friendly, asking if it would be okay just to go for a swim. They didn't buy it. They arrested her and soon caught her friends as well. All three were taken for questioning. For hours, they were locked in a basement with no light, a thick stench, and nowhere to sit. Two men, both soaking wet, had also been thrown in this basement, having been caught trying to make the same crossing. Emmi had heard disturbing rumors about the Soviets' treatment of prisoners, women especially. "Our biggest fear was hearing the dreaded call, 'Woman, come!', which we had heard so often in Berlin," she wrote. "It had driven many acquaintances of ours to reach for a razor blade in despair."[12]

When the time finally came for questioning, Emmi, Charlotte, and Lotti all stuck to the same simple story. They'd only wanted to have a quick swim before another day of looking for work. Supported by a witness statement from Viktor's wife, they were released—but they were also ordered to leave Neu Kaliss and go back to Berlin before dawn the next day. For Charlotte and Lotti, this close shave was enough to kill their resolve. They did as they were told. But Emmi had no intention of going back. "Not for anything in the world," she wrote. "What would I do in Berlin? My children were consumed with anxiety about me, and I about them."[13] She pretended to be too ill to travel and went back to Viktor's house, where she made a new plan to cross the river.

On the night of June 28th, she went to the Elde with Hanno, Viktor's seventeen-year-old nephew, who sometimes swam underwater from one side of the river to the other if an urgent message had to be delivered. She hid in the doorway of a factory that backed on to the river while he started talking to a Soviet soldier patrolling the area. He soon managed to distract the soldier, who turned and walked away. Then he gave a hand signal to Emmi behind his back, and she knew that it was time to go. With a small bundle of belongings wrapped in a moth bag and balanced on a wooden board, she went to the riverbank and "slid into the water like an eel."[14] No sooner than she was in, another Soviet soldier appeared on a nearby bridge. Hanno turned and went to distract him, while Emmi did her best to make as few ripples as possible. She kept swimming until she got to a small island midway through the river. It was covered with stinging nettles. She crawled through them on her belly, dragging her bag behind her, until she reached the water again. When finally she got to the other side, she felt like she "could have kissed the ground—it was the ground where my children were."[15] But her joy was short-lived. As she stood up, she made eye contact with an English soldier who'd been watching her make the crossing through his binoculars. For a long, painful moment, she thought that she'd be arrested again. Instead, he applauded, offered to help carry her backpack, and showed her to the nearest village. She slept there for a few hours before hitting the road again, taking a military car to Hamburg, then a vegetable truck to Lübeck, then hitchhiking the rest of the way to Stawedder. The final steps of this epic journey brought her to the house where her children were staying. Physically and emotionally exhausted, she peered in through a window and saw the three of them sitting around a dining table. "At that point," Emmi wrote, "I couldn't hold back anymore . . . Then came the question, 'Where's Papa?' That was the most dreadful moment, the one that I had feared more than any other. I answered: 'Papa is far ahead of us. . . .'"[16]

*

In March 1958, a letter from an imprisoned convict was delivered to public prosecutors in Stuttgart. It gave a tip-off about Wilhelm Boger, who'd allegedly worked for the SS in Auschwitz. They started a half-hearted investigation that spent months drifting aimlessly through different legal authorities. Later that year, in another German city over a hundred miles away, a group of office workers was caught singing antisemitic songs at a Christmas party. Their office managed reparation money for victims of the Nazis. Among the people who read the scandalized reports about this in the local newspaper was Emil Wulkan, an Auschwitz survivor whose own claims for reparations had gone nowhere. He contacted the newspaper and asked if they could help him. When a journalist responded, he revealed that he had a stash of incriminating documents about Auschwitz that he'd rescued from a burning building at the end of the War. The journalist persuaded him to give them to the authorities, and in January 1959, they landed on the desk of Fritz Bauer in Frankfurt.

Fritz Bauer was one of the most formidable public prosecutors in Germany. He was also a Jew who believed that his country hadn't fully confronted its past.

He used Emil's documents to claim jurisdiction over every ongoing Auschwitz investigation, including the one into Wilhelm Boger, which he soon remolded into something much bigger: an investigation that would put Auschwitz itself on trial. In the past, wrote Ronen Steinke, one of Bauer's biographers, trials involving Auschwitz had only revealed parts of the truth. Bauer was determined to tell "the historical truth of Auschwitz as a whole."[17] Over the next two years, he built a team of prosecutors that interviewed more than a thousand Auschwitz survivors.[18] They also investigated nearly 300 people suspected of committing crimes in the camp. These suspects were divided into groups and subgroups and eventually whittled down to a core of just over twenty defendants. On December 20th, 1963, proceedings against them began in the so-called Frankfurt Auschwitz Trial.

*

On April 23rd, 1964, Emmi Bonhoeffer's friend Ursula Wirth told her about a newspaper article on the treatment of survivors at the Frankfurt Auschwitz Trial. "While other foreign guests were being met at the airport, ushered to their hotels, and catered to with all kinds of ado [. . .] no-one was paying the least attention to those who were arriving, summoned from all over the world, and especially from Poland, to testify as witnesses," Emmi wrote in a letter to another friend.[19]

Emmi and Ursula wanted to do something to help the witnesses. They knew that they couldn't do it alone, though, and so they began working with two other friends, Barbara Minssen and Hilde Müller. The four of them asked the public prosecutor's office for permission to contact the witnesses. They got an enthusiastic response: as well as being given the witnesses' addresses, they were also given schedules for the trial hearings. They were even given some funding.[20] Ultimately, they built a partnership with The Red Cross in Frankfurt. As an international, apolitical organization, it gave their group a degree of legitimacy that it didn't have before. More and more people began to offer help. The group expected all new recruits to be able to form personal relationships quickly, to show sympathy in ways that were sincere and spontaneous, and to be sensitive enough to recognize each individual witness' needs. They also had to be willing to drop personal commitments at a moment's notice. "Above all," Barbara wrote, "those who take on this task must be deeply convinced of the necessity of these trials, and they must feel responsible for what has happened."[21]

The group began just by attending the trial—three times a week, from 8:30 a.m. until 4:30 p.m. each time. Emmi believed it was essential to understand the facts and the atmosphere in which the witnesses had to testify. "If you want to help someone," she wrote, "you must first understand what they're going through."[22] Once they were all more familiar with the trial, they began mailing a letter to introduce themselves to the witnesses. It said:

> We've learned that we may soon be able to welcome you to Frankfurt. We imagine that this journey will be a great emotional burden for you, and that it will be twice as difficult for you to find your way in unfamiliar circumstances. We'd therefore like to offer our help. There's a German Red Cross office on Platform 1 at the Frankfurt am Main train station, which is open day and night. Our staff can advise and support you in every way. In addition, citizens of Frankfurt have offered to be at your disposal if you have any desire to see more of the city or its surroundings. It goes without saying that these are people who, through their own experiences, have a full understanding of your situation.[23]

No one had ever tried to help Holocaust survivors like this before. There wasn't a playbook for what Emmi's group was doing, and, at first, they made mistakes. One woman was hosting some Polish survivors before they testified. She didn't want to seem indifferent or disinterested, and she wanted her children to learn something from them—so she asked them a few questions about Auschwitz. Once they started talking about it, they couldn't stop, and then they couldn't sleep. The next day, one of them collapsed in the stand.[24]

The group soon refined their process. They met the witnesses when they got to Frankfurt at the train station or the airport, then took them straight to a hotel. They always made sure that a hotel room had been reserved in advance. Each witness was given a folder with brochures about Frankfurt, a map, and free tickets for the theater and the zoo. If the witness wanted, someone from the group would stay with them overnight. Otherwise, they'd be met the next morning and taken to the court. Then they were kept company until it was their turn to testify. Someone from the group would eat lunch with them, and they would help them to collect their travel expenses. If the witness wanted, after they'd testified, they arranged walks, sightseeing tours, and similar activities. They helped religious witnesses to observe the sabbath by connecting them with Jewish families in Frankfurt. And their efforts didn't end with the trial. In some cases, they helped with medical needs, ensuring that the witnesses got the prescriptions that they needed. People from impoverished countries in the Eastern Bloc got hearing aids, eyeglasses, and other things that they couldn't find at home. Sometimes the group called in favors. Other times, they stretched the law. Ursula Wirth said that "for years, we were able to send a woman with a lung disease the best medicine, which she couldn't get in Poland. Only secretly through illegal channels, of course—hidden in packages somehow, or via travelers."[25] In other cases, they fundraised to help the survivors realize their career goals and to rebuild their lives.[26] The group never described any of this as "care work." They didn't want anyone to compare it to things like making food in an old folks' home or to accommodating refugees. They *were* giving the witnesses food and accommodation—but they saw it less as "care work," more as a type of help that was fundamentally "mental-spiritual."[27] One member said that their goal was to build "fraternal solidarity" with the witnesses.[28]

The group didn't keep detailed records of their work, but Barbara Minssen thought that they ended up helping around 170 people.[29] They also inspired similar groups to form across Germany. In 1965, Alfons Erb, the president of Pax Christi, an international Catholic peace movement, wrote to Emmi to thank her for everything that she'd done for the survivors in the Frankfurt Auschwitz Trial. "You have truly served peace with your actions," he said. He also laid out his plans for his own organization to work with other witnesses in other upcoming war crimes trials. "We have seen how important and good it is for these deeply wounded people to find individuals in the country where they were mistreated who can earn their trust and make peace with them," he said.[30]

As for Wilhelm Boger, he was sentenced to life in prison after being found guilty of murdering at least 114 people in Auschwitz and of being an accessory to the murder of at least a thousand more. He died behind bars in 1970.

*

"I came to the study of Nazi Germany partially for personal reasons," Devin Pendas tells me. He teaches history at Boston College, and he's the type of professor that every student hopes for: knowledgeable, able to explain complex ideas clearly, and never far away from a good pun or joke. He's a leading expert on the history of legal trials, and on German war crimes trials in particular. "My mom's side of the family is German," he continues, "and they all emigrated to the United States around 1900. My grandfather was a great guy, but he was reactionary as hell. He got badly injured in the Second World War fighting against the Nazis. For the luck of the draw, though . . . " He allows the sentence to ebb to an unspoken conclusion. "As an undergraduate, I became interested in perpetrator psychology and motivation. Then, in grad school, I became interested in the postwar era. The way I articulate it these days—the question that interests me—is: 'Now what?' This horrible thing has happened, the War is over, now what do we do about it?"

Devin was the co-editor of a book about historic trials called *Political Trials in Theory and History*.[31] Its case studies run from the trial of Socrates in Athens nearly two and a half thousand years ago, to the United States' monopoly trial against Microsoft at the dawn of the twenty-first century. I ask what special ingredients a trial needs to become historic.

"You have to think about it in two dimensions," Devin says. "The first dimension is the crime that's being adjudicated. Perhaps it's something that is itself historic, it changed society somehow. You can also have historic trials that don't adjudicate historic crimes. The OJ Simpson trial is a classic example. A man murdering his ex-wife is, sadly, not a historic crime. That trial *became* historic because of the way it embedded itself in American culture—which leads us to the second dimension. A trial can be historic, even when the crime isn't, because it touches a cultural nerve, either domestically or globally. But truly historic trials, like the Frankfurt Auschwitz Trial," he says, pausing for a short moment, "have both dimensions. The crime of adjudication is of manifest historical significance, and it's approached in a way that touches cultural nerves inside and outside the courtroom."

We begin talking about the witnesses in Frankfurt, and how they were treated. Devin succinctly underlines just how difficult it was for them.

"They were asked to go to Germany and to talk about how Germans did all these terrible things. And they were asked to talk about it in German, in a room full of Germans, with the men who tortured and tormented them sitting across the courtroom glaring at them the whole time. There was very little understanding of how difficult it would be for them to testify under such circumstances. In terms of mental health support, this was early. There were really no provisions at all, and it quickly became apparent that the court's setup wouldn't work. I mean, it's psychologically *horrible* for the witnesses. And that wasn't all. Witnesses in a criminal trial are cross-examined. The defense's job is to say, 'There are reasons to doubt your testimony'. Now imagine that you're a Holocaust survivor. You're saying something like, 'Yes, this is what happened;

and yes, that's the man, I saw him drag my children to the gas chamber'. Then an attorney says something like, 'Were you wearing your glasses? Are you sure it was on the 22nd? Because records show that your train arrived on the 23rd. Are you lying?' I can only imagine how horrifying that would be. And that's the attorneys who are just doing their job. Some attorneys in the Frankfurt Auschwitz Trial were clearly Nazi sympathizers, one or two were flat-out Nazis. Their cross-examination was much more hostile, sometimes antisemitic. And so, you know," he says, taking a breath, "what a nightmare for the survivors."

Emmi Bonhoeffer was aware of all this, even if the court wasn't. On May 3rd, 1964, she wrote to a friend, saying that it simply hadn't occurred to anyone "to consider what it must mean to these people twenty years after their horrible ordeal [. . .] so suddenly to have to unearth it all once more, recall it to the last detail, and afterward have to be alone with it, alone here in this country that they had known at its worst."[32] In another letter written later that year, she said that one survivor had told her that they wouldn't have come if they'd have known that they'd be interrogated by someone defending the person who'd abused them.[33]

As our conversation comes to an end, I ask Devin what he thinks we can learn from the legacy of the Frankfurt Auschwitz Trial today.

"Two things come to mind," he says. "First, as I always tell my students, nobody ever thinks that they're the bad guy. Political evil is usually done by people who think that they're doing the right thing. So, it's imperative to step back from your own life and your own politics, and to interrogate your sense of what's good—because it's not self-evident. Second, don't assume that you alone know right from wrong, and that anyone who disagrees with you can only be doing so out of malicious motives. The world is a complicated place. It's important that you recognize that *you* are as vulnerable to making bad decisions, and to supporting evil in the name of what you think is good, as anybody else."

*

There's a wealth of literature about Dietrich Bonhoeffer, Klaus's brother. He was a Christian theologian, a prolific writer, and a member of anti-Nazi resistance circles who was imprisoned in 1943 and eventually murdered in the Flossenbürg concentration camp in 1945. He's been described as "one of the most celebrated and debated theologians of our age," and as "a figure of global importance."[34] His relatives haven't been written about as much—and Emmi, hardly at all. Dr. Jutta Koslowski is a leading expert on the Bonhoeffer family, having written the first biography of Klaus, and having edited collections of previously unpublished works by other family members. But she tells me, with an unassuming laugh, that her interest in them began by coincidence.

"I went to a conference of the International Bonhoeffer Society," she says. "The keynote speaker canceled suddenly. A scholar called Ferdinand Schlingensiepen jumped in—he knew so much, he didn't even need to prepare! It was extremely impressive. I chatted with him after his keynote, and then, after the conference, I read his biography of Dietrich Bonhoeffer. It made many references to the memoirs of Dietrich's younger sister, Susanne, which were unpublished. Later, I wrote to Professor Schlingensiepen and said, 'This material is so interesting, would it be possible for me to see it?' But he told me that the manuscript had been dispersed. So, I began detective work to restore it. It took more than two years, but in the end I was successful. The memoirs contained 600 pages, and I found 599 of them—in attics, in boxes, and in archives. It was published in 2018. Then people started writing to me with new information, which led to some follow-up research projects. The most important was my book about Klaus—Susanne and Dietrich's older brother, and Emmi Bonhoeffer's husband."[35]

We discuss Dietrich's prominence in Holocaust education and remembrance today. "If we could get in a time machine and visit the 1940s," I ask, "and meet the Bonhoeffer family, and tell them that, in the twenty-first century, one of them is remembered more prominently than the others—would it surprise them?"

"Yes, it would," she says. "The very first publications, which came out in 1946, were about Klaus and Dietrich, in that order. Klaus was older, and he was even more outspoken in his opposition to the Nazi regime. He was the one who encouraged Dietrich to join them!"

"Why then has it played out in the way that it has?"

"I think it's coincidental. What do you need to become so prominent?" she asks, rhetorically. "A good biographer." She goes on to tell me about Eberhard Bethge, a close friend of Dietrich's who created an archive of material about him, and who wrote a massive biography about him that's still in print today. "He really was an ideal custodian for this huge archive which he created. The others lacked such a biographer. My personal opinion," she continues, "is that we should talk about the family as a whole—as a system, a subversive system that made opposition to Hitler possible."

"What was it about this family that made them into a 'subversive system' during the Nazi regime? Why them and not another family?" I ask.

"I'm convinced, from my research, that the factors existed long before the Nazi regime emerged. What were they?" she asks, rhetorically again. Then she says, slowly, "Education, combined with liberalism, togetherness, and a critical spirit. There's one example that I like to give in my lectures. The Bonhoeffers had a family resort in a rural area in Germany. They went there often. They spent their time together, they clung to each other in a special way. Father and mother, they traveled on the train in first class. The eight children, they traveled in fourth class. Not because their parents couldn't afford to put them in first class. In their parents' opinion, traveling in fourth class was part of a child's education. So, they're on this train, and it's cold, everybody's shivering. There was an old peasant woman who was very stubborn, and who refused to close the window. In that moment, Klaus stood up and said that he was an eye doctor. He looked at this woman's eyes, and said, 'It's very dangerous for you to sit by an open window, your eyes are about to be infected, so I advise you strongly to close it.' And she closed it. A small example, but it shows something important," she says, smiling widely. "Klaus wasn't going to travel with the window open. He and his siblings didn't confront the woman, they didn't say 'we're the majority, you have to close it.' They looked for a way around her. They were used to behaving as dissidents."

Our conversation moves to Emmi Bonhoeffer and to the fact that so little has been written about her, especially in English. Listening to Jutta speak, it occurs to me that little has been written about the women who resisted Nazism in general. I ask her, is it possible that Emmi is less familiar to us today simply because she was a woman?

"Yes," she says, decisively. "Society as a whole has diminished female contributions to resistance against Nazism. This is why I highlight the role of the female family members in my research and publications. They deserve it, and it's been noticed too little until now. This is not only true for Emmi Bonhoeffer, but for a brilliant woman like Christine von Dohnanyi, who was really very active together with her husband, Hans. Her contribution has also been marginalized." (Christine was one of Klaus's and Dietrich's sisters, and Hans was a jurist and another member of the resistance. He was murdered in the Sachsenhausen concentration camp in April 1945, having been detained there since April 1943.) "And, of course," Jutta continues, "Susanne Bonhoeffer. Of the eight Bonhoeffer children, it was she who wrote a vast biography—not of one person specifically, but of the whole family. Why was it not published, why was it almost lost in attics and boxes? I think it's partly because she was a woman."

Our conversation pulls toward Emmi's legacy and its meaning for today. Jutta is clear that she'd have no interest in being memorialized and that she'd tell us that learning about resistance in the past is only worthwhile if it leads to action in the present. "Emmi might ask: 'Why are you celebrating me? Are you trying to hide away from the challenges of your own time? What are you doing *now*?'"

*

Was it a form of resistance for Emmi Bonhoeffer and others to help the Holocaust survivors who testified at the Frankfurt Auschwitz Trial?

She only ever described her actions in terms of responsibility. "I always felt," she said in an interview, "that we have a duty to the survivors of the Holocaust to listen carefully to what they have to say and at least try to share their suffering in retrospect."[36]

Devin Pendas had another way to describe her actions, though, and it stuck with me.

"One thing that's central to the Holocaust is the dehumanization of the Jewish victims," he said. "Alon Confino out at UMass Amherst wrote an interesting book a few years back called *A World Without Jews*, in which he made a point that I think is crucial: the Nazis wanted not just to kill Jews, but to kill *Jewishness*. They wanted to kill everything that they associated with the so-called 'Jewish spirit,' which was everything that they hated. Cosmopolitanism, liberalism, pluralism, and so on. In the Frankfurt Auschwitz Trial, Emmi Bonhoeffer was trying to forge a human connection with Jewish survivors, as a German. She was trying to claw back the dehumanization and the destruction of Jewishness in the Holocaust. And so, I think that in that regard, it was an important form of resistance—and atonement."

9

Gitta Sereny

The Journalist Who Interviewed a Nazi Mass Murderer

June 27th, 1971, Düsseldorf, Germany

It was nearly 5:00 p.m. when the interview finally ended. Franz Stangl helped the journalist to collect her papers, and he insisted on carrying their coffee cups when they left the makeshift interview room. As usual, he was dressed smartly in a button-down shirt and gray flannels, and he seemed cheerful as they made their way through the prison's corridors. They met a guard who opened a security door to the outside world to let the journalist leave. Franz inhaled deeply.

"Nice air," he said. "Let me smell it for a moment." Then he joked with the guard, "I'll be glad to see the lady out."

The journalist walked through the security door. Behind her, buttons were pressed, and the door slammed shut. She turned and looked at Franz through the little window embedded in it. She waved him goodbye, and he smiled and waved back.

Within twenty-four hours, he would be found dead in his cell.[1]

*

Even as a child, Gitta Sereny regularly traveled across Europe alone. She was born in Vienna in 1921 but attended boarding school in England, and she went back and forth between them at the start and end of semesters and holidays. At the end of summer 1934, she was on a train that broke down in Nuremberg, a city in southern Germany. With its quaint medieval buildings and a storied history that went back to the Roman Empire, it was easy for far-right nationalists to imagine that Nuremberg represented a glorious past that had been lost in the modern age. The Nazis indulged in nostalgia for this imagined past almost obsessively. This is one reason that they held their annual Party rally in Nuremberg. The rallies were enormous events, filled with speeches, military parades, and heavily choreographed ceremonies and rituals. They were meant to cement Hitler's leadership by showing the world that he had unified Germany.[2]

The 1934 Rally was in full swing when Gitta's train broke down. People from a charity—Gitta thought it was the Red Cross, or maybe a Nazi equivalent—volunteered to look after her. They kept her entertained by taking her to the rally. Looking back nearly sixty years later, she recalled feeling overcome. She was too young to understand the speeches, but the synchronized marching, the smiling faces, and the spectacular lighting were all very exciting. "One moment I was enraptured, glued to my seat," she wrote. "The next, I was standing up, shouting with joy along with thousands of others."[3]

The next time Gitta saw a big Nazi event was in March 1938, by which time she was seventeen. It was in Vienna, in the shadows of the imposing Hotel Imperial. Germany had just incorporated Austria into its territory—an event known as the *Anschluss*, or the "annexation." This created an entity that the Nazis called "Greater Germany" and narrowly avoided war between the two countries.[4] Gitta joined the crowds waiting to hear Hitler speak on the Imperial's balcony. Again, later in life, the first thing that she recalled was excitement. She wondered, "What was it that made me join the mindless chorus around me, welcoming this almost motionless figure to our Vienna?

What was it in him that drew us? What was it in us—in me too, that day—that allowed ourselves to be drawn?"[5]

The next day, Gitta was out walking with a friend when they saw some men in brown uniforms and swastika armbands. They surrounded a dozen people who were on their knees, scrubbing the sidewalk with toothbrushes. Onlookers laughed at the spectacle. As they got closer, Gitta spotted her family doctor, who was Jewish, among the people with toothbrushes. Incensed, she and her friend confronted the uniformed men. "It was extraordinary," she wrote. "Within two minutes, the jeering crowd had dispersed, the brown guards had gone, the 'street cleaners' had melted away."[6]

But the victory was small and short-lived. Gitta's mother was engaged to Ludwig von Mises, a famous Austrian-Jewish economist who taught in Switzerland and who was high on the Nazis' wanted list. Soon after the *Anschluss*, she heard a rumor that the Nazis would tempt him back to Austria by taking her hostage. It was enough to convince her to flee with Gitta and join her fiancé abroad. Gitta was a rebellious teenager, though, and she was unhappy in Switzerland. She soon decided to run away—first to London, then Paris. For months, she lived a bohemian life on the road, taking charge of her own education by going to lectures at the Sorbonne and to classical music festivals, enrolling in typing classes, and talking her way into mentorships with actors and actresses.

To a point, her mother and stepfather tolerated these adventures. But they ordered her to return to Switzerland when Germany invaded Poland in 1939. She refused. Then they tried to force her hand by cutting off their financial support. It didn't work. Gitta was content being penniless, sleeping on friends' sofas and walking everywhere. She was a teenager in love, she wrote, "with an English boy, with France, and with my studies. Nothing would have made me leave."[7] In the end, the feud resolved itself. Five months into 1940, Germany invaded and occupied France, and so Gitta was stuck there. Her mother and stepfather fled Europe for the United States without her.

Gitta spent the early years of the War in Villandry, a village near the city of Tours, where she volunteered as a nurse and worked for a charity that helped abandoned children. She also got involved in minor acts of resistance, like hiding downed British airmen. After one such incident—in which she disguised an airman as a nurse to help him to evade capture—a friendly German officer showed up at her home just before dawn to warn her that she'd be arrested later that day. With little more than soap, a toothbrush, and a change of clothes, she went to Paris, then Marseilles, and then the Pyrenees, where she hiked over the mountains into Spain. After cutting across Spain into Portugal, she took a ship from Lisbon to New York. For the next few years, she traveled the United States, lecturing about the War in schools and colleges, and making anti-Nazi propaganda for the Office of War Information. She returned to Europe when the War was coming to an end, working with the United Nations to help relocate displaced children.

In the decades after 1945, Gitta married the American photographer Donald Honeyman, had a son and a daughter, and wrote a novel called *The Medallion*. She and her young family moved back and forth between the United States, England, and France before settling in London in the 1960s. It was only in 1966, by which time she was in her mid-40s, that Gitta decided to become a journalist. Her first articles were for small publications, but they caught the attention of John Anstey, the editor of a prestigious British journal called the *Daily Telegraph Magazine*. He wasted no time striking a deal for her to write for the *Magazine* exclusively.

Gitta went on to become one of the most influential journalists of the twentieth century. One of her biggest stories appeared in the *Magazine* in 1971. She'd been going back and forth to Germany for years, sometimes on assignment, sometimes at her own expense, to attend the trials of Nazi war criminals. She explained her reason for attending them bluntly: "I needed to know."[8] They frustrated her. For one thing, she thought that they weren't adding anything to what was already known about the Holocaust. She wanted deeper questions to be asked about the perpetrators. Had something in their personalities or their inner lives made them commit such terrible crimes? The men and women concerned gave no clue from the docks. They were "similarly primitive, and of similarly limited intelligence," she wrote.⁹ The premise of the trials also frustrated her. As she wrote in a letter of 1975, "It is virtually impossible to judge men correctly on the basis of isolated acts. Both the courts and the public see such people only within a context of isolated criminal acts, and not of their whole lives."¹⁰ She began to dream about uncovering a perpetrator who was less "primitive"—someone who'd been involved in the Holocaust, but who was also intelligent, willing to talk, and capable of self-reflection.

Gradually, Gitta developed this dream into an idea. She made herself known to the people spearheading the trials, building a network of contacts and becoming friendly with famous German prosecutors like Alfred Spiess (who led a trial of SS men from Treblinka) and Adalbert Rückerl (who ran The Central Office of the State Justice Administrations for the Investigation of National Socialist Crimes, or "The Central Office" for short). Alfred Spiess telephoned her in London one day in October 1970. He believed he'd found the person she was after.

That person was Franz Stangl, whom Alfred was prosecuting in Düsseldorf. Franz had worked on the Nazis' euthanasia program, which murdered tens of thousands of disabled German citizens and emaciated concentration camp inmates. He then became an extermination camp commandant, first in Sobibor and then Treblinka. At the end of the War, he fled to Brazil via Syria, where the Jewish Nazi hunter Simon Wiesenthal tracked him down in 1967. He was arrested and extradited to Germany, where he was charged with co-responsibility for the murders of 400,000 people in Treblinka alone.¹¹ (Over his career, though, the total number of men, women, and children murdered would certainly have been close to a million.)

The day after this phone call, Gitta flew to Düsseldorf to see Franz in court for herself. Her first impression was that he was "more complex, more open, serious and even sad than any of the others." He struck her as "the only man with such a horrific record who appeared to manifest a semblance of conscience."[12] She flew to Düsseldorf again in December for the end of the trial (he was found guilty and sentenced to life imprisonment). This time, she met his wife, Thea, who'd come from Brazil to support him. She took the chance to share her ideas with someone who had direct access to him. On the morning that she was due to leave for England, Thea came back to her with word that her husband was willing to be interviewed. Gitta still had to convince the German judiciary, the Düsseldorf prison authorities, and John Anstey and the *Daily Telegraph Magazine* about the project, though. Winter passed and a new year began before she met Franz for the first time on the morning of Friday, April 2nd, 1971.

The prison governor brought her to a room deep inside the prison. Normally, it was used by lawyers to gather their thoughts. Barred windows looked out onto the prison yard. It was dreary, but Gitta thought that it was perfect for what she wanted to do. It was "impersonal, neutral, with nothing in it to please or edify, but equally nothing to distract the eye or the mind."[13] When Franz arrived, he bowed his head toward the governor, shook his hand, and made small talk about the prison classes that he planned to take that spring. By this time, he'd been locked up for four years, mostly in solitary confinement. He wore a white button-down shirt and a necktie, and he spoke quietly and courteously. Gitta sensed something imposing about him. It felt like he was controlling everything that was happening. But as soon as the prison governor left them alone, his composure vanished.

He started complaining about his trial. Gitta sat back and let him speak. She'd already heard these complaints, from him and from other Nazi war criminals besides. "He had done nothing wrong," she wrote contemptuously. "There had always been others above him; he had never done anything but obey orders; he had never hurt a single human being. What had happened was a tragedy of war."[14] He'd already appealed his life sentence, and, as he droned on, Gitta realized that he'd only agreed to meet because he thought that she might be able to help him somehow.

Two and a half hours passed. Before they stopped for a lunch break, Gitta put her cards on the table. She told Franz that she wasn't interested in the rights and wrongs of what he'd done. What she wanted was for him to *really* talk to her. "To tell me about himself as a child, a boy, a youth, a man; to tell me about his father, his mother, his friends, his wife and his children; tell me not what he did or did not do but what he loved and what he hated and what he felt."[15] She told him that she was passionately anti-Nazi, but she also promised to record everything that he said faithfully. Her goal, she said, was simply to try and understand him.

A guard knocked on the door to take Franz away for lunch. Without a word, he got up, bowed to Gitta, and left. She wasn't sure if she'd see him again, and he was gone for hours. When he did finally come back, he'd taken off his necktie and loosened the top button of his shirt.

"I've thought about what you said," he began, his voice sounding unsteady. "I hadn't understood before—I hadn't understood what you wanted. I think I understand now . . . I want to do it. I want to try to do it . . . ."[16]

For seventy hours spread across two weeks, Gitta interviewed Franz Stangl about his life. They revealed his emotional distance from his father, a military man who'd beat him to a pulp for even small misdemeanors. They also revealed his love of the zither, an ancient European musical instrument; his brief career as a master-weaver, which he quit for fear that factory work was harming his health; and his shifting, complicated relationship with Catholicism. Gitta recorded his evasiveness whenever they spoke about the most appalling parts of his past, and the changes in the sound of his voice and the look on his face. Throughout, Franz insisted that he'd never hurt anyone personally and that he'd never known what his orders involved until it was too late. Gitta put up with these lies and half-truths because she wasn't trying to find out what he'd done. That was for the courts. She was trying to find out who he was, and how he'd ended up running two Nazi extermination camps.

The most extraordinary part of their interviews came right at the end.

Gitta brought their final conversation back to an outrageous suggestion that Franz had made in an earlier one: that perhaps there was divine purpose to the Holocaust, because it gave the Jews "an enormous jolt to pull them together, to create a people, to identify themselves with each other."[17] She asked him if he thought that this "jolt" had come from God. He said that it had and that God had been in Treblinka. "Otherwise," he asked, rhetorically, "how could it have happened?"[18] At this point, their conversation fell into a rabbit-hole about the nature of God. When Franz suggested that "God" might be a goal for humans to try and achieve, Gitta sensed an opportunity. In his case, she said, that goal should be to seek truth. He asked what she meant.

"Face up to yourself," she said. "Perhaps as a start, just about what you have been trying to do in these past weeks."

With these words, Franz must have realized that every effort he'd made to deceive or mislead Gitta had failed. But he reiterated that his conscience was clear. This time, Gitta didn't push back. For a moment, he carried on muttering about never having hurt anyone, and then silence filled the room.

"But I was there," he said. "So yes, in reality I share the guilt . . . Because my guilt . . . My guilt . . . Only now in these talks . . . Now that I have talked about it all for the first time . . . ." He stopped. Then he concluded, quietly and half-heartedly, "My guilt is that I am still here. That is my guilt."[19]

He died nineteen hours later. At first, Gitta assumed that he'd taken his own life, but a postmortem showed he'd had a heart attack. His heart was weak, and most likely he would have died around this time no matter what. "But I think he died when he did because he had finally, however briefly, faced himself and told the truth," she wrote later. At the end of their interviews, for one short moment, "he became the man he should have been."[20]

Gitta carried on researching Franz Stangl's life and crimes after her 1971 article for the *Daily Telegraph Magazine* was published. She went to Rome to dig into the Catholic Church's role in helping him escape from Europe. She traveled to Brazil to spend time with Thea Stangl and their family. And she tracked down and interviewed other Nazi war criminals who'd worked with Franz in Treblinka. Her research culminated in an extraordinary book called *Into That Darkness*, which came out in 1974.

*

The Central Office, whose investigations led to many of the trials that Gitta attended in the 1960s and 1970s, still exists today. Their team is much smaller than it was then, but they continue to hunt Nazi war criminals with the same vigor. I ask Thomas Will, the Head of the Office and a man who's sometimes called "The Last Nazi Hunter," how they find people who've been on the run for decades. He wears a crisp suit, and thick, black-framed glasses sit comfortably on his face.

"We decide to investigate a certain concentration camp," he tells me. "Then we try to find as many of the people who worked there as guards, or as secretaries, or so on, as we can. The next step is to go and search for them. If we find one alive, then we try to get as much information as possible about him or her. When were they on duty, and what happened during that time? Was there a phase of systematic killing—and if so, how did it unfold? Once we've put all that information together, we send it to a competent public prosecutor's office. Then the prosecutor decides whether to pursue or close the case. They may come to the suspect's house with a warrant or interview them first," he says, matter-of-factly.

He goes on to tell me about the multitude of sources that The Central Office uses to uncover their targets, from genealogy archives to medical records. I ask him what he thinks of Gitta Sereny's project to understand Franz Stangl, which was deeply personal—especially compared to his process, which sounds so impersonal. He says that he hasn't read her book. There are many other books and movies that try to understand Nazi war criminals, I say. Does he think that such projects can ever be successful?

"Not every effort will fail. Ordinary men can become killers, there is a lot written about that," he says. Then he adds, decisively, "But it's not my work. I'm only interested in the crimes that people have committed. Not in why they committed them. Determining their motives is a matter for the criminal trial."

In the 1970s, in the Düsseldorf prison where Franz Stangl was held, Gitta met members of staff who said that it was pointless to chase Nazi war criminals so long after their crimes had been committed.[21] I ask Thomas if he still encounters that attitude today.

"In Germany, we have . . . " he says. Then he sighs heavily and rebegins. "Among the public, we hear voices that ask, 'Why are you still chasing these people?' There are others who say, 'You must always go on.' But for us, there is no decision to make. The question isn't The Central Office's question. It's not possible for us to put the matter down—to not investigate—because the law is very clear. It says that there is no statute of limitations on these crimes. Despite old age, if someone is healthy enough, then he or she must be prosecuted. If we find someone who is suspected of murder, then we must conduct a criminal investigation. More often than not, our work isn't successful. It takes us a long time, and we have many failures. And from one year to the next, success becomes harder to find."

"What, then, keeps you going?" I ask.

"We all are clear that we want to complete our mission as soon as possible. These crimes were so incredible . . . ," he says. "It is our duty to the victims."

Before we close our conversation, I ask Thomas what he thinks people can learn from The Central Office and its legacy for today.

"We hope to interest as many people as possible in our message that criminal prosecution must never stop for someone who has committed mass crimes, not for their whole life," he says. Then he looks at me despondently. The question seems to have taken him by surprise. "But I don't know how it's possible for us to be heard in these times when people will not hear. There are more and more authoritarian states now, a lot of them. Think about Russia.

Think about the populists and the far right in Europe and worldwide, too—it's growing. If people don't want to hear, then they will not understand, and they will not learn."

*

Mandy Honeyman is Gitta Sereny's daughter. She's easy to talk to—so much so that I'm comfortable sharing that I sometimes find her mom's books frustrating to read. Gitta lets Franz Stangl tell lies until it feels like his lies are radiating off the page. She explains her reasons for this in *Into That Darkness*: it was "essential to let him develop his story in his own way, without showing obvious skepticism or interrupting with critical comments."[22]

I tell Mandy that I feel like her mom must have been a patient person.

"I don't know . . . ," she says, slowly and thoughtfully. "I don't know if I would say that. She had a method, and I don't know if 'patient' is the word that I'd apply to it. It's more that she knew what her objective was."

She goes on to describe her mom's method for interviewing Franz. The interviews weren't recorded. The portable cassette recorder was still relatively new technology in the early 1970s, and Gitta didn't have one. Besides, she'd learned journalism the old-fashioned way.

"She wrote notes in journalists' notepads," Mandy explains. "And she had piles and piles and piles of them, and they were unreadable, except by her. She wrote notes continuously while people were talking to her. You have to try and imagine that. She didn't just sit back and listen, knowing that everything was being recorded and that she could go back to it later. She had to write it all down."

I asked Mandy what her family's home life was like while her mom was interviewing Franz. Did the project cast a shadow over them?

"Really, the impact was after," Mandy says. She goes on to speak candidly about some of the challenges that she faced in her childhood and her teenage years, during which time it sounds like her relationship with her mom was often strained. "She became very ill. It went on for about two years, one thing straight after another. It was awful for her. And I think it was all about the stress from Stangl. It was *awful*," she says again, with emphasis.

"Does that mean that she carried something of him with her, even after he was dead?" I ask.

"I think that the best way for me to answer is to say that she hadn't trained as a psychotherapist, even though she'd read a lot. If you haven't trained, and if you don't go to psychotherapy yourself, then you have no way of being able to disperse horrible stories from your mind."

Gitta died in 2012, a little over a decade ago. The world has changed so much since then. I'm curious to know what she might have made of contemporary political and social events, like the rise of far-right populism in Europe and the United States, or the war in Ukraine.

"Well, a lot of things happened in her lifetime, too," Mandy says. "We had several nuclear crises and the Vietnam War. So, I can't—I find—I think . . . " The sentence falls apart. She pauses for a moment before starting over, speaking more slowly and solemnly than before. "I can't answer for her, and it would be wrong for me to try and answer for her—to put words in her mouth."

This throws me. I tell Mandy that I'd planned for my final question to be about the advice that her mom might have given for the partisan times that we're living in right now. "Let me try and rephrase it," I say. But I'm thinking on the spot, and I can only come up with a watered-down version. "What advice did she have for people generally?"

"Well, she didn't dole out advice unless people came to her asking for it," she says. It feels like our interview is going to fizzle out. But after a short pause, Mandy adds, "I think it would be to read, actually." Now she picks up a pen from her desk and waves it enthusiastically, like a conductor with a baton. "You know what, that would be it! I don't mind putting that in her mouth, I really don't. I can't imagine that she wouldn't come up with reading as the *best* solution for understanding life." She leans into the word *best* in a way that sounds wistful, even longing. "To read what people have written—and not in 280 characters of a single Tweet. To really read books, you know? To read books and poems as a way of understanding, deeply, the experiences that other people have had. I'm pretty sure that she'd say that happily," she concludes. "And I can't think of anything else that any of us can say to try and help people make their own minds up, or to grasp the difference between what's true and what isn't."

*

Dorothy Rabinowitz, a Pulitzer Prize–winning journalist, thought that *Into That Darkness* was a failure.[23] Gitta had revealed nothing about Franz Stangl's character, she said, and it was naïve for her to think that she could do so by interviewing him, his family, and other former Nazis. His confession was hollow. He knew that Gitta expected it of him, and so he forced himself to cough up a few words. Worst of all, Gitta had befriended him, losing sight of his hundreds of thousands of victims in the process.

Even if you don't feel as strongly as Rabinowitz, *Into That Darkness* does pose some difficult questions. Did Franz really die because he confessed his guilt, for example? Gitta wants us to think so. If you examine his last words closely, though, he doesn't really confess anything. He doesn't admit that he was wrong, and he only says that he *shares* the guilt—which quietly pushes it toward other people. Even if his confession were more convincing, the idea of any confession being terrible enough to kill the confessor sounds like something from a fairytale. But Gitta believed it could happen. "No man who *actually participated* in such events," she wrote about the Holocaust, "can concede guilt [. . .] and consent to remain alive."[24] Writing in 1978 about the ill health of Albert Hartl, another Nazi war criminal, she said, "Too extraordinary, how many men connected with these awful events, are dying of heart failure!"[25] Others, like Rabinowitz, questioned whether her relationship with Franz had spilled over into friendship, and whether she'd enabled him to blindside her.

At first, such questions got under Gitta's skin. She kept reviews of *Into That Darkness*, sometimes underlining parts that irritated her, scribbling question marks, or writing things in the margins, like "out of context," "non sequitur," and "not true."[26] She also worried that extracts printed in newspapers had "misrepresented the meaning of the book as a whole."[27]

As she got older, though, she seems to have become more willing to engage with her critics. Speaking in 2000, by which time she was nearly eighty, she said that it would have been impossible to pursue her goals without building relationships with her interviewees. Lies were inevitable. The interviewee had been lying to themselves for years, after all, because "the truth cannot be faced, cannot be lived with." It was up to the interviewer to recognize and deal with them. She also admitted that interviewing someone like Franz was "difficult, demanding, and immensely costly, to yourself and to others"—nudging, perhaps, at the strains in her family life that Mandy had told me about.[28]

In her obituary for Gitta, Diana Athill, her friend and the editor of *Into That Darkness*, said that "when she probed darkness, it was in order to illuminate."[29] Many others have tackled the Holocaust with the same goal. But *Into That Darkness* is unique because it was the only time that a journalist interviewed a Holocaust perpetrator with the aim of understanding them.

Was that an act of resistance?

On October 4th, 1943, Heinrich Himmler spoke at a meeting of senior SS men in Posen, a city in Nazi-occupied Poland. For the first time, he openly addressed the extermination of the Jews. Two days later, he gave a similar speech in the same city, this time for administrative and political leaders. Germany's War effort was collapsing, and Himmler had become both hellbent on expanding the genocide of Europe's Jews and jittery enough to start spreading incrimination for it. "We can mention it now among ourselves quite openly and yet we shall never talk about it in public," he told his audience. "I'm referring to the evacuation of the Jews, the extermination of the Jewish people. Most of you will know what it is like to see 100 corpses lying side by side or 500 or 1,000 of them." Then he ordered, "This is an unwritten—never to be written—and yet glorious page in our history."[30] In his analysis of these speeches, Richard Evans concluded that Himmler and the Nazis believed that the Holocaust was a crime. A necessary crime, perhaps, but still a crime. "Why, otherwise," he asked, "would the history books to be written in the future never dare to mention it?"[31]

Himmler is said to have called Franz Stangl "the best camp commandant in Poland."[32] He was dependable, loyal, and obedient. Decades after the War, though, he was persuaded to help an attempt to write the "page of history" that Himmler had forbidden. Maybe Gitta's methods were questionable, and maybe her ambition exceeded her reach—and maybe her end product was flawed because of it. Yet, she successfully cast light on events that the Nazis intended to remain forever in darkness. In this sense, she'd resisted them.

10

Shoah

The People Who Got Nazi War Criminals to Discuss Their Crimes on Camera

Altötting, Germany, Early 1976

Claude Lanzmann took a deep breath and knocked on the door.[1] The house was nestled in an unassuming Bavarian town, with cobbled roads, statues of military heroes, and churches with ornate steeples. Claude and his research assistant had traveled across Europe to get here.

After a long moment, Franz Suchomel answered the door. He was in his late sixties, but his flabby jowls and his pronounced wheezing made him seem older. Quickly, Claude explained why they'd come.

"I've read the evidence that you gave at the Treblinka trial," he said, forcing himself to speak in broken, heavily accented German. He was almost fluent, but pretending otherwise was an important part of his act. "I have not come out of a psychological interest, nor am I a judge, a prosecutor, or a Nazi-hunter. You have nothing to fear from me."

Claude was still getting his project off the ground, but he could already sense when his subjects were uncomfortable. Like many in his position, the sound of the unknown knock at his door had terrified Franz since 1945. Claude swallowed his disgust. For his plan to work, he knew that he had to manipulate his target by appealing to his vanity, and by making him feel like a great teacher. He kept talking, subordinating himself and offering Franz a role in history.

"I believe that we desperately need your help," Claude said. "We don't know how to raise our children. The young generations of Jews do not understand how this immeasurable catastrophe could have happened, how six million of our people could have allowed themselves to be massacred without response." It seemed to be working. Franz was clearly tempted by the idea of being a lead witness. "I would also consider it appropriate," Claude added, trying to seal the deal, "that you be reimbursed for your time and effort." Franz's eyes whirled with greed. The offer of money was enough to convince him to start talking.

Claude paid several visits to Altötting over the coming weeks, crossing Europe by train and plane, with one goal: to get Franz Suchomel to appear in his film. Finally, at a meeting that stretched through the night and close to dawn, Franz agreed. There was no time to waste. Claude rushed back to Paris to assemble a camera crew. But a telegram was waiting for him when he arrived—Franz had immediately changed his mind. Apparently, his son-in-law had threatened to divorce his daughter over the film. Claude went to Altötting again. Franz opened the door, instinctively took a step back, and pressed a finger to his lips, telling Claude to keep quiet. It was too late, though. Franz's son-in-law—a large, muscular man in his early thirties—had already realized who was there. He barreled down the stairs and shoved Claude into the street.

"Out! Away!" he yelled, in a thick Bavarian accent. "Leave us in peace! Enough of this old shit!" The two men tussled with Franz trying to get between them, and with his wife and daughter screaming from upstairs. When they finally broke up, Franz begged Claude to leave.

Claude did as he was asked and returned to Paris, downcast but still determined. If he was ever going to get Franz to talk on camera about the hundreds of thousands of people that he'd helped to murder, then he'd have to find another way.

*

Claude Lanzmann's first film, *Israel Why*, premiered at the New York Film Festival in 1973. Critics praised it for being emotive without being openly political. It was "subjective reportage" that assembled a "great chorus of voices," and that sank into the contradictions of its subject, revealing "a society that seethes with as much complexity as America itself."[2]

Soon after, Alouph Hareven, an Israeli government official, commissioned Claude to make a film about the Holocaust. He wanted a complete account of the event from a Jewish perspective—the first film of its kind. "I felt as though I was standing at the foot of some petrifying, unchartered north face, the summit obscured by thick clouds," Claude wrote. "I steeled myself, telling myself that what was being offered was a unique opportunity, one that would require the greatest courage, and that it would be thankless and cowardly not to seize that opportunity with both hands."[3]

Claude was born to a secular Jewish family in a Parisian suburb in 1925. He joined the French resistance against the Nazis as an older teenager, and he studied and taught philosophy in Germany after the War. He went on to become a freelance writer and journalist, eventually serving as the editor of *Les Temps Modernes* (*Modern Times*)—a high-end literary magazine founded by existentialist philosophers including Jean-Paul Sartre and Simone de Beauvoir.

None of Claude's family died in the Holocaust, and before Hareven's commission, all he knew about it was a statistic: six million Jews had been murdered.[4] He spent the summer of 1973 assessing his own ignorance, as he put it.[5] This meant reading as much about the Holocaust as possible. He focused on two studies in particular: Gerald Reitlinger's *The Final Solution* and Raul Hilberg's *The Destruction of the European Jews*. He also began going through the archives of Yad Vashem, the Holocaust museum in Jerusalem, where he was given a tiny office to conduct research. On a set of whiteboards, he drew, erased, and redrew his discoveries, trying to find ways of tying them together. He also employed research assistants—people who were multilingual, and who could help him to conduct interviews in Israel, Germany, Poland, the United States, and elsewhere.

He still didn't have a concept for the film by the end of summer. He'd made some important decisions about it, though. Perpetrators would be interviewed, as well as victims and bystanders, and archive footage of the Nazis' ghettos and camps wouldn't be used. Another important decision came deep in the fall. By then, Claude had met with Holocaust survivors. He felt that he'd heard the same stories over and again. "The arrests, the roundings up, the traps, the 'transports,' the overcrowding, the stench, the thirst, the hunger, the deception, the violence, the selection process on arrival at the camps"—the list went on. It was horrifying and it was important, but he also found it repetitive. The core of the Holocaust was missing: "the gas chambers, death in the gas chambers, from which no one had returned to report."[6]

Some survivors had seen people going into the gas chambers. Others had been forced to remove the corpses from them and to clean them before the next group of victims came. But everyone who went in had died. Claude came to see this as a terrible paradox: no one could describe the experience of the Holocaust's main method of killing. What it was like when the doors closed or when the fumes filled the air, or when the crowds struggled. Such details were irretrievably lost. He described this conclusion in almost religious terms. The Holocaust was fundamentally unknowable. It couldn't be explained, interpreted, or understood. It was a "relentless black sun" that had "erected a ring of fire around itself."[7] By the end of 1973, he'd resolved that the subject of his film would be "death itself, death rather than survival," and it would attempt to "take the place of the non-existent images of death in the gas chambers."⁸ Put another way, he deliberately set himself an impossible task.

This decision shaped the way that he spoke to his interviewees, especially the Jewish survivors and non-Jewish bystanders. In a documentary, an interview usually helps us to get to know the interviewee. They tell us about themselves and offer their opinions on whatever the documentary is about. Claude wanted the dead to speak through his interviewees. This meant that he didn't ask them about their own life stories. Instead, he tried to trigger what he called a "reawakening," making them forget about themselves to focus on "the fate of the people as a whole."⁹ To do this, he'd learn as much as possible about them beforehand so that he could dive into their account at any moment. He described this as "coming to their aid"—but he didn't mean it in the sense of helping them. He meant "having the necessary confidence and the knowledge to dare to interrogate, interrupt, get the speaker back on track, [and] ask the right questions at the right time."¹⁰

He also constructed careful types of staging for his interviews. In a sense, to catalyze their "reawakening," his interviewees had to become actors. "They recount their own history," he explained. "But just retelling it is not enough. They had to act it out, that is, they had to give themselves over to it."¹¹ When he interviewed Abraham Bomba, for example—a survivor who'd been forced to cut women's hair before they went into the gas chambers in Treblinka—he did it in a barber's shop. Surrounded by mirrors and chattering customers, Abraham pretends to give a man a haircut while Claude questions him. The setting brings Abraham as close as he could get to reliving his traumatic experiences, which in turn brings him closer to sharing things that he'd never shared before. In another interview, Henrik Gawkowski, a Polish train driver who took Jewish people to their deaths in Treblinka, is made to drive the same train into the same station. According to one film scholar, many of Claude's interviews have an "almost sadistic insistence" about them.¹²

His interviews with perpetrators were slightly different. Just finding a way to film them was an almost insurmountable challenge. At first, he telephoned and told them up front that he was making a film about the Holocaust. "I rarely got the chance to say any more," he wrote. Either they hung up, or they said that he had the wrong number or the wrong person. Sometimes, he heard a spouse in the background telling them to get off the phone.[13] He eventually gave up telephoning and started appearing at homes unannounced. He and his research assistants traveled, often intercontinentally, and to remote, rural locations, without being certain that they even had the right address. If the door wasn't opened on the first try, they'd begin a stakeout, sometimes waiting for hours on end. If it was opened, the conversation usually ended as soon as Claude introduced himself. "To the Germans," he explained, "my name was obviously Jewish."[14] He concluded that he wouldn't get anywhere by being honest. As he put it, "I had to learn to deceive the deceivers."[15]

Claude created a cast of fake identities and a fake historical research center, complete with fake letterhead on fancy paper and envelopes. He even got hold of a fake passport. He learned how to use hidden cameras, which were cutting-edge technology at the time. And he began lying to perpetrators about the purpose of his film. One, Walter Stier, had worked for the German railway (*Reichsbahn*) in the Nazi era. He was responsible for sending Jewish people to extermination camps across Europe. One day, out of the blue, he got a letter from Professor Laborde (a fake identity), telling him that a research assistant at his institute (which didn't exist), Dr. Claude-Marie Sorel (another fake identity), would soon call him and ask for an interview about "the extraordinary way in which the *Reichsbahn* managed to carry out its mission during the War."[16] Everything about the letter was meant to flatter Stier. He was also offered money for his time, and, of course, the letter didn't mention Jews.[17] With a handful of perpetrators, this approach worked. Coupled with an interview technique that Claude described as cold and calm, and by asking questions that didn't seem to have any moral implications, he managed to get Nazi war criminals—Walter Stier included—to describe their actions in unprecedented levels of detail. Some of them were filmed covertly, without their knowledge.

Claude spent two years doing preliminary research. Another four years were spent filming nearly 230 hours of footage in places around the world. Editing began in fall 1979. It was an arduous process that took a further five years.[18] The final product was an epic nine-and-a-half-hour film called *Shoah*, the Hebrew term for the Holocaust. Claude always insisted that it wasn't a documentary. Documentaries entertain us by telling us a story. Voiceovers and dramatic music guide us through that story, while archive footage and reenactments help us to imagine the past. *Shoah* does none of this. For Claude, it was a "true construction of memory."[19] It premiered at the Théâtre de l'Empire in Paris in April 1985 to universal acclaim.

In later life, Claude gained a reputation for chastising anyone who tried to explain, represent, or understand the Holocaust. He accused Steven Spielberg of transgressing and violating it in *Schindler's List*, for example, and of making a cartoon version of it.[20] The journalist Ron Rosenbaum described Claude's response to his seminal book *Explaining Hitler* as "combative," "intemperate," "belligerent," and "annoyed."[21] In one notorious incident in 1990, Claude publicly attacked an Auschwitz survivor, Louis Micheels, at a Yale panel session. Micheels was promoting a short film about Eduard Wirths, an SS doctor in Auschwitz. Claude was appalled by its attempt to explain Wirths' humanity. Among other things, he implied that Micheels was trying to rehabilitate the Nazis. Micheels was "taken aback" and worried that Claude—a tall, physically imposing man who was fond of leather jackets—was so apoplectic "that he might have been about to break down."[22] In 1988, Claude summed up his beliefs in a short, manifesto-like piece called "Here There Is No Why." Among other things, he said that it was "obscene" to ask why the Jews were murdered, and that any project that tried to understand the Holocaust was an "absolute obscenity."[23]

In 2020, over thirty years after *Shoah* was released, and two years after Claude died, a collection of photos that belonged to Johann Niemann, the deputy commandant of Sobibor, was donated to the United States Holocaust Memorial Museum. Before this, there were hardly any known photos of the camp. I sometimes wonder what Claude would have made of them. Perhaps he would have described them as another terrible paradox. Such crisp, clear images of such an unimaginable place ought to be impossible. But within that paradox, there was truth: because even though he was keen on photography and happy to break SS rules about using cameras (they were prohibited in extermination camps), Niemann didn't photograph the gas chambers.[24] The whole collection has just one photo in which historians think that part of the gas chambers' roof *may* be visible.[25] It's grainy and far off in the distance, and it's obscured by dense shrubbery. It would be easy to say that Niemann simply knew better than to create evidence of his crimes. For Claude, though, the photo would surely have felt like vindication—proof that the "relentless black sun" at the heart of the Holocaust was impossible to represent in an image, and proof that documents alone could never have the power of eyewitness testimony.

*

"It's a difficult time," Corinna Coulmas says, solemnly. We've been talking about the rise of populism, and about antisemitism appearing on both the far left and the far right of the contemporary political spectrum. Corinna is seventy-five years old when we speak, but she still leads a busy life in France, working in the performing arts, writing poetry and prose, and teaching children about history and Jewish culture. She has a short, bohemian haircut, and she wears a white woolen sweater that looks understated and glamorous at the same time. She asks, "Do you mind if I eat some chocolate, because—" But she bursts out laughing before she can finish the question.

Corinna had been set to begin a career as a professor. Her doctoral thesis (which was on the history and identity of Jewish communities in Florence) so impressed her examiners that they asked her to join the faculty of the Sorbonne on the spot.

FIGURE 10.1 *Corrina Coulmas. Corinna Coulmas.*

"And then," she says, with a broad smile, "I met Claude Lanzmann." Their paths crossed by chance in the early 1970s at a house party in Paris. Lanzmann had just released *Pourquoi Israel*, which Corinna had seen and loved.

"When he entered the room, I thought, 'well, this man, I have to speak to him.'" There's more laughter as she tells me that she introduced herself in Hebrew, not knowing that he couldn't speak it. (Corinna is a polyglot, fluent in nearly half-a-dozen languages; she speaks English with a cultured European accent that's somewhere between German and French.) She must have made a good impression. A couple of days later, having found out where she lived, Lanzmann showed up at her door unannounced. He told her that he'd recently accepted a commission to make a film about the Holocaust.

"I want to make it at the height of the event—*at the height of the event*," he stressed. He paused before asking, "Do you understand what I mean?" (*Shoah* doesn't cover the story of Hitler's life or the Nazis' rise to power. It starts with Chelmno, the prototype extermination camp.) Corinna tells me that she replied, "'I think I do.' And he said, 'Okay. Let go of everything and start reading about the Holocaust.' And I did that."

At first, I was skeptical about this conversation having been so short and simple. But the more I learned about Lanzmann, the more it seemed that he must have had the charisma of a religious leader; the ability to convince people to change their life's trajectory with one well-spoken sentence, one penetrating stare. Corinna worked on the film for its entire run. She looks to the distance and says, quietly, "It was a long time in my life that I consecrated to the Holocaust. There was no weekend, there was no vacation, there was nothing. It was just plunging into sadness and living with it all the time." "Consecration" was just one of the religious words that came into our conversation. For Corinna, there was something sacred about *Shoah*.

Together with Lanzmann, she worked in archives across Europe and Israel, finding information on potential interviewees. I wondered how they made their decision to look for Nazi war criminals as well as victims and bystanders.

"We didn't even ask ourselves the question," Corinna says. "For us, it was clear that we had to interview from different points of view." Franz Suchomel was one of the first criminals that they contacted. He'd been a guard at Treblinka, and in 1965 he was sentenced to seven years in prison as an accessory to the murder of nearly one million Jewish people. "He'd made a big statement in his trial, we'd read it, and so he was an obvious one to find. But he was only one of 150." Corinna was talking about the long list of Nazi war criminals that they made—150 of them that they would try to convince to be interviewed.

I ask how she managed the first encounter when she visited these people at their homes. How do you begin to convince a Nazi war criminal to appear in a film about the Holocaust? She answers immediately, "You must not come there as Corinna Coulmas." I can imagine her saying this to herself in the mirror every morning before the day began. "You must not say what an impact the Holocaust had on you, or 'my God, how could you?'—no. If you talk about how terrible it was, you won't get anything. But the interviewee also has to understand immediately that you know *everything*. The place, the event, the people. You know everything that happened. And, just as important, you don't judge."

A handful of the 150 criminals agreed to speak with Lanzmann, but not to be filmed. These interviews were filmed with a hidden camera called a "paluche." It sent images to recording equipment being managed by a secret film crew in a van parked nearby.

"I put the paluche in a handbag, and I'd decorated the handbag with silver paper circles," Corinna says. "One circle was in front of the lens. The camera could see through it—but when you looked at the handbag, you only saw the circle. I put the handbag on my knees and directed it at the interviewee. Then Claude started to talk, and I had to find a pretext to go outside and ask the crew if it was working. It was a very poor technique, nothing like today. Then I had to come back and put the handbag back in exactly the same place. It was not easy," she says, laughing. "You know, not to be seen. Especially not by the wives, who observed everything, and who were always wary when their husbands started to speak. They often told me to put the bag down."

I'd read in Lanzmann's autobiography that one of these risky hidden camera interviews went badly wrong. It was with Heinz Schubert, a commander of the *Einsatzgruppen*, the "Special Task Forces" that murdered millions of Jewish people across Poland and Russia in mass shootings. He

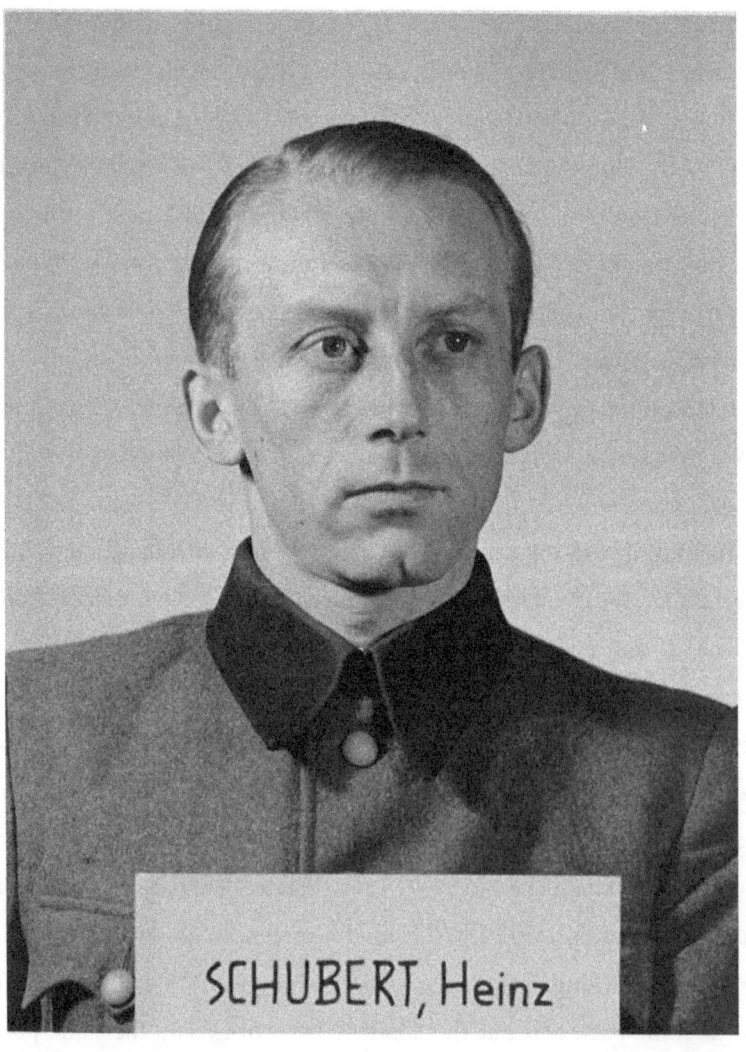

FIGURE 10.2 *Heinz Schubert. United States Holocaust Memorial Museum.*

was sentenced to death in 1948, but in 1951, this was commuted to ten years in prison. Corinna's first memory of the interview isn't how it ended, but how it began.

"Schubert had started to speak," she says lugubriously, perhaps thinking about testimony that had slipped through their fingers. "It was a very hot day, and the crew had taken off their headphones. Schubert's son walked past the van and heard the voice of his father. So, he came in, and –" she makes fists and shakes them above her head. "He was a young man, and strong, and so on. It wasn't very comfortable." This is an understatement. According to Lanzmann's autobiography, Schubert's son and three other young men stormed into the house, battered him and Corinna, and stole the paluche. Bruised and bloodied, they managed to escape to their car, but the Schuberts and their neighbors formed a blockade at the end of the street to stop them from getting away. "The van with the crew left when they saw what happened. Claude was very brave," Corinna says. "He just put the gas pedal down, and well . . . " The memory of the people in the blockade scattering as their car hurtled toward them makes her break into laughter again.

Believing themselves to be the victims of a crime, the Schuberts reported Lanzmann and his entourage to the police, and they turned the paluche over as evidence. Legal concerns aside, the film's shoestring budget meant that they couldn't afford to lose this expensive piece of equipment. By luck, they came up against a sympathetic public prosecutor who gave it back to them. They admitted to him that they'd broken the law, but they also told him who Schubert was and why they were trying to film him. It must have been a difficult landscape to negotiate, I say, never knowing who might beat you up and who might be an ally.

"Of course," Corinna says. "But that was our everyday life, for a long time."

It was easier to get Franz Suchomel to speak. He made it known that he could be bought. For a fee, he'd give an interview—but only for an audio recording, and on condition of anonymity. Lanzmann accepted these terms and secretly broke them to film over four-and-a-half hours of footage with him.

"But it wasn't only about money," Corinna says. "We unlocked the lock that was always there. And you see that violence is *always* connected with lying. You never have violent people who just say, 'Well, I'm violent, and I like. . .' no, no, no," she says, with a few shakes of the head. "They will always find a reason. Suchomel speaks as if he didn't do anything, as if he were just a bystander. He's very much at ease with his role. This man, who said to the women he guided to the gas chambers, 'Quick, little ladies, because the water will get cold!'—you would never think, seeing his interview, that he was concerned. And the *way* he talks," she says. There's a hint of surprise in her voice, even now. "He's actually eager to give all this information! What I realized is that it was never their responsibility. Either, like Suchomel, they said, 'It was terrible, but I was forced to do it,' or they said, 'I didn't know.' But they knew. By 1944, the whole world knew."

"Did you ever meet anyone who didn't fit into either of those categories?" I ask.

"Just one," she says. "Eugen Steimle."

Like Schubert, Steimle was an *Einsatzgruppen* commander. They were unable to film him, but Corinna remembers her initial meeting with him well. Steimle's mug shot, taken for the Nuremberg Trials, shows a man with a fastidiously neat side-parting, an angry glare, and round eyeglasses that go against his square features. He's almost turning his head away from the camera, and his lips are curled downward, giving him a condescending look.

"He was a cultivated bourgeois, a man with a lot of books who was a teacher afterward. I mean, when I think about somebody like that . . . " she trails off for a moment, perhaps picturing Steimle in a classroom full of children. "He received me with tea and chocolate, and he took me from the high: 'Mademoiselle, you're young, you can't understand,' and so on. He always used the German word *Partisanenbekämpfung*"—*crackdown on partisans.*

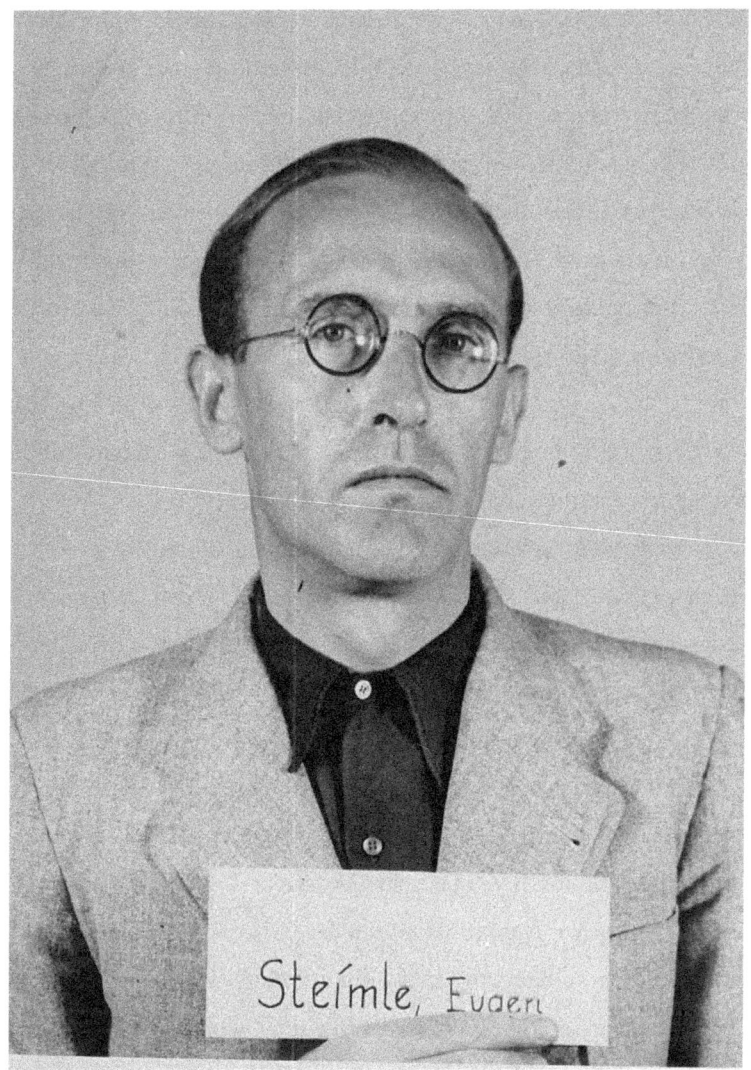

FIGURE 10.3 *Eugen Steimle. United States Holocaust Memorial Museum.*

Something about this word must have triggered Corinna into forgetting her own rules. She tells me that it made her ask him a pointed question about the children who were shot by his troops. But it didn't move him. He just said, "Mademoiselle, you can't imagine how much harm a child can do to the German Army."

"The whole interview was . . . He remained locked. He was a good man who led the crackdown on partisans. There were no Jews, there was no Final Solution, there were no *Einsatzgruppen*. He only tried to help the German Army. He impressed me," she says, "by the negation of everything. He was at ease, totally at ease. The others, when they were lying—which was almost all of them—you could see it. There was some doubt, some place in their mind where they knew. But not him. He was in one piece. He believed in what he said."

"And he showed no trace of antisemitism or belief in Nazism?"

"Nothing, no! It was just a total falsification of history, and he believed it so completely that he was happy. I came with all this evidence about the *Einsatzgruppen*, but there was no way to reach him."

"And no suggestion that he regretted the outcome of the War?"

"No. He wouldn't say that he would be delighted if Hitler had won, not at all. He was just a good German who tried to help the Army. That was his discourse."

This story reveals something important. According to its own leaders, Nazism needs courageous followers to bring the ideology into reality. "Do you believe that fate has chosen you to proclaim the truth?" Hitler asks in *My Struggle*. "If so, then do it [. . .] Replace the flaws of the present with your vision of a better future. If you lack the courage to do this, or if your idea of a better future is unclear even to you, then leave the matter alone altogether."[26] But Nazis only act on their "vision of a better future" when they're certain that they'll come out on top. They're remarkably quick to abandon their supposed vision as soon as the odds are against them. Such cowardice is at the heart of Nazism and all far-right extremism, and it can make it difficult to resist effectively. This may explain why *Shoah* is surrounded by so many ethical questions. Was it acceptable to deceive interviewees and film them covertly, for example? Was it acceptable for a young person like Corinna to endanger herself by coming face-to-face with war criminals?

"We knew that it was the very last moment," she says, with an urgency that still sounds fresh. "Soon it would be finished, there would be no more real testimonies. So, all means were good. All means. We didn't care." Now her voice becomes gruff. She moves to pour herself another cup of tea and reiterates that, when it came to the deception, the lies, and the hidden camera, only one question mattered: will it work? "We didn't have the slightest problem of consciousness about it—no, no," she says. "I was young and alone, so of course it was sometimes frightening. But I didn't think about the legal ramifications. For me, whatever happened, it was really a mission."

I wonder if any of the perpetrators ever tried to sue them after *Shoah* came out, or even just complained. "None of them did anything," Corinna says, with the deep, powerful tone of someone who feels vindicated. "The film came out: nothing. Not one of them." I ask her what that tells us. She thinks about it for a moment and says, "That they wanted to be forgotten."

As our conversation comes to a close, I ask Corinna what she'd like people to take away from *Shoah* when they see it for the first time today.

"To understand that you have a choice," she says. "But that you must choose. At every moment you must choose. Not just when the situation becomes dramatic, but all the time." Then she sits up in her chair a little, and adds, "And when you take the first step of resistance, it can easily become more."

Before we say goodbye, she tells me to rewatch *Shoah*, but to look at it like I'd look at a painting. There's authenticity, depth, and truth in the Holocaust survivors' faces, she says, and lies and falseness in perpetrators' faces. "When a person starts lying, it diminishes their substance, and this you can see. These people are diminished." With survivors, on the other hand, "Even if they've lived through the most terrifying things, there's still something in their eyes that says: 'this is a man.'"

*

"I think of the film crew in a bumpy car, going through rural Poland during the Cold War—it had to feel like they were on a ship in the middle of the ocean. It was so pioneering!" Professor Erin McGlothlin must have seen *Shoah* hundreds if not thousands of times, but she still speaks about it with a smile and a fan's infectious enthusiasm. She goes on, wondering at Claude Lanzmann and his team. "They went out into this nothingness, and they created something, thirty, forty years after the fact. They pulled out this material that wouldn't exist otherwise. It was a heroic effort. It took over a decade, they went broke, Lanzmann was beaten to a pulp—and the constant fundraising, the hustling with governments. Incredible energy was spent getting that footage."

Erin teaches German and Jewish Studies at Washington University in St. Louis, where she's also a Vice Dean. She's a leading expert on Holocaust literature and film, and on *Shoah* in particular, having written a book and several articles about it. Heroism is a word that she uses more than once in our conversation. "*Shoah* was obsessive, it was monomaniacal. It required a kind of singlemindedness, a bulldoggedness—and I admire that," she says with a chuckle.

Lanzmann wasn't the only one who interviewed Nazi war criminals after 1945. Before *Shoah* was made, the BBC interviewed Karl Wolff, a senior SS leader and the Chief of Heinrich Himmler's Personal Staff, for the famous documentary series *The World at War*. As we saw in the previous chapter, the Austrian-British journalist Gitta Sereny interviewed former Nazis extensively, publishing articles and books about Albert Speer, Hitler's favorite architect, as well as Franz Stangl and others. In the 1990s and into the 2000s, the historian Laurence Rees interviewed Nazi war criminals for several books and documentaries. But these interviewers are all empathic, Erin says, or they at least honor certain journalistic conventions. *Shoah*, on the other hand, is "all about strategic or deceptive empathy. Lanzmann *pretends* to empathize, he *pretends* to be an ally, at least when it comes to the perpetrators that he interviewed. And he isn't. He's willing to deceive, to feign ignorance, to flatter the ego. He's not a historian, and he's not a jurist. It's not a court of law, and no rights are being preserved. He doesn't care about any of that. He just does whatever it takes to *get* something, to *provoke* something that isn't a rote response. It's that complete disregard for all conventions, whether ethical, or professional, or even epistemological. He disregards them to get what he wants. We have so few testimonies from perpetrators that are reliable, and so few interviews that probe them. That's what makes *Shoah* so valuable and so fascinating. The perpetrator interviews are tiny blips on a screen of silence and non-response."

The result of all this, Erin concludes, is that *Shoah* confronts us with the perpetrators' humanity in a way that's uniquely unsettling.

"These men are deeply human in their weaknesses. They're egocentric, they're worried about how they look to their colleagues, they puff themselves up with pride about ridiculous things. Their struggle is humanity's struggle. The way in which they present themselves is only too human. It's not monstrous, and it's not bestial. It's terribly, tragically, awfully human."

We chat about our mutual admiration for *Shoah* for a long time; about everything that made it extraordinary, and about the extent of Lanzmann's achievement. Eventually, though, we confront an awkward fact. Relatively few people today have seen the film, and most of the students that we teach don't even know that it exists. It's nowhere near as famous as other Holocaust films, like *Schindler's List* or *The Boy in the Striped Pajamas*. I ask Erin: why?

"Well, it's hard to watch," she says, laughing. "And it's long." At nine-and-a-half hours, *Shoah* is one of the longest films ever made. Still, *Schindler's List* is hard to watch, and it's long, too—obviously not as long as *Shoah*, but still over three hours, I say.

"It has all the Hollywood tropes, though," Erin says. "It's got music and a narrative arc. We know who the hero is, we know who the bad guy is, and we recognize the hero's moment of conversion from lout to rescuer. And we recognize all that because it's Hollywood 101! We've trained our whole lives for it. Whereas *Shoah* can feel . . . " she stops for a moment to search for the right word. "It can feel *primitive*, with its long takes, its long silences, and its long, panning shots of landscapes. It doesn't try to be democratic and appealing. It doesn't guide you, and it doesn't give you any signposting for where it's going or what it's trying to do. With the narrative and visual tools that we have in popular culture, it's hard even to hold onto it. I mean, when I saw it for the first time in college, I thought it was boring. It was only later that I understood how significant it was, that it was a heroic act—because the absolute goal of the Final Solution was for the memory of the victims to be silenced."

*

Would Claude Lanzmann have accepted the idea that *Shoah* was an act of resistance? He tended to make clear cut divisions between those who understood his film and those who didn't. Whatever his answer, I'm sure that he'd have delivered it with his customary zeal. He may have said that not only was *Shoah* an act of resistance, it was resistance in its purest possible form. Equally, though, he may have dismissed the question as a radical misunderstanding, and as "obscene"—a word he often used when criticizing others. I did track down another member of his crew, and this was precisely the line that they took. Speaking with Lanzmann's own quasi-religious fervor, and with one hand drumming on the table for emphasis through much of our meeting, they blew my question out of the water. And it didn't end there. I later received a vitriolic email, written variously in caps, bold, and underlined font, that hammered their point home: *Shoah* was not resistance.

But Erin McGlothlin's words stuck with me for months after our interview. Claude Lanzmann rescued the truth from oblivion. Obviously, he'd pushed back against Nazi war criminals' desire to live in anonymity after 1945, and against their desire for their crimes to be forgotten. But he'd also pushed back against their unspoken desire for their *victims* to be forgotten. Dragging these people out from the shadows, extracting testimony from them, and preserving it was more than an act of resistance against Nazism. It was an act of resistance against history itself.

11

The Holtzman Amendment
The People Who Expelled Nazi War Criminals from the United States

Fall 1973, Detroit, Michigan

Ralph Blumenthal, a journalist with *The New York Times*, walked toward the entrance of a large church compound. He was carrying a tape machine, some clippings from 1940s Romanian newspapers, and a black-and-white photo of a man in an Iron Guard uniform. He may not have known it, but he was on the brink of a story that would change politics in the United States and around the world.

*

Like many European countries, Romania gave birth to a fledgling democracy in the 1920s that crumbled under the weight of authoritarianism in the 1930s. This familiar story intersected with the unique elements of Romania's history. In the early twentieth century, it was at a crossroads between becoming an industrialized, urban nation, like its partners in the West, and its ancient agrarian traditions. In the early stages of the Second World War, it lost a third of its territory, and with it, a third of its population—to the Soviet Union in the east, to Hungary in the northwest, and to Bulgaria in the south.[1] All this culminated in a massive political crisis. On September 6th, 1940, King Carol II abdicated and gave his dictatorial powers to Ion Antonescu, a nationalist and a career military man who'd worked his way to the top of the Romanian Army. He became prime minister and took the additional title of *Conducător*, or "Leader." Then he formed a coalition government with a brutal paramilitary group called the Iron Guard. Both arms of this coalition were antisemitic, but one wasn't antisemitic enough for the other. Where Antonescu wanted an "orderly" solution to "The Jewish Question," with measures like tax hikes, nationalizing Jewish businesses, and putting unemployed Jews in forced labor, the Iron Guard wanted to be more radical. This was just one of the disagreements between them. As their disagreements deepened, Romania came to the brink of civil war.

In private, Hitler told Antonescu to crack down on the Iron Guard. He didn't really care who ruled Romania. He was only interested in the country for its natural resources, which Germany needed for its war effort. To keep supplies steady, he preferred a leader like Antonescu who'd work with him. Not an overcharged paramilitary group so full of revolutionary ideas, and so opposed to the idea of government in general, that they'd never come to heel. But—in a way that characterized his leadership style—he didn't share any of this with the senior members of his Party or with the Nazis whose feet were on the ground in Romania. They were all encouraging the Iron Guard. In the Iron Guard's wish to spark an antisemitic revolution, they saw the reflection of their own ideals.

One of the Iron Guard's most valuable leaders was Viorel Trifa, an educated theologian and historian. He rapidly accumulated power after King Carol II's abdication, mainly with the goal of bringing about "the destruction of the Jewish people."[2] He edited a student newspaper called *Libertatae*, where he wrote antisemitic articles and unfolded his delusional belief in a conspiracy between Jews, Communists, and Free Masons. He was the president of The National Union of Romanian Christian Students, an antisemitic fraternity that was tied to the Iron Guard. And he was a charismatic speaker who knew how to whip up a crowd.

At a rally on December 10th, 1940, Trifa said that Romanian students were antisemitic not for intellectual or scientific reasons but because they "could no longer make a living" in their own country. They had left their villages, which were being "plundered by the Yids," only to find that the big cities were all being "plundered by the Yids," too.[3] Meanwhile, the Iron Guard was becoming increasingly brazen as they ramped up their competition with Antonescu for absolute power, gunning down their political opponents in the street, and terrorizing Jewish people away from their homes and businesses.[4]

When a German officer was murdered outside the Iron Guard's Bucharest headquarters on January 19th, 1941, the situation came to a head.[5] Antonescu blamed the murder on the Iron Guard and seized the chance to kick his rivals out of the coalition government, the police, and the security forces. Meanwhile, the Iron Guard blamed the murder on Antonescu. In this crucible, and dressed in his Iron Guard regalia, Trifa gave one of his trademark incendiary antisemitic speeches to a mass of Romanian students. He traced the War as far back as the French Revolution, and to the three words that inspired it, liberty, equality, and fraternity. These words freed the people from the tyranny of a lone monarch, he argued, only for them to be handed over to "hundreds of thousands" of other tyrants who enslaved them again: the Jews. The premise of the French Revolution was a lie, he said, because "people were never equal." The ideas of liberty, equality, and fraternity had only "served the Kikes." He concluded by heaping praise on Hitler for starting the "huge struggle of National Socialism" and "the fight against Judaism." Even if he'd done nothing else, Hitler "still would have risen to the great peaks of history."[6]

The next day, Trifa published a manifesto that was distributed in Bucharest and in the surrounding provinces. It was also read out over the radio. In it, he called for Jews and Free Masons to be removed from the government. He also accused members of Antonescu's government of being "tools of the Jews"—including Eugen Cristescu, the head of Romania's intelligence service. (It's testament to the paranoia of Trifa's antisemitism that Cristescu was himself a vicious antisemite who was later convicted of war crimes.) The manifesto went on to demand the formation of an Iron Guard government. That night, posters were plastered across Bucharest on Trifa's orders, blaming the German officer's murder on Jewish people. Trifa then led a parade through the streets to call for the death of the Jews, and to celebrate Hitler and Mussolini.[7] His voice was one of many in the Iron Guard's antisemitic chorus. By this time, the Romanian far-right press had spent weeks stirring the public into a frenzy over the need to solve the Jewish Question in their country. As one historian wrote, "Clear indications of what was about to take place were evident almost daily. The writing was on the wall."[8]

On January 21st, 1941, the Iron Guard moved to seize power from Antonescu. They went on an antisemitic rampage in the process, including a pogrom in Bucharest that was one of the most appalling in history. Emil Dorian, an eyewitness, wrote in his diary that he couldn't create a complete list of the crimes in this pogrom, because more were coming to light all the time. "Shop after shop with shutters wrenched off their hinges, windows smashed, walls burned, rooms emptied," he wrote. "It is impossible to tell what had been there before. The mind cannot grasp how looting bands were able to wreak such utter destruction in so short a time." Corpses littered the streets. In many cases, their bodies had been desecrated. "Before the victims were killed, their noses were smashed, their limbs broken, their tongues cut out, their eyes gouged."[9] Other eyewitnesses told of Jewish homes, temples, and stores being looted and burned in the city. They told of mass shootings taking place in the forests, of jewelry being stolen from the dead, and of corpses being mutilated. They told of Jewish people being forced to drink gasoline and of children being tortured in front of their parents.[10] About sixty Jewish people were killed in a slaughterhouse, where they were hung from butcher's hooks. According to one report, three of them had "their abdomen cut deep" before their killers "took out their intestines and knotted a tie at the neck of each one of them."[11] The rest were probably skinned alive before they died.[12] Richard Evans wrote that even the Germans could be shocked by the antisemitic violence in Romania, citing one Nazi who described seeing (and tolerating) "unspeakable atrocities" there.[13]

This orgy of violence lasted for three days. The Iron Guard was so blinded by its own antisemitism, its leaders believed that Jewish people had secretly taken control of everything—even the Romanian Army. The Army didn't take kindly to the suggestion that it was just a puppet, and it threw its weight behind Antonescu, who quickly regained control of the country. Thousands of members of the Iron Guard were rounded up and arrested in the aftermath. But nine of its leaders took sanctuary in the German embassy, including Viorel Trifa, before heading to Germany itself.[14] The Nazis granted them an unusual form of asylum, keeping them in concentration camps but in remarkably good conditions, as sort-of celebrity prisoners. Meanwhile, back in Romania, Trifa was sentenced to life in prison *in absentia*. He had to live nomadically in the years after the War, moving from one country to another across Europe. He worked in secretarial roles in the Romanian Orthodox Church, and as a college lecturer. Then, in 1950, he made an extraordinary decision to start a new life overseas.

*

Ralph Blumenthal was raised in uptown Manhattan, where he studied at City College as an art major. He aspired to become a painter or a sculptor. In his freshman year, though, he visited the offices of *The Campus*, City College's student-run newspaper. "And very quickly," he tells me, "I got hooked into journalism." Ralph rose through the ranks of *The Campus* and stayed an extra half-year at City College to work as its editor-in-chief. "I learned more editing

The Campus than I did at *The New York Times*. It was very hands on, and there was no manual," he says. "I had to figure out things for myself. I just threw myself into it." After further study at Columbia Journalism School, Ralph became a copy boy at *The New York Times*. "It was a menial job, but it gave me access to the paper," he says. He went on to become one of their leading voices, and to build a journalistic career that's lasted more than forty years. Among his many achievements are his exposes about Nazi war criminals living in hiding in the United States.

Ralph's account of how these exposes began goes back to 1964. On July 14th that year, *The New York Times* published a story by Joseph Lelyveld called "Former Nazi Camp Guard is Now a Housewife in Queens."[15] It was about Hermine Braunsteiner-Ryan, a convicted war criminal who came to live in New York City. She'd been an SS guard, first in Ravensbruck, a women's concentration camp, and then in Majdanek, a hybrid concentration and extermination camp, like Auschwitz, where some 80,000 people were murdered. Russell Ryan, an American electrical engineer, had met her after the War while he was on holiday in Austria—by which time she'd already been in and out of prison. They got married and moved to the United States in 1959, where she became a citizen on January 19th, 1963. (She was eventually extradited to West Germany, tried anew for war crimes, and sentenced to life imprisonment.[16])

Ralph tells me that he was deeply affected by Lelyveld's story—and that Hermine Braunsteiner wasn't a one-off. Thousands of former Nazis had come to the United States after 1945. Some got in through official, organized routes, like "Operation Paperclip." When the War was nearing its end, the Allies set their sights on the new era ahead, and on potential future conflicts. They would need the best and brightest minds to keep pace with each other. Paperclip aimed to recruit German scientists and technicians, bringing them to the United States for an arms race with the Soviet Union. Many of them had designed cutting-edge weaponry for the Third Reich, using their expertise in aerodynamics, jet engines,

FIGURE 11.1 *Ralph Blumenthal. Deborah Blumenthal.*

and rockets. (The name "Paperclip" supposedly came from the practice of attaching paperclips to the folders of Germans whose visa applications had been flagged for fast-tracking.[17] The British also acquired German scientific expertise through projects like Operation Backfire. The historian Mary Barbier compared the tug-of-war between the two nations for Germany's best scientists to a draft process in professional sport.[18]) Officially, Operation Paperclip was a secret. It was impossible for so many Germans to show up in the United States without the public noticing, though. Over time, through a drip-drab of information, the government tried to put a positive spin on what they were doing. They led the public to believe that the scientists coming to the country had never bought Nazism or been involved with the Party. In truth, many of them had been in the SS or the SD, and Operation Paperclip involved serious ethical malpractice—from creating fake resumes to wiping names from the Central Registry of War Criminals and Security Suspects (CROWCRASS).

Beyond official, organized routes into the United States, like Paperclip, Nazi war criminals with the right mix of guile and luck were able to connive their way into the country. John Demjanjuk, for example, participated in the murder of thousands of Jewish people at Sobibor, and later enjoyed a career as an autoworker in Cleveland. Refugee officials didn't notice that he fudged his life story in his visa application, because they "had to process millions of forms, didn't have time to check details, and had no access to records."[19] After arriving in the United States, people like Demjanjuk were usually able to live prosperously and undisturbed. According to the writer Richard Rashke, there were four reasons for this. First, as immigrants went, most Americans felt that former Nazis were preferable to either Jews or Communists. Second, the United States government didn't want to spend time pursuing former Nazis when they could be pursuing Cold War objectives. Third, America had its own wartime secrets that it wanted to keep under wraps. Last, and perhaps most important, the average American simply didn't care if they lived next door to a former Nazi, so long as they behaved themselves.[20]

Throughout our conversation, Ralph keeps coming back to Charles Allen, a journalist who was one of the first to uncover the country's Nazi secret in a 1963 pamphlet called *Nazi War Criminals Among Us*. "He tracked a lot of them early on," he says, admiringly. "It was very innovative reporting." He got pulled into the field himself in the early 1970s when he met Anthony DeVito and Vincent Schiano, two agents at the Immigration and Naturalization Service

(INS) who quit after the Hermine Braunsteiner story. They accused the INS of covering up such cases for years.[21] "They told me that they were investigating Nazi war criminals who had found their way into the country with some kind of official help. It was very mysterious," Ralph says. He began writing stories about the government not being forthcoming in these cases. It was during this time that he met Simon Wiesenthal, the famous Nazi hunter. Wiesenthal told him that he was tracking a Romanian bishop living in Detroit who may have participated in the Holocaust. His name was Valarian Trifa.

Ralph began digging into Trifa's past, using YIVO, the Institute for Jewish Research—an archive and library in downtown Manhattan. By sifting through old Romanian newspapers with the help of a translator, he established that *Valarian* Trifa was *Viorel* Trifa—the Iron Guard leader who'd catalyzed the brutal Bucharest pogrom in 1941.

"So, I compiled some clippings, and I went to see him," Ralph says, nonchalantly. "I didn't warn him in advance. I just went out there and got him cold."

I try to slow our conversation for a moment. I want to know more about this meeting and how it unfolded. What do you say to a suspected Nazi war criminal after taking him by surprise on his doorstep?

"I remember distinctly," Ralph says. "I asked him, was he a member of the Iron Guard? He said, 'no.' Then I showed him a picture from a Romanian newspaper of him in the Iron Guards' uniform. He said, 'Well, I wore the uniform, but I wasn't really in the Iron Guard.' Then I showed him a clipping with the speech he made denouncing the Jews. He said, 'Well, I gave the speeches, but I *had* to give them.'" Sounding exasperated by the memories, Ralph adds, "He always had an answer for everything. But, eventually, I got him to admit that it was him, and that those were his words."

This impromptu doorstep interview became the foundation of an in-depth story that was published on the front page of *The New York Times* on December 26th, 1973. Ralph tells me that it caused an uproar. For one thing, unlike

Hermine Braunsteiner-Ryan, Viorel Trifa didn't come to the United States by marriage and live a quiet life in the suburbs. He abused immigration laws that were meant to help displaced War victims, and within a year he'd become a bishop of the Romanian Orthodox Church in America. This role turned him into a community leader and a significant public figure. On May 11th, 1955, for example, he gave the opening prayer at the United States Senate, at the invitation of Richard Nixon, who was then Vice President.[22] In this prayer, among other things, he beseeched God to grant the Senators "the wisdom, the understanding, the ability, and the power to govern this beloved country of ours."[23]

After his story about Trifa was published, Ralph started to get tips about other Nazi war criminals living in hiding in the United States. "One by one," he says, "I told the stories of what they had done, and I questioned in *The Times* why they had been let in to the country." These criminals included people like Boļeslavs Maikovskis, Karlis Detlavs, and Bronius Kaminskas. One of his biggest breakthroughs—he calls it "the capstone" of his reporting on Nazi war criminals—came in summer 1985, when he was asked to join the international effort to find Joseph Mengele, the SS physician infamous for conducting human experiments at Auschwitz. Ralph worked with other reporters, and with forensic scientists and pathologists, to discover that Mengele had drowned after a heart attack while swimming in the ocean in 1979. They found his grave in Sao Paulo, Brazil, and they exhumed it, putting decades of speculation to rest.

I ask Ralph if he was ever concerned about his safety while pursuing these people. Some of them were mass murderers. And some, like Mengele, had embedded themselves in networks of Nazi sympathizers.

"I don't remember thinking about it at the time," Ralph says, dismissively. "They were pretty powerless. Mostly they were afraid of being identified."

I share with Ralph that Corinna Coulmas had said similar things about the Nazi war criminals that she met. Then I wonder aloud if the war criminals had shared anything else in common. Ralph quickly offers up two other traits.

"First, they tried to be better Americans than any other Americans," he says. "They were so grateful to have refuge, and they had to pass as Americans to stay hidden. They were the first to run the flag up the flagpole every morning, they saluted it, and they sang the national anthem—all because they were hiding their terrible pasts. Second, they vociferously denied that it was their fault. They would make up stories about being anti-Nazi and about saving Jews. The truth only came out," he adds, now speaking slowly, as if the words themselves were heavy, "through a lot of very, very difficult digging."

"Wasn't it strange that so many of them chose to come to America?" I ask. After all, in the Nazi imagination, the United States was one of two great enemies—the other being the Soviet Union. (They saw the two nations as opposite sides of the same coin: the Soviet Union was the home of "racial degeneracy" and "Jewish Bolshevism," while America was the home of "cultural decadence" and "Jewish capitalism.")

"America was very appealing," Ralph says. "It was a place to live freely. The spotlight was off them, they could make a lot of money, and they could be accepted. And they were anti-Communist, so they were in-tune with the mood of the 1950s. They weren't carrying the Nazi ideology of racial purity with them. They were happy to leave it behind and start a new life."

I ask how Ralph's readers reacted to his stories.

"There were still a lot of Nazi sympathizers in Germany. They were saying, 'We lost and we atoned, and we made reparations to Israel and the Jews. When will it be enough?' But I had encouraging responses back in New York. I got friendly with people in the government who were working on these cases, and eventually The Office of Special Investigations was set up."

The Office of Special Investigations, or OSI, was created as a branch of the Justice Department by Congresswoman Elizabeth Holtzman in 1979. It worked to uncover other Nazi war criminals living in the United States. Thousands of investigations led to over 300 successful prosecutions and 70 deportations. (The Justice Department's most recent scalp was Karl Friedrich

Berger—a former guard at the Neuengamme concentration camp, who was deported to Germany in 2021 at the age of ninety-five.)

Ralph speaks fondly of the relationship that he struck up with Martin Mendelson, one of the OSI's first leaders.

"He was very helpful to me. And you know," he adds, "there's always a symbiotic relationship between government investigators and the newspapers when they're pursuing the same thing. Newspapers are looking for stories, and investigators are looking for support."

Pursuing Nazi war criminals would have been hard for anyone, but I suspect that it must have been especially hard for Ralph: I know from his writing that he's Jewish. In 2016, he published a *New York Times* article about his family's history.[24] His parents emigrated from Europe to the United States in 1929. After his mom died in 1984, he found a collection of letters and documents from his aunt and uncle, Hella and Szilard Diamant. They'd lived in Berlin in the 1930s. With "the tightening Nazi dragnet" slowly destroying their lives, they tried to join their relatives in the United States in 1938 and 1939—but they'd left it too late. Ralph had always "sensed a world of danger in whispered conversations" at home, and he and his sister had been "especially spooked by a black lacquer wardrobe in a dark hallway" of their apartment, where their mom had kept the belongings that Szilard and Hella had optimistically sent ahead. In the process of trying to find out what had happened to them, he unearthed relatives that he didn't know about—in the United States, and as far away as Israel and Australia. Eventually he discovered that Szilard most likely died in the Majdanek extermination camp. But Hella survived the War, after close brushes with both Auschwitz and Sobibor. She used a fake identity to hide out in Warsaw, where she pretended to be a Catholic, before starting a new life in Australia in the 1950s. The story of Ralph's family is the story of the Holocaust in microcosm: loved ones ripped apart and scattered across the world, their identities erased, carrying secrets that couldn't be spoken aloud.

As he talks about what it meant to be a Jewish reporter investigating Nazism's legacy, he pulls back as far as 1961, when he went traveling abroad, first to Germany, and then to Israel. "The Eichmann trial was on in Jerusalem," he remembers. "You could just line up in the morning and go in—it was extraordinary. I'll never forget it. I saw him in the dock, and it helped to form my consciousness about Nazi war criminals." Then he continues, coolly, "But I approached every story I ever did with a kind of detachment. You set out to be fair and rigorous, you do fact-checking, and you give everybody a fair shake. I never felt that I was on a personal crusade, or that it was a mission, or anything like that."

*

Elizabeth Holtzman was first elected to Congress in 1972 when she was thirty-one years old, making her the youngest Congresswoman in history. (Her record stood for decades until Elise Stefanik, and then Alexandria Ocasio-Cortez, set new precedents in 2014 and 2018 respectively.) Born in New York and educated at Harvard, she served four terms in the House of Representatives before becoming District Attorney of Kings County, and then the Comptroller of New York City. Throughout her career, she championed civil rights, women's rights, and rights for immigrants and refugees. Now in her early 80s, she still works as Counsel and Co-Chair of the Government Relations Group at the New York-based law firm Herrick. She responded to my request for an interview immediately, but months passed before we spoke.

When our Zoom call finally comes, the Congresswoman is seated at her desk, flanked by piles of books. Still more books are heaped on an imposing bookshelf in the background. I begin by asking when she first became aware that Nazi war criminals were living in the United States. Like Ralph Blumenthal, she remembered reading about Hermine Braunsteiner-Ryan in the *New York Times*, at which time she was in her early 20s.

"But the story just came and went," she says. "It seemed like a one-off, an anomaly. It was only later, when I was elected to Congress, that someone came to see me in my DC office and revealed that the problem was much, much bigger. The man who came was somehow connected to the Immigration Service. He told me that the Service had a list of fifty-three Nazi war criminals living in the United States, and that the government was doing nothing about it. He spoke in a clear, simple way." (Then, she jokes, "He didn't talk about lasers beaming onto him." I wonder if this is a sideswipe at Marjorie Taylor Greene, the Republican Congresswoman who speculated, in 2018, that "Jewish space lasers" had caused wildfires in California.) "He seemed like a normal person. But I still couldn't quite believe what he was telling me. It was shocking; it was horrifying. Tens of thousands of Americans had died fighting Hitler in the Second World War; hundreds of thousands were wounded. Why would our government allow Nazi war criminals to live in the United States undisturbed? It made no sense to me. But I couldn't put it out of my mind," she says, becoming more and more animated as she tells the story.

"I was a member of the House Immigration Subcommittee which had scheduled a hearing with the Immigration Commissioner not long after that encounter. And I thought to myself, 'I'll just ask the Commissioner about the list then.' So, when the hearing took place, I asked whether it was true that the Immigration Service had a list of Nazi war criminals living in the United States. The Commissioner said, 'Yes, I have a list—fifty-three people.' I almost fell off my chair. Then I asked, "Well, what are you doing about it?" At that point, I got a bureaucratic cloud of words. And so, I started my own inquiry."

Congresswoman Holtzman soon discovered that the Immigration Service was keeping only the slightest of tabs on the Nazi war criminals that they knew about in the United States. There were records of who they were and where they lived, but little else.

"It turned out that the Immigration Service never did any investigations into the accusations that had been made against the fifty-three persons. They never did any investigations to determine whether the allegations were true; they never went to Europe or Israel to get documents or find witnesses," she says, sounding increasingly irate. She leans forward in her chair and adds, "They did *nothing*," landing heavily on the final word. "But I took action. After discussions with my staff and pondering a proper strategy, I held a press conference in which I disclosed the fact that the United States government had let accused Nazi war criminals reside in the country undisturbed, and I attacked the government for its inaction on them. I knew that this was a critical disclosure because it would mobilize public opinion in favor of prompt efforts to bring the accused Nazis to justice. Fortunately," she adds, dryly, "Nazi war criminals weren't popular in the United States at that time. Given that many years had elapsed since the Second World War, I knew that investigating the Nazi war crimes accusations would be complicated and difficult. So, I also called for the creation of a special unit, with specially trained staff, to seek and obtain evidence on a worldwide basis and to determine whether the people on the list had committed war crimes."

In 1978, the Holtzman Amendment passed. It made it illegal for Nazi war criminals to enter or remain in the United States, and it provided a legal framework for their deportation. Then, in 1979, The Office of Special Investigations was created as part of the Department of Justice to enforce the Amendment.

Like Ralph Blumenthal, Congresswoman Holtzman is Jewish. We talk about her background and how it interwove with her pursuit of Nazi war criminals. She tells me about her family's history, the pogroms that her mother's family survived in Europe, and the antisemitism that she experienced growing up in New York.

"I knew what it was like for Jews to plead for their lives, and I knew what antisemitism was," she says. "On the way to Hebrew school, when I was child, there were kids who called us names and wanted to beat us up. I remember seeing signs on Long Island that said, "Restricted: No Jews, Negroes, or dogs allowed." And I knew about the Holocaust and the destruction that had taken place. Six million Jews were killed, hundreds of thousands of Roma and Sinti people were killed, and millions of non-Jews were killed, all because of Hitler's bigoted rage. It made no sense for America, a country that stood for human rights, to allow these Nazi murderers to live here in peace and security. By its inaction, the United States was condoning their war crimes and their acts of inhumanity. How could we allow our country to do that?" she asks. The question feels less directed at me, more at the past itself. "We couldn't." She pauses before concluding, "So, that's why I acted."

I ask if her actions met with any opposition.

"Some of the émigré groups were hostile; some were relatives of the alleged Nazis, some were supportive of Nazi ideology, and some were just misinformed. I remember receiving a phone call after my first press conference about Nazi war criminals in the United States. A guy with a thick New Jersey accent said, 'Ms. Holtzman?'"—she imitates the accent perfectly—"I said, 'Who is this?' He said, 'You wanna stay alive, you stay outta Bayonne!'"

The memory makes her laugh, but I'm shocked.

"Didn't phone calls like that make you concerned for your safety?" I ask. She snaps back with an answer that's pointed and brief.

"I wasn't concerned. The work was too important."

I'd read Congresswoman Holtzman's autobiography before our conversation. It's called *Who Said It Would Be Easy?*, and it tells the swashbuckling story of her political. One line had really stuck with me. She wrote that, after the Watergate scandal and the discovery that Nazi war criminals were living in the United States, she found herself filled with longing for "the affirmation of decency in our government."[25] It made me think of more recent troubles in the United States' political life, like the lie that the 2020 election had been stolen, or the storming of the Capitol on January 6th. As our interview wraps up, I say that we're no closer to achieving "the affirmation of decency in our government" today than we were when her book was published in 1996. What, I want to know, can any of us do about it?

"The story about Nazi war criminals shows that you can make a difference, even years later, against an intractable problem," she says. "You can't lose your optimism about bringing about justice. You have to be involved. Try to get members of Congress to do what they need to do. Go to their district offices, meet with them, talk to them. Same with Senators. It won't always work. In fact, it won't work most of the time. But if all of us aren't involved, good things won't happen. It's the responsibility of all of us to make democracy work. I really believe that politics follows Newton's basic laws of motion: an object at rest will stay at rest unless pressure is applied to move it. Nothing will happen unless you apply pressure to make something happen. Putting that pressure on is what it means to work for justice, and it involves talking to people in positions of power and enlisting as much of the public as possible as allies."

With that, our conversation comes to an abrupt conclusion. Congresswoman Holtzman has to rush to her next meeting.

*

A denaturalization suit was filed against Valerian Trifa soon after the publication of Ralph's 1973 article. It sat in court files for years, not least because the Romanian government refused to share evidence from its national archives. Then, in 1979, Trifa came into the orbit of The Office of Special Investigations. Congresswoman Holtzman lobbied for trade benefits to be withheld from Romania until their government cooperated with the investigation, and quickly the doors to their archives were opened. Trifa faced a trial to lose his US citizenship on October 14th, 1980. Then, less than two months before the trial started, he stunned everyone involved by voluntarily surrendering his naturalization certificate.

"He and his lawyers issued a book-length sob story of this Romanian nationalist and theologian, persecuted no end by the United States government," wrote the attorney Allan Ryan, a Justice Department lawyer and later a Harvard professor who prosecuted many Nazi war criminals in the 1980s.[26] Trifa's motive soon became clear. Once the deportation papers were filed, he appealed against his own surrender—a last-ditch effort to bury his trial in legal limbo. To some extent, it worked. A full year passed before the appeal was dismissed, during which time he continued to enjoy his freedom. Then, when the trial finally started, on October 4th, 1982, he tried to strike a deal. He'd admit to entering the United States illegally and accept deportation if all other charges against him were dropped. The OSI refused. Turning down a certain win was a gamble, but they feared that Trifa would try to spin it by telling the media that "he was an innocent Romanian patriot, unable to fight the United States government forever, forced to agree to deportation on a technicality only to save his Church the expense of defending him."[27]

The trial continued. With each day, more details about Trifa's violent antisemitic past became public. On October 7th, desperate to bring it to an end, he admitted everything: he'd abused the Displaced Persons Act, he'd lied to obtain a United States visa, and he'd been a leader in the Romanian Iron Guard. If the trial ever put any strain on him, Allan Ryan wrote, it didn't show. Unlike others, even when he was being cross-examined, "it was not at all difficult to see him as the demagogue, the smooth-talking instigator of disorder that left blood on everyone's hands but his own, the ambitious editor of bigotry and cunning."[28]

Later in 1982, Trifa finally left the United States and went to Portugal. But he lied on his visa application there, too. The Portuguese began their own deportation proceedings against him. He died in 1987, at the age of seventy-two, while those proceedings were still ongoing.

12

Formers

The American Neo-Nazis Who Turned on Their Beliefs

"I went to a Shabbat service in Temple Judea at Palm Beach Gardens. It was the most fun I've had in a while," Arno Michaelis says. He's tall and broad-shouldered, and he speaks with a distinctive, gruff voice. He's been telling me about a recent work trip to Florida, where he gave presentations on antisemitism with the Holocaust educator Tamara Meyer and then attended synagogue afterward. "There was an amazing cantor, and an amazing rabbi, and it was a musical Shabbat. They had greatest hits by Jewish artists, with a Shabbat spin on them. The opening song was 'Temple Judea' to the tune of 'Copa Cabana,'" he says. Then he sings, "At the Temple, Temple Judea!" before bursting into laughter. "It was awesome. I was singing along with everybody else." His enthusiasm is infectious, but my guard is up. I've also heard him scream the N-word and sing songs about exterminating Jews.

*

Some of the most vigorous resistance to Nazism today comes from people who used to be in violent far-right groups but who became disillusioned, left, and began helping others to leave too. These people sometimes call themselves

"Formers." In 2011, a handful of them started the nonprofit organization Life After Hate. It currently has a network of over fifty people helping others to leave the violent far right and other extremist groups across the United States. Patrick Riccards is their first executive director who's not a Former. He has a clean-shaven head and a gaze that's resolute and intense.

"I've spent most of my life building and fixing nonprofits and other organizations. That's what brought me here," he tells me. "It's also personal, because I'm the father of two children of color. For me, the question is always: how do we make society a little bit safer?" He starts our conversation by telling me what happens when someone comes to Life After Hate for help. They'll try to understand what brought "the client," as he calls them, to this point in their life. They'll also try to figure out the client's immediate needs. Most of them are still wrestling with a strong desire to harm others, or themselves, or both—and so the first step is usually to get them working with a psychologist or therapist.

"But we're unable to provide that kind of help ourselves," Patrick says. "We're not a clinic. So, how do we find the right licensed professional?" The question lingers for a moment, and then the challenges that face him and his clients seem to creep over him like clouds. "As you can imagine, there are plenty of licensed professionals who mean well, and who have experience dealing with trauma. But not many have had a white supremacist—a violent white supremacist, at that—sitting two feet from them in their office. How do we make the right connection? And how do we help clients find tattoo removal services," he continues, "because they've realized that it's impossible to get a job or rent an apartment with a swastika on their neck?"

As well as working with a psychologist or therapist, clients meet weekly with a case manager and an "Exit Specialist." The Exit Specialist is a Former, a peer adviser who can "talk about what has to be talked about," as Patrick puts it. "It's easy to give a client clinical instructions about what they should be doing. It's different to have somebody who's served prison time for hate crimes who's prepared to share from their experiences—and, more importantly, who can provide insight into the client's life that they can't see at that moment."

I ask if there's such a thing as an average client. The question makes Patrick laugh.

"Well, we often come across folks who believe that they're unicorns, both in terms of what drew them into extremism, and what's drawing them to get out. They believe that nobody else has experienced what they've experienced. Our team knows far better. There's rarely a day when we hear something that we haven't heard before. Even so, there is no average client," he says, still smiling. "It always takes people by surprise. There's a view that they must all be like Edward Norton's character in the movie *American History X*."

He's read my mind. Norton plays a shaven headed, muscular white man with a swastika tattooed on his chest, which is exactly what I think of when I picture Life After Hate's clients.

"*American History X* was partially based on one of our founder's lives, at least in terms of what happened to him in prison. But the rest is fictitious," Patrick continues. "About 50 percent of our clients are women, despite every violent extremist group in the United States being steeped in misogyny. About 20 percent identify as LGBTQ+, despite extremist groups being steeped in homophobia. We have members of white supremacy groups who are Black or Latino. It always surprises people," he says again, before taking a momentary pause. "You know, this used to be a much simpler space, with racism directed at the Black community and antisemitism directed at the Jewish community. That was the basis of everything. Today, if you want to be anti-Black, anti-Latino, anti-immigrant,"—he speaks faster and faster as this list unfurls—"anti-Asian, anti-Islam, anti-government, you name it, I can find a hate group for it. As society's hate diversifies, there's a diversity of people who embrace it."

As Patrick seems to anticipate, this isn't what I'm expecting to hear. Why would women, or members of the LGBTQ+ community, or people of color,

I ask, join angry white men in violent extremist groups that are governed by racism, sexism, misogyny, and homophobia?

"It's a mistake to believe that people join these groups because of the ideology," he says. "You'll always have people who were raised in families of hate—people who were taught to be misogynistic or antisemitic or racist. For them, joining an extremist group is a natural progression. But we see far more individuals who suffered trauma in childhood, and who think that society doesn't understand them. As a result, they're constantly looking for a sense of place and a sense of belonging, and extremist groups are adept at recruiting them. Anyone who seems lost or detached from something—whether it's their family, their school, their church, or their community—is easy prey."

As well as exploiting people's trauma, he says, violent extremist groups also know how to exploit a toxic sense of entitlement that he believes is spreading across our society.

"A growing number of folks feel that they're not getting what they deserve. They don't have the job they want, or the girlfriend, or the car, or the house. Somebody must be to blame. Extremist groups are particularly good at delivering the right flavor of hate in such cases. 'You didn't get into the college you want?'" he says. He shifts his posture and changes the tone of his voice, imitating an extremist recruiter. "'It must be down to affirmative action! You didn't get the job you want? It must be all those illegals!'"

"Surely the extremist groups care about their ideology, though?" I interject.

"They don't recruit on the basis of ideology," he says again, this time more firmly. "Think of the average sixteen, seventeen-year-old boy who spends most of his time gaming on Twitch. Prime recruitment ground for right-wing extremist groups. They want guys who play *Call of Duty* on Twitch. They love guys who play *Call of Duty*, almost as much as they love recently discharged veterans. In the beginning, it's all about praising somebody who's got a lot of self-doubt. 'I can't believe what a great gamer you are!'" he says, throwing his arms up and speaking as if he were a recruiter again. "'You're incredible, I'm surprised you're not a pro! How can your mom say that you spend too much time gaming? This is what you should do!'" Then he leans forward and adds a sinister inflection to his voice. "'By the way, me and my buddies get together and play all the time. We'd love for you to join us. You're so good, you'd be great for our group!'"

He takes a breath and sits back again.

"So, they join. Over time, they get pulled in deeper, still before the ideology is even there. They're asked to leave everything behind. Their parents and siblings, their clergy and community—everything. The extremist group becomes both parent and priest. The individual realizes that to stay with their new family, they have no choice but to take on the ideology. Then it's only a matter of time before they begin to believe it."

The process that Patrick is describing reminds me of the professional development I've done while working in K-12, specifically on how to identify children who are being sexually abused. I share this point of comparison and say that extremist recruitment sounds predatory.

"It is," he says decisively. "They find people who are easy marks, who've had trauma, and they figure out how to take advantage. They're so good at discovering our weaknesses, our insecurities, and our desires. Do they ever fulfill them? Probably not. Which is why so many people eventually want to get out. But they know exactly how to recruit. At the end of the day, it's only about building numbers."

I ask if any of Life After Hate's clients ever relapse.

"I wish I could tell you that the process is linear," he says, heavily. "But it's not. Something could happen in your life, or in the news, and you're triggered. I've heard our process compared to a twelve-step program, to cult deprogramming, and to domestic abuse counseling. It's not linear. There will be setbacks, there will be gains. And, for the average client, it typically takes 18 to 24 months to truly disengage."

Patrick is Life After Hate's sole public face. Go to their website and you won't see anyone who's on the Board of Directors or anyone who works as a case manager or an Exit Specialist. Even in private meetings with clients, case managers and Exit Specialists only use their first names. The organization used to have an office in Chicago, but now they do everything virtually—partly because they got too many "drop-bys," as Patrick casually calls them, from extremist groups. Today, those same groups are trying to hack their database instead. In addition to all that, because of its focus on the far right, Life After Hate lost federal grant funding under the first Trump Administration. Patrick also has stories of his public appearances being protested by far-right groups from The Proud Boys to Moms for Liberty.

"Doesn't all of that make you worry for your personal safety?" I ask.

"Well yeah, I do get death threats," he says, almost lackadaisically. "Most of them come online, and I vet them with law enforcement. Usually, I don't have to worry about them. Every so often, though, you get one that's serious. But it's part of the job, and it means that you're being effective. My objective is to put every far-right extremist group out of business. I want to make it impossible for them to recruit or to raise money, and I want as much transparency and sunshine as possible in this country, so that we recognize these groups as a clear and present danger, and so we see them for what they are: domestic terrorists. I'm very open about saying that publicly."

Our conversation turns to Nazism's enduring appeal. Isn't it strange, I ask, that an ideology that wrought so much destruction in the twentieth century is still alive in the twenty-first?

Patrick's response ebbs like a river through one issue after another: governmental failure to treat post-traumatic stress disorder among United States veterans, many of whom were trained to wage war on Islamic communities overseas; the twin failures of US law enforcement to weed out recruits who harbor hatred, and to address the hatred already within their ranks; and the explosion of social media, which he thinks makes us feel stronger and bigger than we really are, and which forces us continually to raise the stakes in pursuit of likes and views. More than anything else, though, he points back to the sense of entitlement that's swamped us, and to the accompanying urge to blame others for the shortcomings in our own lives.

"If people don't evolve with society, they get left behind. Then they ask, 'who's to blame?' They can blame critical race theory, or 'wokeism,' or the transgender or LGBTQ+ communities, or immigrants. They just keep finding blame. They never take personal responsibility. It's why accountability is so important to what we do at Life After Hate. I don't ask our clients to go public with their pasts, or to flog themselves on the steps of whatever church they wronged. But they have to understand what they've done," he says, now speaking more slowly and emphasizing each word. "They have to see the damage that they've caused. They have to take responsibility for it, and they have to pledge to themselves, 'never again.' That's how they move beyond it."

He sighs and pauses deeply before continuing.

"But the answer to your question—the reason that Nazism hasn't gone away, and that it continues to grow—is because we still haven't addressed it," he says. "How many times have I had a conversation in which somebody asks me, 'Are these people worth it? With all the challenges that we're facing, with our schools, our healthcare, and our jobs, is it really worth our time and money to help *these* people?' We failed to realize the cost of not helping them, and we've begun to see the results of that failure over the last decade. For so long, we wanted to ignore Nazism and far-right extremism. We wanted to believe it was a fringe issue, that we weren't talking about *that* many people, and that they were relics of the past."

As our conversation comes to an end, I ask Patrick what he's learned about resisting Nazism and other forms of extremism from his work at Life After Hate.

"We deal with a lot of family, friends, and loved ones who are concerned that somebody they care about is falling into the violent far right. One thing that we always have to make clear is that it's not a time for condemnation," he says. "It's not a time to say, 'Don't you realize how wrong this is, don't you realize how stupid this is? Your grandmother would be horrified!' That's not the response. The response is asking them to explain *why* they think what they think, and *why* they're doing what they're doing," he says, leaning on the word "why" each time. "To help them articulate it. To help them explore if it's something they truly believe, or if it's something they're just following. You have to be willing to have those discussions. Often, in moments of clarity, people who are moving toward the violent far right will realize that the things they're saying aren't true. So, it's not a matter of telling them that they're wrong," he concludes. "It's about explaining other perspectives and asking them *why*."

*

Arno Michaelis was the lead singer of a white power band called Centurion. Their eponymous first album, which came out in 1994, sold 20,000 copies globally. By the standards of white power music, it was a massive hit. He was also a leader of a white supremacist group called The Northern Hammerskins. Today, though, he's one of the most prominent Formers in the United States.

Arno was born and raised in Mequon, an affluent town north of Milwaukee. "Looking back," he wrote in his autobiography *My Life After Hate*, "I don't see any valid excuse for how fucked up I turned out."[1] His childhood wasn't impoverished or violent, but his father struggled with alcohol addiction, and he argued constantly with his mother. As a result, their home could sometimes feel loveless. "In the absence of love's light," Arno concluded, "hate can be exciting, seductive. It beckons you and sends torrid, empty power coursing through your veins."[2]

By kindergarten, Arno was "an accomplished bully," and by sixth grade, he was "out of control."[3] His behavioral issues developed in tandem with a love for the heroes in violent Greek and Norse myths, and in medieval European folklore. Arno couldn't remember which came first, his "fascination with the idea of waging war or the anger that drove it."[4] In seventh grade, a group of "jocks," as he calls them, beat him up and cut off his rat-tail (a mini ponytail that was fashionable for men in the 1970s and 1980s). Beyond being hurt and humiliated, he felt abandoned by the group of friends who watched without helping. The group happened to be multiracial. It's a sad story, but plenty of people get bullied at school without later joining violent far-right extremist groups. Arno acknowledges this in *My Life After Hate*, conceding that "the assault should have taught me empathy for the people I had persecuted over the years. But that's not what happened. I turned in the wrong direction. Suddenly it was 'those Black guys' who didn't come to my aid [. . .] Simmering anger turned to rage. Soon, Arno the class bully turned into Arno the racist street fighter."[5]

As an older teenager, Arno found his way into Milwaukee's underground punk scene, which was chaotic and violent.[6] He started drinking, his high-school grades fell, and he became distant from his family. During phases of living away from home with the punks he met, he got his first tattoos, one of which was the twin bolts of the SS—"Not because it meant anything to me at that point, but just because it looked cool."[7] Punk's political spectrum ran from the far left to the far right. Arno gravitated toward the far right, which overlapped with the world of white power skinhead gangs. Before long, he'd started a white power gang of his own. In May 1988, his gang accepted an invitation from the Hammerskins, a much bigger movement based in Texas, to become their northern branch. Arno was now responsible for recruiting across the whole of the Midwest. "Our political agenda was inspired by the doctrine of the Führer himself," he wrote. "Preserve and promote the white race by any means necessary, even if it meant killing our enemies."[8] Some of the most infamous white supremacists in the United States, like David Duke, Ben Klassen, and Tom Metzger began to court him. Over time, though, the far right's fantasies about an all-white future seemed increasingly unrealistic, and Arno grew bored of them because of it. On top of that, the birth of his daughter in 1992 triggered a slow-burning series of epiphanies. What would her life be like without a father, if he died or got imprisoned?

Being a parent also forced him to socialize outside the cloistered world of white supremacy. He left Centurion and spent less time with his gang. He also got pulled into early 1990s rave culture, which revived the spirit of the 1960s, and which had no place for hatred or violence. "I began to see the futility, the absolute madness, of hating based on someone's race or religion or sexual orientation," he remembered.[9] By 2004, he'd given up alcohol. Soon after that, he began to develop an idea for a digital magazine dedicated to both victims and perpetrators of hate. He finally launched it on Martin Luther King Jr. Day in 2010, and it grew faster than he could ever have expected.

Today, nearly fifteen years later, Arno is a nonprofit leader, author, and filmmaker. We spend a lot of time at the start of our conversation talking about his books and about our respective approaches to educational school programs. He tells me that his programs have been protested in the past and that some people have accused him of still being a racist. I latch onto this and ask him how he responds.

"When I started doing this work, I saw a problem with it," Arno explains. "Why should I be congratulated for no longer attacking people because of the color of their skin? But then I realized, my work isn't about who I was. It's about who I am—and I have the ability to reach people that others may not, because of my lived experiences."

The focus of Arno's work today is violent extremism in a broad sense. It takes in the far right as well as other violent ideologies rooted in everything from far-left politics to religion. I ask him what special ingredients or circumstances draw people to far-right groups, rather than groups like Antifa or ISIS.

"Honestly, in my experience, it's kind of a roll of the dice," he says. "I've worked on multiple cases where young people have bounced from white nationalism to Antifa and back. I have a case later this afternoon that's like that," he says, with a heavy sigh. "This guy was getting involved in extremist Islamist stuff, and now he's back to Confederate secession from the United States. It's really more about their unresolved trauma than the flavor of the ideology." This reminds me of what Patrick Riccards had said to me.

As well as reading Arno's books, I also listened to Centurion's albums before we spoke. Not because I wanted to call him out on them—he calls out his past by himself anyway—but simply because I felt that I had to. They surprised me. The lyrics' hateful subject matter aside, they were more sophisticated than I'd expected. The rhyme schemes were tight, the syllabic rhythms were carefully measured, and the songs' concepts were sometimes quite abstract. The sound wasn't far from the nu-metal bands that were big when I was a teenager in the 2000s, like Korn, Limp Bizkit, or Slipknot. I'd thought that Centurion's albums would make me angry. Mostly, though, they just made me sad: they represented a terrible waste of talent. I shared these reflections with Arno.

"Did you ever listen to those big nu-metal bands and think, 'that could have been me'?" I ask.

"Oh, totally—I still love—I've loved—" Even though we're talking about what might have been, the shift toward music makes him overflow with excitement. "I've been head-over-heels in love with music my entire life. I still am. I spend hours a day listening to music." He tells me about the bands that he's listened to recently and about all the playlists that he's built. Then he comes to the story of Centurion's collapse. In part, it happened because the band members all started smoking cannabis. This represented an ideological breach with the white power movement, which saw cannabis as a "Black drug." But they were also cheated by the same movement that their music championed.

"We had a contract with Resistance Records that said we were supposed to be paid $3 per CD we sold," Arno tells me. "And we found out we'd sold 20,000 CDs. Here's me and my guys, we're all broke as fuck, and we're all working menial, minimum wage jobs. We all had young families. We were living between raindrops, trying to scrape by, and suddenly we realized, 'Hey, Resistance owe us twelve grand a piece!' Back then, twelve grand seemed like a million dollars to me. I was floored. So, I got on the phone with the label's owner, and I asked him where our money was. He said, 'What are you guys, a bunch of *Jews*?!'" Arno says, spitting out the word "Jews." "This is all about money to you? We need the money to put out more music and to fund the movement!"

He lets out an exasperated laugh before continuing.

"I thought, 'Are you fucking kidding me?' I was so pissed, and so was everyone in the band. After that, we renamed ourselves Lycanthrope, and we cut a new demo of four songs that were run-of-the-mill metal—violent but not racial. We weren't under the illusion that we'd be the next Metallica, but we thought that we were good enough to make a living, touring and selling records. We definitely aspired to escape the white power yoke and just be a typical band."

But it never happened for them.

While looking up Centurion's albums, I saw recent comments describing Arno as a sell-out and a "race traitor," among other things. People out there are still mad that he left the far right, even though he left over twenty years ago. I share this with him and ask if he ever worries about his own safety.

"Nah," he says, breezily. "I really don't give a shit. I'm proudly a 'race traitor,' and I hope to create more 'race traitors' everywhere I go. When I'm traveling, I'm going to enjoy it, and I'm going to experience that place fully, whether it's Morocco or Berlin or Dubai. I'm not going to look over my shoulder, and I'm not going to allow people to terrorize me from behind a keyboard."

As we talk about it more, though, his breeziness begins to fade. He tells me that he and his family have had death threats in the past. One that came via email around 2012 included his home address, plus the personal details of the relatives who were living with him. He showed the email to the police, but whoever sent it had covered their tracks too thoroughly to be traced.

"So, I put myself back in my old boots, and I thought, 'If I was coming for you, the last thing I'd do is send you an email,'" Arno snorts. "I'd just show up on your doorstep one morning. For a while, that helped me to get past it and the other threatening messages. But then there were other times when I'd dwell on that, and I'd think, '"I haven't got any death threats in a while, is that a bad sign?'" He laughs again before describing the Buddhist ideals that guide him today. "I'm not going to worry about what might happen. Death comes with all mornings: that would be true whether I was a former Neo-Nazi or not. You might get hit by a car, struck by lightning, killed in a terrorist attack. Who knows? You can't let the specter of death diminish the quality of the life that you're living in the moment."

Our conversation moves toward the lessons that people can learn from his story. What does he want the readers of my book, I ask, to know about resisting Nazism?

"That violence is the ultimate capitulation," he says. "If I think about resistance, then I think about resisting the provocation to violence. When I talk to young men who are pounding their chests and ready to throw a fist at anyone who looks at them funny, I say, 'That doesn't impress me. I've done that myself, and it doesn't take a lot of courage. What does take courage—*true courage*,'" he stresses, "'is responding to aggression with compassion.'" He also thinks that Neo-Nazism and far-right extremism can be resisted with what he calls "gray areas"—spaces in which we expose ourselves to cultures, opinions, and traditions other than our own. "What the far right needs to operate and thrive is certainty. All violent extremism is rife with certainty. It's very binary: black-white, one-zero, good-evil, us-them. There's no gray areas. Violent extremism can't function in gray areas. It can't function if there's curiosity or wonder. It can only function with certainty."

There's a cottage industry of tell-all books by Formers. Some of them remind me of *The Wolf of Wall Street*, the 2013 movie about the real-life convicted conman Jordan Belfort. It starts as a salutary story about greed, but it inadvertently ends up glamorizing Belfort's excessive lifestyle while sidelining his victims. In a similar way, Formers' books can start as salutary stories about extremism but end up glamorizing violence. Accidentally or otherwise, the Former presents themselves as an antihero on a voyage of self-discovery, which leaves their victims as anonymous tools of that self-discovery.

Much of Arno's work is different because he actively collaborates with victims of violent extremism, giving them a voice and a chance to share their story. He co-wrote his book *The Gift of Our Wounds* with Pardeep Singh Kaleka, whose father was murdered in a 2012 mass shooting at a Sikh Temple in Oak Creek, Wisconsin, for example. He also appears in the documentary *Refuge*, in which he orchestrates a meeting between a man working to leave the Ku Klux Klan and a Kurdish-Muslim immigrant. But he wrote his first book, *My Life After Hate*, on his own. I told him that one chapter—a graphic account of a violent assault that he once committed—had left me uncomfortable. Not because it was violent, but because I felt it sidelined the victim.

"There is definitely a danger of voyeurism," Arno concedes. "A danger of exploitation. We always need to remember throughout these stories that there are real people who suffered because of it. And honestly, that wasn't lost on me when I was writing *My Life After Hate*. I felt like shit quite often."

Some of my friends and colleagues were concerned when I told them that I'd contacted a Former, even if the Former in question had spent the best part of twenty years speaking against extremism. Before the interview, one of them, a trained counselor, said to me, "If it feels like the conversation is going too well—if it feels like he's *charmed* you—then you should take a step back. It probably means that he's a sociopath."

All through our time together, Arno strikes me as being authentic, honest, and sincere. But he isn't charming. Not in the sense that my colleague meant it, at least: someone who can see inside you and figure out what you want to hear, and then say it as if it had come to them naturally, all to take control of the conversation—and of you.

We eventually got into the extraordinary backstory of Life After Hate. Arno took the lead in founding it in 2011, off the success of his digital magazine. Within a few years, though, he was fired by his own Board of Directors, all of whom were also Formers. There was more in-fighting among the board after he'd gone. In 2019, they ended up in court, with one Former being sued by the others over petty disputes about who created which programs, slogans, and social media profiles. I'd read Arno's account of his firing in *The Gift of Our Wounds*, and I'd read through the 2019 court papers. For me, the takeaway was that people can leave far-right groups, and that they can abandon Nazi ideology—but reentering society is a much bigger challenge. Most Formers were traumatized to begin with, and then they lost significant parts of their youth to a cult-like movement that deliberately interrupted their social-emotional development and deepened their trauma. They're unlikely to have learned the "soft skills" that most of us take for granted, like how to vent frustration constructively, or how to get through the daily grind.

Arno accepts these points and speaks magnanimously about the people who fired him. While he doesn't want to be known as the founder of Life After Hate anymore, he wishes the organization and his ex-partners well.

By now, we've been speaking for hours.

"The fact is," he says, still with the same energetic earnestness that he had at the start of our interview, "we all got involved in hate groups because we're fucked up. We're broken people. And just because we left the hate groups, it doesn't mean that we're no longer fucked up. It only means that we've moved from one stage of our lives to another. I'm better now than I was five years ago, and I was better five years ago than I was ten years ago. So, I'm on a good trajectory. But I still have a lot of issues, and I'm the first to admit it. I'm never going to be fully healed. I'm going to be working on myself till the grave."

As Arno says these words, I feel myself holding back tears. For perhaps the first time while I've been writing this book, I realize that Nazi ideology endangers its own followers as well as its enemies.

Conclusion

Ralph Rehbock tells me that he always ends his school presentations by issuing the students a challenge and then by sharing his family photos with them. Not photos from the 1930s or 1940s, but from the recent past. One—which is of a baby-naming ceremony that took place in 2015—shows seven beaming great-grandparents sitting next to each other in a synagogue with their descendants standing behind them. I ask him, why does he think that it's important for students to see photos like this?

"Because they need to know that Hitler did not win," he says emphatically.

Ralph is a Holocaust survivor. Born in Gotha, Germany, in 1934, he's lived in Chicago, Illinois, for over eighty years. His family immigrated to the United States just before the Second World War began, thanks to his mother's cousin who lived in the country and who sponsored them.

On November 9th, 1938, they went from Gotha to Berlin, where they had an appointment to collect their immigration papers from the United States Embassy the next day. But the 9th and 10th would be inscribed in history as the November Pogrom, or *Kristallnacht*.

"The night of November 9th," Ralph says, "We could see the flames of the synagogue across the street out of our hotel window."

Meanwhile, in Gotha, the Gestapo was knocking on the door of their home. His father—a businessman who owned a metalwork factory—was one of around 30,000 Jewish men who were earmarked for arrest. Their housekeeper telephoned the family in Berlin to tell them not to come home. Fearing that the line was tapped, she used a code phrase that Ralph's father had given her just in case: "the English lesson has been canceled." It was a narrow escape. The arrested men were detained in the concentration camps in Buchenwald, Dachau, and Sachsenhausen. Hundreds of them died. The family eventually got their immigration papers on November 11th. Ralph's father went immediately to London while his mother packed up their belongings for shipment to their new home. They never returned to the factory, which the Nazis forcibly acquired.

Ralph remembers the sight of the burning synagogue, but the rest of the details that he's sharing with me he only heard from his mother much later in his life. In 1986, when she was nearly eighty years old, she gave a video interview to a fledgling local Holocaust survivor's group in Chicago. (This group has since blossomed into the Illinois Holocaust Museum and Education Center, one of the biggest Holocaust museums in the United States.)

"She spoke for several hours, in great, great detail," Ralph says, proudly. "She told of her personal, individual experiences of what happened in Germany after 1918: the hyperinflation, the Depression, the political parties that sprung up in the 1920s, the 1933 election, the Nazis' seizure of power, and the Nuremberg Laws, all building up to the moment that she asked for help from her cousin in America."

"Had she ever spoken about the family history before then?" I ask.

"Not at all," he says. Then he says it again, emphasizing each individual word and taking pauses between them. "*Not—at—all*. She didn't tell the story, and my father didn't tell the story. One night in 1978, my children, who were in high school, said to my father, 'Grandpa, tell us about how you left Germany.' I think that they were asking for a homework assignment of some kind. So, they went upstairs to one of their bedrooms, and my mother followed and took over—as she always did! That was our first glimpse of this story, but another eight years passed before it was told more fully."

The interview that Ruth Rehbock, Ralph's mother, gave in 1986 can still be seen online at the United States Holocaust Memorial and Museum's website.

Even after that interview, though, there were details that she never shared. It was only when she died in 2000 that the family found a letter from her sister, Ralph's aunt, hidden in a sock drawer. Dated January 10th, 1943, it was a harrowing goodbye mailed from Berlin just before she was deported to Auschwitz, where she was murdered.

Ralph got involved in Holocaust remembrance and education in the 1980s. These fields were growing in Illinois at the time, driven by Neo-Nazis who'd spent the late 1970s trying to hold demonstrations in Skokie, a predominantly Jewish neighborhood. One local survivors' group began sending letters to synagogues, asking for fellow survivors to come and join them. Ralph went to one of their meetings and found that he was much younger than everyone else there.

"I started talking about living in Germany, and about how we were able to get out by virtue of a sponsor," he says, "and one lady jumped up and said, 'You are not a survivor!'" He repeats this line with emphasis and a pause between each word, just as he had before. "'We all suffered greatly, we were all in camps'—words to that effect. I very well could have turned around and left."

This is a sad reminder of how long it took the world to define the Holocaust, let alone the meaning of "Holocaust survivor." Raphael Lemkin, a Polish lawyer, coined the word "genocide" in 1944, partly to describe the mass murder of Europe's Jews. In Israel especially, by the late 1940s, the mass murder was often described with the Hebrew word "Shoah," which means "calamity" or "catastrophe." Both terms are still in use today. But it was only in the late 1970s that the word "holocaust" gained a capital "H" and became a universal term for the event. (It'd been used in English to describe tragedies since the nineteenth century, and it comes from the Greek word *holokauston*, which means "completely burnt sacrificial offering.") For decades after the War, a "Holocaust survivor" was generally assumed to be a person who'd survived one of the Nazis' camps. Today, though, a survivor is considered any person, Jewish or non-Jewish, who was "displaced, persecuted, or discriminated against due to the racial, religious, ethnic, social, and political policies of the Nazis and their collaborators between 1933 and 1945."[1]

"I contacted the people who were trying to build a museum instead," Ralph continues, "and I said, 'I know that you have school groups come to hear stories, and I have a story to tell.' I started speaking for them, and their museum grew, and because I had an automobile, I could drive to schools that couldn't come to the museum. And I'm still doing that today, under the auspices of the Illinois Holocaust Memorial Museum and Education Center, where I'm a Vice President."

When we speak, Ralph is one month shy of his ninetieth birthday. I say that most people his age are just enjoying their retirement. Why is he still driving himself around Chicago and telling his story to any young people who will listen?

"Lies are being spewed on social media," he says energetically. "And so many people believe what they see on those platforms. It's not just America; it's worldwide. Some of it is stuff that Hitler began spewing back in the 1920s: that all Jews have huge noses, that they drink the blood of children, that they wrote the *Protocols of the Elders of Zion* . . . " His voice trails away, and then he begins again. "It's all fantasy. Fantasy, fantasy, fantasy. The children hear so much of it, and there seems to be nobody around to counter any of it."

Just as we're about to wrap up our interview, I realize that I never asked Ralph about the challenge that he issues to students at the end of all his talks.

"Whether your family has any connection to the Holocaust or not," he says, "take your mobile device, get together with your parents and grandparents, and get all their stories down—so that you can begin to understand from whence you came."

*

A resister is someone who works to create change in the face of injustice. To do that, their first step is always to build their own expertise. They work to understand what needs to be changed, how it needs to be changed, and what the world will look like after the change has been made. For this reason, above all else, resisters are critical thinkers. They're driven by a need to know the truth, no matter how painful or uncomfortable it may be. They put their opinions aside and challenge their own assumptions at every turn.

A resister's bravery is defined by this combination of desires: to create change for everyone and to better themselves individually. And to create change for everyone, the resister must have a deep sense of common humanity. This is why they almost never use violence. (The only person in this book who used violence directly was Alexander Pechersky—but that was in the indescribable, unimaginable circumstances of a Nazi extermination camp.) It's also why many of the resisters in this book were passionate about the arts in one way or other. Creativity can be a form of resistance because it connects us to our own humanity, and to the humanity of others. This is worth remembering in the twenty-first century, a time when the arts seem to be under constant attack.

A resister's goals are usually arrestingly simple. They want to do something useful and meaningful, and they want to live in a decent world. When their actions are successful, they don't seek credit or praise. That's partly because they rarely work alone. The most effective forms of resistance almost always seem to be collective and collaborative. Equally, resisters don't just give up if their actions are unsuccessful. Their commitment to their goals and ideals is more important to them than winning or losing.

Nazism is the opposite of all this. Like all forms of far-right extremism, it requires its followers to shut down their critical thinking skills and to forget their humanity. This enables them to buy into a fantasy about being better than everyone else. Better because of their gender, nationality, sexual orientation, race, or religion. As a fantasy, Nazism isn't driven by facts and truth. It's driven by opinion—what its followers think *should* be true, what they *want* to be true. They prefer shouting matches and physical violence to real debate, because real debate quickly exposes how nonsensical their ideology is. It's easy to mistake this preference for shouting and violence for bravery. But it's just bullying, and bullying is always cowardly—because bullies only show strength when they know that they'll win before the fight has begun. Hence, perhaps, the far right targets minorities who are already downtrodden and ostracized.

This book wasn't only meant to be about the past. It was meant to be about the present, too. My greatest hope is that the stories within it have given some flickers of light to illuminate the darkness in our own time. Perhaps these flickers will show us new ways of moving forward, and new ways of resisting.

NOTES

Introduction

1. The quotations at the head of this book come, respectively, from Hannah Arendt, *Men in Dark Times* (New York: Harcourt Brace and Company, 1968), ix; and Frédéric Gros, *Disobey! The Philosophy of Resistance*, trans. David Fernbach (New York: Verso, 2020), 5.

2. Richard J. Evans, *The Third Reich in Power, 1933–1939: How the Nazis Won Over the Hearts and Minds of a Nation* (New York: Penguin, 2006), 44–5.

3. See Detlev J. K. Peukert, *Die Edelweißpiraten. Protestbewegungen jugendlicher Arbeiter im "Dritten Reich." Eine Dokumentation* (Köln: Bund-Verlag GmbH, 1980), 236.

4. Gros, *Disobey!*, 5.

Chapter 1

1. I would like to express my gratitude to Dr. Ann Robertson, author of *Karikatur im Kontext. Zur Entwicklung der sozialdemokratischen illustrierten satirischen Zeitschrift Der Wahre Jacob zwischen Kaiserreich und Republik* (Peter Lang: Frankfurt am Main, 1992). Both Dr. Robertson's book and her generous correspondence helped to shape this chapter.

2. Franz Schoenberner, *Confessions of a European Intellectual* (New York: Collier Books, 1965), 12.

3. Schoenberner, *Confessions*, 17.

4. See, for example, Richard J. Evans, *Hitler's People: The Faces of the Third Reich* (New York: Penguin, 2024), 11; or Peter Longerich, *Hitler: A Life*, trans. Jeremy Noakes and Lesley Sharpe (Oxford: Oxford University Press, 2019), 6.

5. Christian Weikop, "Introduction," in *The Oxford Critical and Cultural History of Modernist Magazines*, Volume III, Part 2, ed. Peter Brooker, Sascha Bru, Andrew Thacker, and Christian Weikop (Oxford: Oxford University Press, 2019), 699.

6. Albert Langen, untitled editorial note, in *Simplicissimus*, June 27, 1896 (Year 1, no. 13), 6. For the "divided society" in Germany at the turn of the twentieth century, see

Ulrich Herbert, *A History of 20th-Century Germany*, trans. Ben Fowkes (Oxford: Oxford University Press, 2019), 17.

7   Schoenberner, *Confessions*, 2.

8   Schoenberner, *Confessions*, 2.

9   Richard Evans, *The Coming of the Third Reich: How the Nazis Destroyed Democracy and Seized Power in Germany* (London: Penguin, 2004), 293.

10 Evans, *Hitler's People*, 264.

11 Quoted in Benjamin Carter Hett, *The Death of Democracy: Hitler's Rise to Power and the Downfall of the Weimar Republic* (New York: Henry Holt and Company, 2018), 182.

12 See the indexes on http://www.der-wahre-jacob.de/ (accessed March 9, 2023).

13 Ann Taylor Allen, *Satire and Society in Wilhelmine Germany: Klatteradatsch and Simplicissimus, 1890–1914* (Lexington, KY: The University Press of Kentucky, 1984), 214.

14 Translation taken from Evans, *The Third Reich in Power*, 144.

15 David Welch, *The Third Reich: Politics and Propaganda* (New York: Routledge, 2002), 44.

16 Peter Krain, *Willibald Krain. Als Künstler Gefeiert—Verboten—Vergessen* (Norderstedt: BoD—Books on Demand, 2007), 6.

17 Quoted in Schoenberner, *Confessions*, 5.

18 See Thomas Theodor Heine, *I Wait for Miracles*, trans. Clara G. Stillman (New York: Greenburg, 1947).

19 Walter Trier, *Nazi-German in 22 Lessons, Including Useful Information for Führers, Fifth Columnists, Gauleiters and Quislings: Reprint of a Pamphlet from 1942*, trans. Jon Cho-Polizzi (Berlin: Favoriten Presse, 2022), unnumbered pages.

20 Otto M. Nelson, "*Simplicissimus* and the Rise of National Socialism," *The Historian* 40, no. 3 (May 1978): 441–62 on 461.

21 These two cartoons are "The Hitler Trial—or, how Kahr Saved the Fatherland," *Simplicissimus*, March 17, 1924 (Year 28, no. 51), front cover; and "Munich Circus: Adolf and August," *Simplicissimus*, April 11th, 1927 (Year 32, no. 2), 16.

22 Paula Schwerdtfeger, *Raum—Zeit—Ordnung. Kunstausstellungen im Nationalsozialismus* (Köln: Böhlau, 2023), 61.

23 See The Wiener Holocaust Library, *Eyewitness Account by Susanne Veit of her "Illegal" Life in Berlin*, P III d. No. 536; Viviane Béragnes, *La caricature antihitlérienne dans la presse satirique allemande de 1923 à 1933* (Toulouse:

Université Toulouse le Mirail—Toulouse II, 2012), 3; and Arno Lustiger, *Rettungswiderstand. Über die Judenretter in Europa während der NS-Zeit* (Düsseldorf: Wallstein Verlag, 2011), 58-9.

24 Schoenberner, *Confessions*, 8.

25 Schoenberner, *Confessions*, 306.

26 Schoenberner, *Confessions*, 2.

27 Peter Burke, *Eyewitnessing: The Uses of Images as Historical Evidence* (New York: Cornell University Press, 2008), 9.

28 Franz Schoenberner, *You Still Have Your Head: Excursions From Immobility* (New York: Macmillan, 1957), 13.

29 Schoenberner, *You Still Have Your Head*, 13.

30 Schoenberner, *You Still Have Your Head*, 13.

31 Schoenberner, *You Still Have Your Head*, 15.

32 Schoenberner, *You Still Have Your Head*, 15.

33 Schoenberner, *You Still Have Your Head*, 3.

Chapter 2

1 Sebastian Haffner, *Defying Hitler: A Memoir*, trans. Oliver Pretzel (New York: Farrar, Straus and Giroux, 2002), 79.

2 Haffner, *Defying Hitler*, 80.

3 Haffner, *Defying Hitler*, 97.

5 Haffner, *Defying Hitler*, 3.

6 Haffner, *Defying Hitler*, 16.

7 Haffner, *Defying Hitler*, 68-9.

8 Haffner, *Defying Hitler*, 104.

9 Haffner, *Defying Hitler*, 107.

10 Haffner, *Defying Hitler*, 137.

11 Haffner, *Defying Hitler*, 138.

12 Haffner, *Defying Hitler*, 146.

13 Haffner, *Defying Hitler*, 157.

14 Haffner, *Defying Hitler*, 140.

15 Haffner, *Defying Hitler*, 144.

16 Haffner, *Defying Hitler*, 189–90.

17 Haffner, *Defying Hitler*, 194.

18 Haffner, *Defying Hitler*, 221.

19 Haffner, *Defying Hitler*, 229.

20 Haffner, *Defying Hitler*, 230.

21 Haffner, *Defying Hitler*, 236.

22 Haffner, *Defying Hitler*, 248.

23 Haffner, *Defying Hitler*, 241.

24 Haffner, *Defying Hitler*, 272.

25 Haffner, *Defying Hitler*, 267.

26 Evans, *The Third Reich in Power*, 550.

27 Jürgen Peter Schmied, *Sebastian Haffner. Eine Biographie* (Munich: C. H. Beck, 2010), 58.

28 Fredric Warburg, *All Authors Are Equal: The Publishing Life of Fredric Warburg, 1936–1971* (London: Hutchinson & Co, 1973), 6.

29 Schmied, *Haffner*, 42.

30 Schmied, *Haffner*, 79.

31 Schmied, *Haffner*, 81.

32 Schmied, *Haffner*, 64–5 and endnote on 513.

33 Jutta Krug, *Sebastian Haffner als Engländer maskiert. Ein Gespräch mit Jutta Krug über das Exil. Mit einer Nachbemerkung von Uwe Soukup* (Stuttgart: Deutsche Verlags-Anstalt, 2002), 28–30.

34 Schmied, *Haffner*, 42.

35 See Sebastian Haffner, *Das Leben der Fußgänger. Feuilletons 1933–1938*, ed. Jürgen Peter Schmied (Munich: Deutscher Taschenbuch Verlag, 2004).

36 Haffner, *Defying Hitler*, 4.

37 Evans, *The Third Reich in Power*, 213–14, quote on 214.

38 Haffner, *Defying Hitler*, 185.

Chapter 3

1. Lisa Pine, *Education in Nazi Germany* (Oxford: Berg, 2010), 27.
2. The examples that follow are a condensed form of Richard Evans's investigation into how the Nazis changed school curricula. See Evans, *Third Reich in Power*, 265.
3. Evans, *Third Reich in Power*, 272.
4. Evans, *Third Reich in Power*, 273.
5. The teacher's report is reproduced in Peukert, *Die Edelweißpiraten. Eine Dokumentation*, 4.
6. Detlev J. K. Peukert, trans. Richard Deveson, *Inside Nazi Germany: Conformity, Opposition, and Racism in Everyday Life* (New Haven, CT: Yale University Press, 1987), 164.
7. See, among others, Jan Krauthäuser, Keno Mescher, and Betsy de Torres, *Edelweißpiratenfestival. Eine Dokumentation in Text, Bild und Ton* (Köln: Dabbelju Verlag, 2016), 10; and *Encyclopedia of German Resistance to the Nazi Movement*, ed. Wolfgang Benz and Walter H. Pehle, trans. Lance W. Garmer (New York: Continuum, 1997), 148; Gertrud Koch and Regina Carstensen, *Edelweiß. Meine Jugend als Widerstandskämpferin* (Hamburg: Rowohlt Taschenbuch Verlag, 2006), 87–90.
8. Michael H. Kater, *Hitler Youth* (Cambridge, MA: Harvard University Press, 2006), 138.
9. Quoted in Peter Finkelgruen, *"Soweit er Jude war ... " Moritat von der Bewältigung des Widerstandes—Die Edelweißpiraten als Vierte Front in Köln 1944*, ed. Roland Kaufhold, Andrea Livnat, and Nadine Englhart (Norderstedt: BoD—Books on Demand, 2020), 67.
10. Detlev Peukert, *Inside Nazi Germany*, 157.
11. In Peukert, *Die Edelweißpiraten. Eine Dokumentation*, 73.
12. In Peukert, *Die Edelweißpiraten. Eine Dokumentation*, 4.
13. In Peukert, *Die Edelweißpiraten. Eine Dokumentation*, 76.
14. In Peukert, *Die Edelweißpiraten. Eine Dokumentation*, 31–2.
15. Peukert, *Die Edelweißpiraten. Eine Dokumentation*, 28–30. Translation from Patricia Heberer, *Children During the Holocaust* (Lanham, MD: AltaMira Press, 2011), 254–56.
16. In Peukert, *Die Edelweißpiraten. Eine Dokumentation*, 80–1. Translation in Heberer, *Children During the Holocaust*, 256.
17. In Peukert, *Inside Nazi Germany*, 160.

18 All quotations from this memorandum come from the English translation in *The Third Reich Sourcebook*, ed. Anson Rabinbach and Sander L. Gilman (Berkley: University of California Press, 2013), 860–1.

19 Koch and Carstensen, *Edelweiß*, 62–3.

20 Koch and Carstensen, *Edelweiß*, 77.

21 Koch and Carstensen, *Edelweiß*, 92.

22 Koch and Carstensen, *Edelweiß*, 93.

23 Koch and Carstensen, *Edelweiß*, 88.

24 Finkelgruen, "Soweit er Jude War . . . ," 280.

25 Koch and Carstensen, *Edelweiß*, 128.

26 Fritz Theilen, *Edelweißpiraten*, ed. Matthias von Hellfeld (Frankfurt am Main: Fischer Taschenbuch Verlag, 1987), 18.

27 Theilen, *Edelweißpiraten*, 18.

28 Theilen, *Edelweißpiraten*, 21.

29 Theilen, *Edelweißpiraten*, 38.

30 Theilen, *Edelweißpiraten*, 76.

31 Theilen, *Edelweißpiraten*, 88–97.

32 Theilen, *Edelweißpiraten*, 147.

33 Krauthäuser et al., *Edelweißpiratenfestival*, 23.

34 Benz and Pehle, *Encyclopedia of German Resistance*, 148.

35 See Francesca Weil, *Uns geht es scheinbar wie dem Führer . . . Zur späten sächsischen Kriegsgesellschaft* (1943–1945) (Göttingen: Vandenhoeck and Ruprecht Verlage, 2020).

36 See *Kindheiten im Zweiten Weltkrieg*, ed. Francesca Weil, André Postert, and Alfons Kenkmann (Halle: Mitteldeutscher Verlag, 2018).

Chapter 4

1 For a full account of this meeting, see Saul Friedländer, *Kurt Gerstein: The Ambiguity of Good*, trans. Charles Fullman (New York: Alfred A. Knopf, 1969), 122–7.

2 I'm grateful to Dr. Jürgen Kampmann at Eberhard Karls Universität Tübingen for offering his expert guidance on the German Evangelical Church in the early twentieth century.

3   Friedländer, *Kurt Gerstein*, 34.

4   Friedländer, *Kurt Gerstein*, 37.

5   Friedländer, *Kurt Gerstein*, 43.

6   Evans, *Third Reich in Power*, 310.

7   Henry Friedlander, *The Origins of Nazi Genocide: From Euthanasia to the Final Solution* (Chapel Hill, NC: University of North Carolina Press, 1995), 1.

8   Ernst Klee, ed., *Dokumente zur "Euthanasie"* (Frankfurt am Main: Fischer Taschenbuch Verlag, 1985), 232.

9   Friedländer, *Kurt Gerstein*, 100.

10 Friedländer, *Kurt Gerstein*, 208.

11 Friedländer, *Kurt Gerstein*, 108.

12 Friedländer, *Kurt Gerstein*, 113–14.

13 Heinrich Himmler, *Der Dienstkalender Heinrich Himmlers 1941/42*, ed. Peter Witte, Michael Wildt, Martina Voigt, Dieter Pohl, Peter Klein, Christian Gerlach, Christoph Dieckmann, and Andrej Angrick, with a foreword by Uwe Lohalm and Wolfgang Scheffler (Hamburg: Hans Christians Verlag, 1999), 233.

14 See Robert Gerwarth, *Hitler's Hangman: The Life of Heydrich* (New Haven, CT: Yale University Press, 2011), 206–7.

15 Himmler, *Dienstkalender*, 234.

16 Chris Webb, *The Belzec Death Camp: History, Biographies, Remembrance* (Stuttgart: ibidem Press, 2016), 94–5.

17 Alan Elsner, "Unearthing the Horror of Belzec: In Poland, a Forgotten Nazi Camp Becomes Hallowed Ground," *Washington Post*, September 21st, 2023, https://www.washingtonpost.com/archive/lifestyle/2003/12/28/unearthing-the-horror-of-belzec/dba80037-b9cf-43f8-9680-cd855798c146/

Chapter 5

1   There's no definitive account of the Sobibor Uprising. As is to be expected, the details differ slightly from one testimony to the next. The account offered here draws on various sources, and principally on the books by Yitzak Arad, Tovi Blatt, Miriam Novitch, and Jules Schelvis referenced below; and on Chris Webb, *The Sobibor Death Camp: History, Biographies, Remembrance* (New York: Columbia University Press, 2017).

2   Yitzak Arad, *Belzec, Sobibor, Treblinka: The Operation Reinhard Death Camps* (Bloomington, IN: Indiana University Press, 1999), 137.

3   Quoted in Miriam Novitch, *Sobibor: Martyrdom and Revolt, Documents and Testimonies*, preface by Leon Poliakov (New York: Holocaust Library and Schocken Books, 1980), 90.

4   Novitch, *Sobibor*, 94.

5   For a full account of this incident, see Arad, *Belzec, Sobibor, Treblinka*, 307.

6   Interview with Alexander Pechersky quoted in Jules Schelvis, *Sobibor: A History of a Nazi Death Camp*, ed. Bob Moore, trans. Karin Dixon (Oxford: Berg, 2007), 93.

7   Quoted in Arad, *Belzec, Sobibor, Treblinka*, 307–8.

8   Arad, *Belzec, Sobibor, Treblinka*, 299.

9   This is an abridged version of the exchange quoted in Arad, *Belzec, Sobibor, Treblinka*, 309.

10 Schelvis, *Sobibor*, 152.

11 Schelvis, *Sobibor*, 154.

12 Arad, *Belzec, Sobibor, Treblinka*, 154–5.

13 Arad, *Belzec, Sobibor, Treblinka*, 324.

14 Arad, *Belzec, Sobibor, Treblinka*, 330.

15 Quoted in David Cesarani, *Final Solution: The Fate of the Jews 1933–1949* (New York: St. Martin's Press, 2016), 649.

16 Arad, *Belzec, Sobibor, Treblinka*, 363.

17 Franz Stangl, quoted in Gitta Sereny, *Into That Darkness: An Examination of Conscience* (New York: Random House, 1983), 261.

18 These numbers are from Schelvis, *Sobibor*, 167–8 and 182. According to him, forty-seven of the Sobibor escapees survived the War. Arad estimated that there were fifty to seventy. See *Belzec, Sobibor, Treblinka*, 364.

19 Arad, *Belzec, Sobibor, Treblinka*, 376.

20 Yitzhak "Antek" Zuckerman, *A Surplus of Memory: Chronicle of the Warsaw Ghetto Uprising*, ed. Barbara Harshav, with a foreword by Zivia Lubetkin (Berkley, CA: University of California Press, 1993), 20.

Chapter 6

1   See Rudolf Höss's unforgiving portraits of Glücks and Maurer in Höss, *Death Dealer: The Memoirs of the SS Kommandant at Auschwitz*, ed. Steven Paskuly, trans. Andrew Pollinger (Boston: Da Capo Press, 1996), 257–60 and 301–4 respectively.

2 Walter Lüdde-Neurath, *Unconditional Surrender: A Memoir of the Last Days of the Third Reich and the Dönitz Administration*, trans. Geoffrey Brooks (London: Frontline Books, 2010), 106–7.

3 Höss, *Death Dealer*, 178.

4 Peter Longerich, *Heinrich Himmler*, trans. Jeremy Noakes and Lesley Sharpe (Oxford: Oxford University Press, 2012), 3.

5 Winston Spencer Churchill, *The Second World War, Volume II: Their Finest Hour* (London: Cassell & Co. Ltd., 1949), 337.

6 For a full list of the Field Security Sections that were active during the Second World War, including the places and dates that they were active, see Anthony Clayton, *Forearmed: A History of the Intelligence Corps* (London: Brassey's, 1996), 264–76.

7 Clayton, *Forearmed*, xvi.

8 See Jock Haswell, *British Military Intelligence* (London: Weidenfeld and Nicolson, 1973), 171.

9 Eric Mockler-Ferryman, "The Introduction," in *FSS: Field Security Section*, ed. Robin Steers (Bexhill-on-Sea: Olivers Printers Limited, 1996), unnumbered page.

10 Christopher Andrew, *The Secret World: A History of Intelligence* (New Haven, NJ: Yale University Press, 2018), 1.

11 See Christopher Moran, *Classified: Secrecy and the State in Modern Britain* (Cambridge: Cambridge University Press, 2013), 165.

12 Robin Steers, *FSS: Field Security Section* (Bexhill-on-Sea: Olivers Printers Limited, 1996), 8–19.

13 IWM, Documents.12841, 96 FSS security intelligence report, July 30, 1945, 1–2.

14 96 FSS report, December 13 (2), 1945, 3.

15 96 FSS report, July 30, 1945, 4.

16 96 FSS report, July 31, 1945, 1.

17 96 FSS report, August 5, 1945, 2.

18 96 FSS report, August 12, 1945, 1.

19 96 FSS reports, August 26, 1945, 1.

20 Deposition of Anton Oswald on June 14, 1946, in Daniel Blatman, *The Death Marches: The Final Phase of Nazi Genocide*, trans. Chaya Galai (Cambridge, MA: The Belknap Press of Harvard University Press, 2011), 225–7.

21 See 96 FSS report, August 20t, 1945, 1; and 96 FSS report, August 26, 1945, 1.

22 See Eleonore Lappin-Eppel, *Ungarisch-jüdische Zwangsarbeiter und Zwangsarbeiterinnen in Österreich 1944/45. Arbeitseinsatz, Todesmärsche, Folgen* (Berlin: Lit Verlag, 2010), 368.
23 96 FSS report, May 8, 1946, 5.
24 IWM, Documents.16378, John C. Clark, unpublished memoir, 32.
25 Clark, memoir, 33.
26 Clark, memoir, 37.
27 Ernst Klee, *Das Personenlexicon zum Dritten Reich. Wer war was vor und nach 1945* (Frankfurt am Main: S. Fischer Verlag, 2003), 616.
28 IMW, Documents.16378, John C. Clark, unpublished SD report, 1.
29 Clark, memoir, 1.
30 Clark, memoir, 1.
31 MIM, 92 FSS arrest report for Rudolf Höss, 1.
32 MIM, 92 FSS arrest report for Rudolf Höss, 1.
33 Thomas Harding, *Hanns and Rudolf: The True Story of the German Jew who Tracked Down and Caught the Kommandant of Auschwitz* (New York: Simon and Schuster, 2013), 238–9.
34 IWM, K10/629, 2.
35 Höss arrest report, 1.
36 Harding, *Hanns and Rudolf*, 240–3.
37 See Helen Burchell, "The Northampton Shoemaker who Caught the Auschwitz Commander," *BBC News*, November 11, 2023, https://www.bbc.com/news/uk-england-northamptonshire-66875251 (accessed May 10, 2024).
38 Höss arrest report, 1.
39 Clark, memoir, 38.
40 Clark memoir, 38.

Chapter 7

1 For Leon Bass's account of this incident, see Leon Bass, *Good Enough: One Man's Memoir on the Price of a Dream* (Lawrenceville, NJ: Open Door Publications, 2011), 115–17.
2 See Nina Kaleska, *Nelli's Journey: From the Depths of Evil to Reconciliation and Beyond* (Pittsburgh, PA: Dorrance Publishing, 2005), esp. Chapter Two.

3   Bass, *Good Enough*, 15.

4   Bass, *Good Enough*, 26.

5   Bass, *Good Enough*, 28.

6   Matthew F. Delmont, *Half American: The Epic Story of African Americans Fighting World War Two at Home and Abroad* (New York: Viking, 2022), xiv.

7   Bass, *Good Enough*, 29.

8   Bass, *Good Enough*, 36.

9   Bass, *Good Enough*, 36.

10 Bass, *Good Enough*, 38.

11 This comment was made in a speech given to the House of Commons on January 18, 1945. Quoted in Anthony Beevor, *Ardennes 1944: Hitler's Last Gamble* (London: Viking, 2015), 356.

12 Bass, *Good Enough*, 47.

13 Bass, *Good Enough*, 46–7.

14 *The Buchenwald Report*, trans., ed., and with an introduction by David A. Hackett, foreword by Frederick A. Praeger (Oxford: Westview Press, 1995), 1.

15 Nicholas Wachsmann, *KL: A History of the Nazi Concentration Camps* (New York: Farrar, Straus and Giroux, 2015), 99.

16 Richard Evans, *The Third Reich at War: How the Nazis Led Germany from Conquest to Disaster* (New York: Penguin, 2009), 522.

17 Evans, *Hitler's People*, 404.

18 Bass, *Good Enough*, 52.

19 Bass, *Good Enough*, 53.

20 Bass, *Good Enough*, 53.

21 Bass, *Good Enough*, 55.

22 Bass, *Good Enough*, 55.

23 Bass, *Good Enough*, 66.

24 Bass, *Good Enough*, 115.

25 Bass, *Good Enough*, 116.

26 Bass, *Good Enough*, 116.

27 Bass, *Good Enough*, 117.

28 Leon's talk at this conference can be seen online at the US Holocaust Museum, https://collections.ushmm.org/search/catalog/irn1002693.

29 Bass, *Good Enough*, 127.

30 Delmont, *Half American*, xii.

31 Robbie Waisman with Susan McClelland, *Boy from Buchenwald: The True Story of a Holocaust Survivor* (New York: Bloomsbury, 2021).

32 David Bercuson and Douglas Wertheimer, *A Trust Betrayed: The Keegstra Affair* (Garden City, NY: Doubleday & Company, Inc., 1985), 29.

33 Bass, *Good Enough*, 128.

34 Bass, *Good Enough*, 128–9.

35 Bass, *Good Enough*, 129.

Chapter 8

1 This exchange is documented in Bernd Naumann, *Auschwitz: A Report on the Proceedings Against Robert Karl Ludwig Mulka and Others Before the Court at Frankfurt*, trans. Jean Steinberg, with an introduction by Hannah Arendt (New York: Frederick A. Praeger, 1966), 122–3.

2 Sigrid Grabner and Hendrik Röder, eds., *Emmi Bonhoeffer. Bewegende Zeugnisse eines mutigen Lebens* (Hamburg: Rowohlt Taschenbuch Verlag, 2006), 79.

3 Grabner and Röder, *Emmi Bonhoeffer*, 64.

4 United States Holocaust Memorial Museum RG-50.423.0007, *Oral History Interview with Emmi Delbrück Bonhoeffer*, 7:08–27.

5 Jutta Koslowski, *Wer War Klaus Bonhoeffer? Annäherungen an einen unbekannten Widerstandskämpfer* (Gütersloh: Gütersloher Verlagshaus, 2023), 259.

6 Klaus would be responsible for running Germany's civil aviation in the aftermath of the coup. See Koslowski, *Wer War Klaus Bonhoeffer?*, 326.

7 See Ian Kershaw, *Hitler 1936–1945: Nemesis* (New York: W. W. Norton & Company, 2001), 693.

8 Quoted in Koslowski, *Wer War Klaus Bonhoeffer?*, 803.

9 Grabner and Röder, *Emmi Bonhoeffer*, 81.

10 Dorothee von Meding, *Courageous Hearts: Women and the Anti-Hitler Plot of 1944*, trans. Michael Balfour and Volker R. Berghahn (New York: Berghahn Books, 1997), 22.

11 Cited in Jutta Koslowski, "'Dieses lächerliche Hindernis nehmen . . .' Aus dem Erlebnisbericht von Emmi Bonhoeffer über ihre gefährliche Reise im Sommer 1945," *Zeitzeichen*, 4/2022, 47–9 on 48.

12 Koslowski, "'Dieses lächerliche Hindernis nehmen . . . ,'" 49.

13 Koslowski, "'Dieses lächerliche Hindernis nehmen . . . ,'" 49.

14 Koslowski, "'Dieses lächerliche Hindernis nehmen . . . ,'" 49.

15 Koslowski, "'Dieses lächerliche Hindernis nehmen . . . ,'" 49.

16 Grabner and Röder, *Emmi Bonhoeffer*, 91.

17 Ronen Steinke, *Fritz Bauer: The Jewish Prosecutor Who Brought Eichmann and Auschwitz to Trial*, trans. Sinéad Crowe with a foreword by Andreas Vosskuhle (Bloomington, IN: Indiana University Press, 2020), 132.

18 Devin O. Pendas, *The Frankfurt Auschwitz Trial, 1963–1965: Genocide, History, and the Limits of the Law* (Cambridge: Cambridge University Press, 2010), 2.

19 Emmi Bonhoeffer, *Auschwitz Trials: Letters from an Eyewitness*, trans. Ursula Stechow (Richmond, VA: John Knox Press, 1967), 12.

20 Merle Funkenberg, *Zeugenbetreuung von Holocaust-Überlebenden und Widerstandskämpfern bei NS-Prozessen (1964–1985). Zeitgeschichtlicher Hintergrund und emotionales Erleben* (Giessen: Psychosozial-Verlag, 2016), 110.

21 Cited in Funkenberg, *Zeugenbetreuung*, 109.

22 Cited in Grabner and Röder, *Emmi Bonhoeffer*, 111.

23 Funkenberg, *Zeugenbetreuung*, 111.

24 Bonhoeffer, *Letters*, 29–30.

25 Funkenberg, *Zeugenbetreuung*, 115–16.

26 Funkenberg, *Zeugenbetreuung*, 119.

27 Renate Reinke, cited in Funkenberg, *Zeugenbetreuung*, 11.

28 Alfons Erb, cited in Funkenberg, *Zeugenbetreuung*, 11.

29 Funkenberg, *Zeugenbetreuung*, 112.

30 Funkenberg, *Zeugenbetreuung*, 122.

31 Jens Meierhenrich and Devin O. Pendas, eds., *Political Trials in Theory and History* (Cambridge: Cambridge University Press, 2016).

32 Bonhoeffer, *Letters*, 12.

33 Bonhoeffer, *Letters*, 22.

34 Michael Mawson and Philip G. Ziegler, "Introduction," in *The Oxford Handbook of Dietrich Bonhoeffer*, ed. Mawson and Ziegler (Oxford: Oxford University Press, 2019), 1.

35 Koslowski, *Wer War Klaus Bonhoeffer?*

36 Von Meding, *Courageous Hearts*, 27.

Chapter 9

1 Gitta Sereny, *Into That Darkness*, 365.

2 See Evans, *Third Reich in Power*, 123.

3 Gitta Sereny, *The German Trauma: Experiences and Reflections, 1938–2001* (New York: Penguin, 2001), 1.

4 See Evans, *The Third Reich in Power*, 646–64.

5 Sereny, *German Trauma*, 5–6.

6 Sereny, *German Trauma*, 6.

7 Sereny, *German Trauma*, 10.

8 Sereny, *German Trauma*, 87.

9 Sereny, *German Trauma*, 88.

10 Gitta Sereny, Letter to Professor Thompson, March 22, 1975 (The Wiener Holocaust Library, Gitta Sereny Collection, 2244/1/2/1/14).

11 Klee, *Personenlexicon*, 596.

12 Sereny, *German Trauma*, 89.

13 Sereny, *Into that Darkness*, 21.

14 Sereny, *Into that Darkness*, 22.

15 Sereny, *Into that Darkness*, 23.

16 Sereny, *Into that Darkness*, 25.

17 Sereny, *Into that Darkness*, 360.

18 Sereny, *Into that Darkness*, 363.

19 Sereny, *Into that Darkness*, 364.

20 Sereny, *Into that Darkness*, 366.

21 Sereny, *Into that Darkness*, 24.

22 Sereny, *Into that Darkness*, 31. The italics are in the original.

23 Dorothy Rabinowitz, "Into That Darkness (book review)," *Commentary* 59, no. 5 (May 1, 1975): 75–8.

24 Sereny, *Into that Darkness*, 39.

25 Gitta Sereny, Letter to Robert Graves, October 3, 1978 (The Wiener Holocaust Library, Gitta Sereny Collection, 2244/1/2/1/56).

26 See Gitta Sereny's annotated copy of Thomas Walker, "Treblinka: Two Men in White," review of *Into That Darkness* in *Forum World Features* (The Wiener Holocaust Library, Gitta Sereny Collection, GS, 2244/1/2/1/2).

27 Gitta Sereny, Letter to Doctor Dickson, March 22, 1975 (The Wiener Holocaust Library, Gitta Sereny Collection, 2244/1/2/1/15).

28 Gitta Sereny, "Questioning the Perpetrators," in *Lessons and Legacies V: The Holocaust and Justice*, ed. Ronald Smelser (Evanston, IL: Northwestern University Press, 2002), 194.

29 Diana Athill, "The Gitta Sereny I Knew," *The Guardian*, June 21, 2012, February 2nd, 2023, https://www.theguardian.com/books/2012/jun/21/diana-athill-gitta-sereny-knew.

30 Translation from Longerich, *Himmler*, 689.

31 Evans, *Third Reich at War*, 615.

32 Klee, *Personenlexicon*, 596.

Chapter 10

1 For Claude Lanzmann's account of his first meetings with Franz Suchomel, see Lanzmann, *The Patagonian Hare: A Memoir*, trans. Frank Wynne (New York: Farrar, Straus and Giroux, 2012), 445–8.

2 Nora Sayre, "Film Fete: 'Israel Why,'" *New York Times*, October 8, 1973, 40.

3 Lanzmann, *The Patagonian Hare*, 411.

4 Lanzmann, *The Patagonian Hare*, 412.

5   Marc Chevrie and Hervé le Roux, "Site and Speech: An Interview with Claude Lanzmann about *Shoah*," in *Claude Lanzmann's* Shoah: *Key Essays*, ed. Stuart Liebman (Oxford: Oxford University Press, 2007), 38.

6   Lanzmann, *The Patagonian Hare*, 419.

7   Lanzmann, *The Patagonian Hare*, 517; and Geoffrey Hartman, *The Longest Shadow: In the Aftermath of the Holocaust* (Bloomington, IN: Indiana University Press, 1996), 84.

8   Lanzmann, *The Patagonian Hare*, 419.

9   Lanzmann, *The Patagonian Hare*, 423.

10 Lanzmann, *The Patagonian Hare*, 429–30.

11 Chevrie and le Roux, "An Interview with Claude Lanzmann," 44.

12 Aaron Kerner, *Film and the Holocaust: New Perspectives on Dramas, Documentaries, and Experimental Films* (New York: Continuum, 2011), 209.

13 Lanzmann, *The Patagonian Hare*, 442.

14 Lanzmann, *The Patagonian Hare*, 443.

15 Lanzmann, *The Patagonian Hare*, 449.

16 Lanzmann, *The Patagonian Hare*, 450.

17 Lanzmann, *The Patagonian Hare*, 451.

18 This timeline comes from Jennifer Cazenave, *An Archive of the Catastrophe: The Unused Footage of Claude Lanzmann's Shoah* (Albany, NY: SUNY Press, 2019), xix–xxii.

19 Lanzmann, *The Patagonian Hare*, 469.

20 See *Spielberg's Holocaust: Critical Perspectives on Schindler's List*, ed. Yosefa Loshitzky (Bloomington, IN: Indiana University Press, 1997), 11 and 54.

21 Ron Rosenbaum, *Explaining Hitler: The Search for the Origins of his Evil* (Boston, MA: Da Capo Press, 2014), 257.

22 See Claude Lanzmann, Cathy Caruth, and David Rodowick, "The Obscenity of Understanding: An Evening with Claude Lanzmann," *American Imago* 48, no. 4 (Winter 1991): 473–95; and Rosenbaum, Explaining Hitler, 274.

23 Claude Lanzmann, "Hier ist Kein Warum," *Nouvelle Revue de Psychanalyse*, "Le Mal," 38 (Autumn, 1988), 263.

24 Operation Reinhard staff had to sign a contract that included an "absolute prohibition" on photography inside the Operation Reinhard camps. For a copy of this contract, see Yitzak Arad, Israel Gutman, and Abraham Margaliot, eds., *Documents on the Holocaust: Selected Sources on the Destruction of the Jews of Germany and*

Austria, Poland, and the Soviet Union, trans. Lea Ben Dor (Lincoln, NE: University of Nebraska Press, 1999), 274–75.

25 Martin Cüppers, Anne Lepper, and Jürgen Matthäus, eds., *From "Euthanasia" to Sobibor: An SS Officer's Photo Collection* (Bloomington, IN: Indiana University Press, 2022), 124–25.

26 Adolf Hitler, *Hitler, Mein Kampf. Eine kritische Edition*, ed. Christian Hartmann, Thomas Vordermayer, Othmar Plöckinger, and Roman Töppel, with assistance from Pascal Trees, Angelika Reizle, and Martina Seewald-Mooser (Munich: Institute for Contemporary History, 2016), 349.

Chapter 11

1 Keith Hitchins, *A Concise History of Romania* (Cambridge: Cambridge University Press, 2014), 200.

2 CIA Special Collection, Nazi War Crimes Disclosures Act, Document no. 519bdecf993294098d51469f.

3 Judy Feigin, *The Office of Special Investigations: Striving for Accountability in the Aftermath of the Holocaust*, ed. Mark M. Richard (Washington, DC: U.S. Department of Justice, 2009), 203.

4 See Hitchins, *A Concise History of Romania*, 206, and Dennis Deletant, *Hitler's Forgotten Ally: Ion Antonescu and His Regime, Romania 1940–1944* (New York: Palgrave Macmillan, 2006), 63.

5 Deletant, *Hitler's Forgotten Ally*, 64.

6 Cited in Ralph Blumenthal, "Bishop Under Inquiry on Atrocity Link," *The New York Times*, December 26, 1973, 1.

7 CIA, Special Collection, Nazi War Crimes Disclosures Act, Document no. 519bdecf993294098d51469f, 8.

8 Jean Ancel, *The History of the Holocaust in Romania*, trans. Yaffah Murciano, ed. Leon Volovici, with the assistance of Miriam Caloianu (University of Nebraska Press and Yad Vashem, 2011), 151.

9 Emil Dorian, *The Quality of Witness: A Romanian Diary 1937–1944*, ed. Marguerite Dorian, trans. Mara Soceanu Vamos, with an introduction by Michael Stanislawski (Philadelphia: The Jewish Publication Society of America, 1982), entry on January 24th, 1941, on 139.

10. Carmen Țăgșorean, "Testimony over Time: The Fascist Rebellion in Bucharest in Words and Pictures (January 21–23, 1941)," *Philobiblon* 20, no. 1 (2015): 45–66.

11. CIA, Special Collection, Nazi War Crimes Disclosures Act, Document no. 519bdecf993294098d51469f, 3.

12. Feigin, *The Office of Special Investigations*, 204.

13. Evans, *Third Reich at War*, 231–2.

14. Feigin, *Office of Special Investigations*, 204.

15. Joseph Lelyveld, "Former Nazi Camp Guard Is Now a Housewife in Queens," *New York Times*, July 14, 1964, 10.

16. Robert Wistrich, *Who's Who in Nazi Germany* (New York: Routledge, 2002), 215–16.

17. Annie Jacobsen, *Operation Paperclip: The Secret Intelligence Program that Brought Nazi Scientists to America* (New York: Little, Brown and Company, 2014), 260.

18. Mary Kathryn Barbier, *Spies, Lies, and Citizenship: The Hunt for Nazi Criminals* (Lincoln, NE: Potomac Books, 2017), 232.

19. Richard Rashke, *Useful Enemies: John Demjanjuk and America's Open-Door Policy for Nazi War Criminals* (New York: Delphinium Books, 2013), xiv.

20. Rashke, *Useful Enemies*, 3.

21. Rochelle G. Saidel, *The Outraged Conscience: Seekers of Justice for Nazi War Criminals in America* (Albany, NY: SUNY Press, 1984), 7.

22. Saidel, *Outraged Conscience*, 37.

23. Senate Congressional Record, May 11, 1955 (July 23rd, 2024), https://www.congress.gov/84/crecb/1955/05/11/GPO-CRECB-1955-pt5-4-1.pdf.

24. Ralph Blumenthal, "In Berlin, Unraveling a Family Mystery," *The New York Times*, June 22, 2016 (April 24th, 2024), https://www.nytimes.com/2016/06/26/travel/berlin-world-war-2.html.

25. Elizabeth Holtzman with Cynthia L. Cooper, *Who Said It Would be Easy? One Woman's Life in the Political Arena* (New York: Arcade Publishing, 1996), 93.

26. Allan A. Ryan, Jr., *Quiet Neighbors: Prosecuting Nazi War Criminals in America* (San Diego: Harcourt Brace Jovanovich, 1984), 240.

27. Ryan, *Quiet Neighbors*, 242.

28. Ryan, *Quiet Neighbors*, 243.

Chapter 12

1 Arno Michaelis, *My Life after Hate*, foreword by Angier Aker and Tanya Cromartie (Milwaukee, WI: Authentic Presence Publications, 2012), 35.

2 Michaelis, *My Life after Hate*, 36.

3 Arno Michaelis and Pardeep Singh Kaleka, with Robin Gaby Fisher, *The Gift of Our Wounds: A Sikh and a Former White Supremacist Find Forgiveness After Hate* (New York: St. Martin's Press, 2018), 20, 24, and 27.

4 Michaelis and Kaleka, *The Gift of Our Wounds*, 22–3.

5 Michaelis and Kaleka, *The Gift of Our Wounds*, 29.

6 Michaelis and Kaleka, *The Gift of Our Wounds*, 62.

7 Michaelis and Kaleka, *The Gift of Our Wounds*, 68.

8 Michaelis and Kaleka, *The Gift of Our Wounds*, 80–1.

9 Michaelis and Kaleka, *The Gift of Our Wounds*, 117.

Conclusion

1 This is The United States Holocaust Memorial Museum's current definition of a Holocaust survivor, quoted in Paul R. Bartrop, *Resisting the Holocaust: Upstanders, Partisans, and Survivors* (Santa Barbara, CA: ABC-CLIO, 2016), xxix.

FURTHER READING

This book began with the question that I'm asked most often on The Ninth Candle's programs: "Why didn't more people resist Nazism?" This section is a response to the second-most asked question, which often comes up when we start digging into the details of unfamiliar individuals and events: "How did you find all this stuff?"

The answer is simple: continuous, unending reading. Historians have written a wealth of literature about Nazi Germany and the Holocaust, and it would take many lifetimes to get through all of it. With that thought in mind, I've decided not to include a traditional academic bibliography—a dense list of references to every article, book, and document that I used in my research. (There is a list of works cited, though, which gives the details of everything from which I quoted directly.) Instead, for readers who want to learn more about Nazism and the Third Reich, I'm offering this list of recommended reading. Every book that I've chosen is currently in print and available to buy in paperback for a reasonable price (usually between $20 and $40) from local bookstores or Amazon, or to loan from local libraries. The list isn't meant to be definitive—it's only meant to give a choice of starting points.

Books About Everyday Life in Nazi Germany

Richard Evans, *The Third Reich Trilogy* (2003–2008)

1. *The Coming of the Third Reich: How the Nazis Destroyed Democracy and Seized Power in Germany*

2. *The Third Reich in Power, 1933–1939: How the Nazis Won Over the Hearts and Minds of a Nation*

3. *The Third Reich at War: How the Nazis Led Germany from Conquest to Disaster*

This magisterial trilogy tells the story of Nazi Germany's birth and rise, its time in power, and its ultimate collapse. Written in astonishing historical detail and with an accessible, page-turning narrative, it is suitable for older high school students as well as teachers and general readers. Even though new archival documents have come to light since it was published (as Evans himself has pointed out), it remains an unrivaled overview of the circumstances, social forces, and institutions that produced Nazism in Germany and that drove it forward. Ideally the Trilogy should be read in tandem with Evans's latest book, *Hitler's People* (see below). I probably referred to these four books more than any others while writing *Resisting Nazism*.

Detlev Peukert, *Inside Nazi Germany: Conformity, Opposition, and Racism in Everyday Life* (1987)

Peukert was a brilliant German historian who died in 1990 in tragic circumstances when he was just thirty-nine years old. He was one of the first to try studying Nazi Germany "from the bottom up"—approaching it through the experiences of everyday people, rather than through its leaders. Even though his career was cut short, and even though his book is nearly forty years old, it is still one of the best and most readable accounts of Germans' experiences of Nazism.

Leaders and Followers in Nazi Germany

Richard Evans, *Hitler's People: The Faces of the Third Reich* (2024)

Beginning with a detailed biographical portrait of Hitler himself, Evans spirals outward through the circles of power that surrounded him. He divides these circles into three layers. The innermost layer, the "paladins," consisted of infamous figures like Hermann Göring, Joseph Goebbels, and Heinrich Himmler. The next layer, the "enforcers," consisted of those who worked to solidify Hitler's dictatorship and to bring his most radical visions into reality, like Adolf Eichmann, Reinhard Heydrich, and Julius Streicher. Some (like Streicher) were driven principally by their own ideological fanaticism, others (like Heydrich) by slavish loyalty to those above them. The outermost layer, the "instruments," consisted of opportunists who worked in particular domains and who built a life for themselves in the Third Reich, like Karl Brandt (Hitler's doctor), Ilse Koch (the wife of a camp commandant), and Leni Riefenstahl (the director of *The Triumph of the Will*). Some of the biographies in *Hitler's Faces* are new takes on familiar figures, others are the first of their kind to be written in English. Evans explains and interweaves the personalities and life-stories of the people who put Hitler in power, kept him there, and helped him to wage war and genocide.

Volker Ullrich, *Hitler: Ascent, 1889–1939* and *Hitler: Downfall, 1939–1945* (2013–2020)

Ullrich's two-volume biography is the latest large-scale study of Adolf Hitler. It builds on earlier biographies by historians like Ian Kershaw and Peter Longerich. Ullrich is primarily a journalist, and his writing is gripping and fast-paced. But his study is also serious historical scholarship. He challenges us to see Hitler as a human being, by delving into his personal qualities and his relationships in ways that his predecessors sometimes avoided.

Peter Longerich, *Heinrich Himmler* (2007) and *Joseph Goebbels* (2010)

These books tell the life stories of two of the most significant figures in the Third Reich. Beyond unfolding their biographies, Longerich probes their psyches to try and discover what turned them into the men they became. Joseph Goebbels's exploitation of the mass media—which in his time meant, principally, the radio and the cinema—has become newly relevant in the era of "fake news." Longerich's account of the propaganda empire that Goebbels built, and his analysis of how it worked, is especially impressive.

Books about the Holocaust and the Nazis' Camps

David Cesarani, *Final Solution: The Fate of the Jews 1933–1949* (2016)

There are many pioneering books that tell the story of the Holocaust, including Raul Hilberg's *The Destruction of the European Jews* (1961), Martin Gilbert's *Holocaust: A History of the Jews of Europe During the Second World War* (1987), and a dazzling two-volume study by Saul Friedländer that was a over decade in the making, *Nazi Germany and the Jews: The Years of Persecution, 1933–1939* (1997) and *Nazi Germany and the Jews: The Years of Extermination, 1939–1945* (2007). David Cesarani was a decorated British historian who died shortly before his book about the Holocaust was published. It's one of the most recent in this lineage, and it's both a readable and impressively in-depth study that takes advantage of sources unavailable to earlier scholars.

Peter Longerich, *The Unwritten Order: Hitler's Role in the Final Solution* (2001)

This is a short book based on the expert testimony that Longerich gave at the trial of David Irving, a British Holocaust denier, in 2000. It's also a compelling account of the Holocaust and an explanation of Hitler's role in it. Longerich illuminates the nature of Hitler's leadership, and he shows how he drove the antisemitic and genocidal policies of his regime. After reading this book, one could progress to Longerich's larger and more challenging study, *Holocaust*.

Yitzak Arad, *Belzec, Sobibor, Treblinka: The Operation Reinhard Death Camps* (2018)

This is an updated edition of a book that was first published in 1987. It is still the most detailed and authoritative single-volume study of the three Operation Reinhard extermination camps, where over two million Jewish people were murdered. Packed with eyewitness accounts and extracts from other documents, it reconstructs how these secretive camps worked, and what everyday life inside them was like. It also sheds light on the lives and minds of the perpetrators who ran them.

Nikolaus Wachsmann, *KL: A History of the Nazi Concentration Camps* (2015)

Our memory of the Nazis' concentration and extermination camps tends to concentrate on Auschwitz, and perhaps, secondarily, on a handful of other infamous places, like Buchenwald, Dachau, and Treblinka. But the Nazis' penal system was a dense network of tens-of-thousands of camps. Wachsmann surveys this network in its entirety, using a staggering array of documents and testimonies to portray and analyze the different types of camp, how the camp network evolved, and the many purposes it served in Nazi Germany.

Documents about Nazi Germany

Anson Rabinbach and Sander L. Gilman, *The Third Reich Sourcebook* (2013)

This is the biggest and the most expensive book in my list of recommendations—the paperback edition will set you back about $85 (at the time of writing). It is an invaluable resource, though, especially for teachers who want materials that they can use to build their own inquiry-based lesson plans and curricula about Nazi Germany and the Holocaust. It's an exhaustive and varied collection of documents, organized by topic and translated into English.

Yitzak Arad, *Documents on the Holocaust: Selected Sources on the Destruction of the Jews of Germany and Austria, Poland, and the Soviet Union* (1999)

The 1999 edition is the eighth of this book, a collection of over 200 documents relating specifically to the Nazis' antisemitic policies and the Holocaust. Stretching back to 1920, it shows how these policies took shape and radicalized over time.

Ernst Klee, *"The Good Old Days": The Holocaust as Seen by Its Perpetrators and Bystanders* (1991)

This unique collection of documents and testimonies sheds light on the Holocaust exclusively from the perspectives of the people who carried it out and of those who stood by and watched. It's often extremely difficult to read, but it gives an invaluable, revealing glimpse into the minds of the people who made the Holocaust happen.

Nonfiction Books for Young People about Nazi Germany and Its Legacy

Peter Hayes, *Why? Explaining the Holocaust* (2017)

Although this unique and easy-to-read book is not written for young people specifically, it is a great choice for older high school students. It addresses some of the biggest questions around the Holocaust, all based on the questions that Hayes—who taught history at Northwestern for over thirty years—was asked most often by his own students.

K. R. Gaddy, *Flowers in the Gutter: The True Story of the Edelweiss Pirates, Teenagers Who Resisted the Nazis* (2020)

Nonfiction books about Nazi Germany written specifically for young people can be hard to find. Gaddy's is one of the best. She tells the story of the Edelweiss Pirates with both fastidious historical accuracy and page-turning urgency. The book is augmented throughout with English translations of archival documents, making it an excellent one to include in any middle- or high-school curriculum.

Timothy Snyder, *On Tyranny: Twenty Lessons from the Twentieth Century* (2017) and *On Freedom* (2024)

Timothy Snyder is a history professor at Yale best-known for his epic book *Bloodlands: Europe Between Stalin and Hitler* (2010), a study of the mass murders of civilians that took place under the Nazi and Communist regimes between 1933 and 1945. His two books *On Tyranny* and *On Freedom* are beautifully written miniatures. They offer accessible lessons in which he uses his historical expertise to dig into the meaning of terms like "democracy" and "freedom" and to carve out questions and observations for our own time.

WORKS CITED

Archival Materials

CIA Special Collection, Nazi War Crimes Disclosure Act. Freedom of Information Electronic Reading Room, P.L. 105-246.
Database One, Field Security Section Personnel Listed in the Archive Material. Military Intelligence Museum, Chicksands.
Der Wahre Jacob, http://www.der-wahre-jacob.de/index.php?id=34.
Documents Relating to 64 and 65 Field Security Sections, SOE, 1944–1945. The Imperial War Museum (IWM), Documents.16378.
Eyewitness Account by Susanne Veit of her "Illegal" Life in Berlin. The Wiener Holocaust Library, P III d. No. 536.
Gitta Sereny Collection. The Wiener Holocaust Library, 2244/1/2/1.
Judge, A. F. *The Field Security Sections of the Intelligence Corps 1939 to 1960: A Consolidated Listing and Description of the British Army's Field Security Sections in War and Peace*. The Military Intelligence Museum, Chicksands.
Pamphlet of Standard Instructions for N.C.O.s of no. 7 Field Security Section, Intelligence Corps. The Imperial War Museum (IWM), LBY K. 10/629.
Private Papers of J R Tempest. The Imperial War Museum (IWM), Documents.12841.
Rudolf Höss Arrest Report. Military Intelligence Museum, Chicksands.
Senate Congressional Record, May 11, 1955.
Simplicissimus, http://www.simplicissimus.info/index.php?id=5.

Documents and Critical Editions

Arad, Yitzak, Israel Gutman, and Abraham Margaliot, eds. *Documents on the Holocaust: Selected Sources on the Destruction of the Jews of Germany and Austria, Poland, and the Soviet Union*. Translated by Lea Ben Dor. Lincoln, NE: University of Nebraska Press, 1999.
Hackett, David A., ed. and trans. *The Buchenwald Report*. Oxford: Westview Press, 1995.
Himmler, Heinrich. *Der Dienstkalender Heinrich Himmlers 1941/42*. Edited with a commentary by Peter Witte, Milchael Wildt, Martina Voigt, Dieter Pohl, Peter Klein, Christian Gerlach, Christoph Dieckmann, and Andrej Angrick. Hamburg: Hans Christians Verlag, 1999.

Hitler, Adolf. *Hitler, Mein Kampf. Eine kritische Edition*. Edited by Christian Hartmann, Thomas Vordermayer, Othmar Plöckinger, and Roman Töppel, with assistance from Pascal Trees, Angelika Reizle, and Martina Seewald-Mooser. Munich: Institute for Contemporary History, 2016.

Klee, Ernst, ed. *Dokumente zur "Euthanasie."* Frankfurt am Main: Fischer Taschenbuch Verlag, 1985.

Peukert, Detlev J. K. *Die Edelweißpiraten. Protestbewegungen jugendlicher Arbeiter im "Dritten Reich." Eine Dokumentation*. Köln: Bund-Verlag GmbH, 1980.

Trier, Walter, *Nazi-German in 22 Lessons, Including Useful Information for Führers, Fifth Columnists, Gauleiters and Quislings: Reprint of a Pamphlet from 1942*. Translated by Jon Cho-Polizzi. Berlin: Favoriten Presse, 2022.

Articles, Magazines, Newspapers

Athill, Diana. "The Gitta Sereny I Knew." *The Guardian*, June 21, 2012. https://www.theguardian.com/books/2012/jun/21/diana-athill-gitta-sereny-knew (accessed February 12, 2024).

Blumenthal, Ralph. "Bishop Under Inquiry on Atrocity Link." *The New York Times*, December 26, 1973, 81.

Blumenthal, Ralph. "In Berlin, Unraveling a Family Mystery." *The New York Times*, June 22, 2016, TR1.

Burchell, Helen. "The Northampton Shoemaker who Caught the Auschwitz Commander." *BBC News*, November 11, 2023. https://www.bbc.com/news/uk-england-northamptonshire-66875251 (accessed May 24, 2024).

Esner, Alan. "Unearthing the Horror of Belzec: In Poland, a Forgotten Nazi Camp Becomes Hallowed Ground." *Washington Post*, December 27, 2003. https://www.washingtonpost.com/archive/lifestyle/2003/12/28/unearthing-the-horror-of-belzec/dba80037-b9cf-43f8-9680-cd855798c146/ (accessed August 25, 2024).

Haffner, Sebastian. *Das Leben der Fußgänger. Feuilletons 1933-1938*. Edited by Jürgen Peter Schmied. Munich: Deutscher Taschenbuch Verlag, 2004.

Koslowski, Jutta. "'Dieses lächerliche Hindernis nehmen . . .'. Aus dem Erlebnisbericht von Emmi Bonhoeffer über ihre gefährliche Reise im Sommer 1945." *Zeitzeichen*, 4/2022, 47–9.

Lanzmann, Claude, Cathy Caruth, and David Rodowick. "Hier ist Kein Warum." *Nouvelle Revue de Psychanalyse*, "Le Mal" 38 (Autumn 1988): 263.

Lanzmann, Claude, Cathy Caruth, and David Rodowick. "The Obscenity of Understanding: An Evening with Claude Lanzmann." *American Imago* 48, no. 4 (Winter 1991): 473–95.

Nelson, Otto M. "*Simplicissimus* and the Rise of National Socialism." *The Historian* 40, no. 3 (May 1978): 441–62.

Rabinowitz, Dorothy. "Into That Darkness (book review)." *Commentary* 59, no. 5 (May 1, 1975): 75–8.

Sayre, Nora. "Film Fete: 'Israel Why.'" *New York Times,* October 8, 1973, 40.

Țăgșorean, Carmen. "Testimony over Time: The Fascist Rebellion in Bucharest in Words and Pictures (January 21–23, 1941)." *Philobiblon* 20, no. 1 (2015): 45–66.

Diaries, Letters, and Memoirs

Bass, Leon. *Good Enough: One Man's Memoir on the Price of a Dream.* Lawrenceville, NJ: Open Door Publications, 2011.

Bonhoeffer, Emmi. *Auschwitz Trials: Letters from an Eyewitness.* Translated by Ursula Stechow. Richmond, VA: John Knox Press, 1967.

Churchill, Winston Spencer. *The Second World War, Volume II: Their Finest Hour.* London: Cassell & Co. Ltd., 1949.

Dorian, Emil. *The Quality of Witness: A Romanian Diary 1937–1944.* Edited by Marguerite Dorian. Translated by Mara Soceanu Vamos. Philadelphia: The Jewish Publication Society of America, 1982.

Haffner, Sebastian, *Defying Hitler: A Memoir.* Translated by Oliver Pretzel. New York: Farrar, Straus and Giroux, 2002.

Heine, Thomas Theodor. *I Wait for Miracles.* Translated by Clara G. Stillman. New York: Greenburg, 1947.

Holtzman, Elizabeth, with Cynthia L. Cooper. *Who Said It Would be Easy? One Woman's Life in the Political Arena.* New York: Arcade Publishing, 1996.

Höss, Rudolf. *Death Dealer: The Memoirs of the SS Kommandant at Auschwitz.* Edited by Steven Paskuly and translated by Andrew Pollinger. Boston: Da Capo Press, 1996.

Kaleska, Nina. *Nelli's Journey: From the Depths of Evil to Reconciliation and Beyond.* Pittsburgh, PA: Dorrance Publishing, 2005.

Koch, Gertrud, and Regina Carstensen. *Edelweiß. Meine Jugend als Widerstandskämpferin.* Hamburg: Rowohlt Taschenbuch Verlag, 2006.

Lanzmann, Claude. *The Patagonian Hare: A Memoir.* Translated by Frank Wynne. New York: Farrar, Straus and Giroux, 2012.

Lüdde-Neurath, Walter. *Unconditional Surrender: A Memoir of the Last Days of the Third Reich and the Dönitz Administration.* Translated by Geoffrey Brooks. London: Frontline Books, 2010.

Michaelis, Arno. *My Life After Hate.* Forewords by Angier Aker and Tanya Cromartie. Milwaukee, WI: Authentic Presence Publications, 2012.

Michaelis, Arno, and Pardeep Singh Kaleka, with Robin Gaby Fisher. *The Gift of Our Wounds: A Sikh and a Former White Supremacist Find Forgiveness After Hate.* New York: St. Martin's Press, 2018.

Ryan, Jr., Allan A. *Quiet Neighbors: Prosecuting Nazi War Criminals in America.* San Diego: Harcourt Brace Jovanovich, 1984.

Schoenberner, Franz. *You Still Have Your Head: Excursions From Immobility.* New York: Macmillan, 1957.

Schoenberner, Franz. *Confessions of a European Intellectual*. New York: Collier Books, 1965.
Steers, Robin. *FSS: Field Security Section*. Bexhill-on-Sea: Olivers Printers Limited, 1996.
Theilen, Fritz. *Edelweißpiraten*. Edited by Matthias von Hellfeld. Frankfurt am Main: Fischer Taschenbuch Verlag, 1987.
Waisman, Robbie, with Susan McClelland. *Boy from Buchenwald: The True Story of a Holocaust Survivor*. New York: Bloomsbury, 2021.
Zuckerman, Yitzhak "Antek." In *A Surplus of Memory: Chronicle of the Warsaw Ghetto Uprising*. Edited by Barbara Harshav, with a foreword by Zivia Lubetkin. Berkley, CA: University of California Press, 1993.

Books

Allen, Ann Taylor. *Satire and Society in Wilhelmine Germany: Klatteradatsch and Simplicissimus, 1890–1914*. Lexington, KY: The University Press of Kentucky, 1984.
Allen, Jr., Charles R. *Nazi War Criminals in America: Facts . . . Action. The Basic Handbook*. New York: Highgate House, 1985.
Ancel, Jean. *The History of the Holocaust in Romania*. Translated by Yaffah Murciano and edited by Leon Volovici with the assistance of Miriam Caloianu. Lincoln, NE: University of Nebraska Press, 2011.
Andrew, Christopher. *The Secret World: A History of Intelligence*. New Haven, NJ: Yale University Press, 2018.
Arendt, Hannah. *Men in Dark Times*. New York: Harcourt Brace and Company, 1968.
Barbier, Mary Kathryn. *Spies, Lies, and Citizenship: The Hunt for Nazi Criminals*. Lincoln, NE: Potomac Books, 2017.
Bartrop, Paul R. *Resisting the Holocaust: Upstanders, Partisans, and Survivors*. Santa Barbara, CA: ABC-CLIO, 2016.
Beevor, Anthony. *Ardennes 1944: Hitler's Last Gamble*. London: Viking, 2015.
Benz, Wolfgang, and Walter H. Pehle, eds. *Encyclopedia of German Resistance to the Nazi Movement*. Translated by Lance W. Garmer. New York: Continuum, 1997.
Béragnes, Viviane. *La caricature antihitlérienne dans la presse satirique allemande de 1923 à 1933*. Doctoral thesis. Toulouse: Université Toulouse le Mirail - Toulouse II, 2012.
Bercuson, David, and Douglas Wertheimer. *A Trust Betrayed: The Keegstra Affair*. Garden City, NY: Doubleday & Company, Inc., 1985.
Blatman, Daniel. *The Death Marches: The Final Phase of Nazi Genocide*. Translated by Chaya Galai. Cambridge, MA: The Belknap Press of Harvard University Press, 2011.
Brooker, Peter, Sascha Bru, Andrew Thacker, and Christian Weikop, eds. *The Oxford Critical and Cultural History of Modernist Magazines*. Oxford: Oxford University Press, 2019.

Browning, Christopher R., with contributions by Jürgen Matthäus. *The Origins of the Final Solution: The Evolution of Nazi Jewish Policy 1939–1942*. London: Arrow Books, 2005.

Burke, Peter. *Eyewitnessing: The Uses of Images as Historical Evidence*. New York: Cornell University Press, 2008.

Cazenave, Jennifer. *An Archive of the Catastrophe: The Unused Footage of Claude Lanzmann's Shoah*. Albany, NY: SUNY Press, 2019.

Cesarani, David. *Final Solution: The Fate of the Jews 1933–1949*. New York: St. Martin's Press, 2016.

Clayton, Anthony. *Forearmed: A History of the Intelligence Corps*. London: Brassey's, 1996.

Cüppers, Martin, Anne Lepper, and Jürgen Matthäus, eds. *From "Euthanasia" to Sobibor: An SS Officer's Photo Collection*. Bloomington, IN: Indiana University Press, 2022.

Deletant, Dennis. *Hitler's Forgotten Ally: Ion Antonescu and His Regime, Romania 1940–1944*. New York: Palgrave Macmillan, 2006.

Delmont, Matthew F. *Half American: The Epic Story of African Americans Fighting World War Two at Home and Abroad*. New York: Viking, 2022.

Evans, Richard J. *The Coming of the Third Reich: How the Nazis Destroyed Democracy and Seized Power in Germany*. New York: Penguin, 2004.

Evans, Richard J. *The Third Reich in Power, 1933–1939: How the Nazis Won Over the Hearts and Minds of a Nation*. New York: Penguin, 2006.

Evans, Richard J. *The Third Reich at War: How the Nazis Led Germany from Conquest to Disaster*. New York: Penguin, 2009.

Evans, Richard J. *Hitler's People: The Faces of the Third Reich*. New York: Penguin, 2024.

Feigin, Judy. *The Office of Special Investigations: Striving for Accountability in the Aftermath of the Holocaust*. Edited by Mark M. Richard. Washington, DC: U.S. Department of Justice, 2009.

Finkelgruen, Peter, ed. Roland Kaufhold, Andrea Livnat, and Nadine Englhart. *"Soweit er Jude war . . ." Moritat von der Bewältigung des Widerstandes – Die Edelweißpiraten als Vierte Front in Köln 1944*. Norderstedt: BoD – Books on Demand, 2020.

Friedländer, Saul. *Kurt Gerstein: The Ambiguity of Good*. Translated by Charles Fullman. New York: Alfred A. Knopf, 1969.

Funkenberg, Merle. *Zeugenbetreuung von Holocaust-Überlebenden und Widerstandskämpfern bei NS-Prozessen (1964–1985). Zeitgeschichtlicher Hintergrund und emotionales Erleben*. Giessen: Psychosozial-Verlag, 2016.

Gerwarth, Robert. *Hitler's Hangman: The Life of Heydrich*. New Haven, CT: Yale University Press, 2011.

Grabner, Sigrid, and Hendrik Röder, eds. *Emmi Bonhoeffer. Bewegende Zeugnisse eines mutigen Lebens*. Hamburg: Rowohlt Taschenbuch Verlag, 2006.

Gros, Frédéric. *Disobey! The Philosophy of Resistance*. Translated by David Fernbach. New York: Verso, 2020.

Harding, Thomas. *Hanns and Rudolf: The True Story of the German Jew who Tracked Down and Caught the Kommandant of Auschwitz*. New York: Simon and Schuster, 2013.

Hartman, Geoffrey. *The Longest Shadow: In the Aftermath of the Holocaust*. Bloomington, IN: Indiana University Press, 1996.

Haswell, Jock. *British Military Intelligence*. London: Weidenfeld and Nicolson, 1973.

Heberer, Patricia. *Children During the Holocaust.* Lanham, MD: AltaMira Press, 2011.
Henry Friedlander, *The Origins of Nazi Genocide: From Euthanasia to the Final Solution.* Chapel Hill, NC: University of North Carolina Press, 1995.
Herbert, Ulrich. *A History of 20th-Century Germany.* Translated by Ben Fowkes. Oxford: Oxford University Press, 2019.
Hett, Benjamin Carter. *The Death of Democracy: Hitler's Rise to Power and the Downfall of the Weimar Republic.* New York: Henry Holt and Company, 2018.
Hitchins, Keith. *A Concise History of Romania.* Cambridge: Cambridge University Press, 2014.
Jacobsen, Annie. *Operation Paperclip: The Secret Intelligence Program that Brought Nazi Scientists to America.* New York: Little, Brown and Company, 2014.
Kater, Michael H. *Hitler Youth.* Cambridge, MA: Harvard University Press, 2006.
Kerner, Aaron. *Film and the Holocaust: New Perspectives on Dramas, Documentaries, and Experimental Films.* New York: Continuum, 2011.
Klee, Ernst. *Das Personenlexicon Zum Dritten Reich. Wer war was vor und nach 1945.* Frankfurt am Main: S. Fischer Verlag, 2003.
Koslowski, Jutta. *Wer War Klaus Bonhoeffer? Annäherungen an einen unbekannten Widerstandskämpfer.* Gütersloh: Gütersloher Verlagshaus, 2023.
Krain, Peter. *Willibald Krain. Als Künstler gefeiert – verboten – vergessen.* Norderstedt: BoD – Books on Demand, 2007.
Krauthauser, Jan, Keno Mescher, and Betsy de Torres. *Edelweißpiratenfestival. Eine Dokumentation in Text, Bild und Ton.* Köln: Dabbelju Verlag, 2016.
Krug, Jutta. *Sebastian Haffner Disguised as an Englishman. Ein Gespräch mit Jutta Krug über das Exil. Mit einer Nachbemerkung von Uwe Soukup.* Stuttgart: Deutsche Verlags-Anstalt, 2002.
Lappin-Eppel, Eleonore. *Ungarisch-jüdische Zwangsarbeiter und Zwangsarbeiterinnen in Österreich 1944/45. Arbeitseinsatz, Todesmärsche, Folgen.* Berlin: Lit Verlag, 2010.
Liebman, Stuart, ed. *Claude Lanzmann's Shoah: Key Essays.* Oxford: Oxford University Press, 2007.
Longerich, Peter. *Heinrich Himmler.* Translated by Jeremy Noakes and Lesley Sharpe. Oxford: Oxford University Press, 2012.
Longerich, Peter. *Hitler: A Life.* Translated by Jeremy Noakes and Lesley Sharpe. Oxford: Oxford University Press, 2019.
Loshitzky, Yosefa, ed. *Spielberg's Holocaust: Critical Perspectives on Schindler's List.* Bloomington, IN: Indiana University Press, 1997.
Lustiger, Arno. *Rettungswiderstand. Über die Judenretter in Europa während der NS-Zeit.* Düsseldorf: Wallstein Verlag, 2011.
Mawson, Michael, and Philip G. Ziegler, eds. *The Oxford Handbook of Dietrich Bonhoeffer.* Oxford: Oxford University Press, 2019.
Meding, Dorothee von. *Courageous Hearts: Women and the Anti-Hitler Plot of 1944.* Translated by Michael Balfour and Volker R. Berghahn. New York: Berghahn Books, 1997.
Meierhenrich, Jens, and Devin O. Pendas, eds. *Political Trials in Theory and History.* Cambridge: Cambridge University Press, 2016.

Moran, Chrisopher. *Classified: Secrecy and the State in Modern Britain*. Cambridge: Cambridge University Press, 2013.

Naumann, Bernd. *Auschwitz: A Report on the Proceedings Against Robert Karl Ludwig Mulka and Others Before the Court at Frankfurt*. Translated by Jean Steinberg with an introduction by Hannah Arendt. New York: Frederick A. Praeger, 1966.

Pendas, Devin O. *The Frankfurt Auschwitz Trial, 1963–1965: Genocide, History, and the Limits of the Law*. Cambridge: Cambridge University Press, 2010.

Peukert, Detlev J. K. *Inside Nazi Germany: Conformity, Opposition, and Racism in Everyday Life*. Translated by Richard Deveson. New Haven, CT: Yale University Press, 1987.

Pine, Lisa. *Education in Nazi Germany*. Oxford: Berg, 2010.

Rashke, Richard. *Useful Enemies: John Demjanjuk and America's Open-Door Policy for Nazi War Criminals*. New York: Delphinium Books, 2013.

Robertson, Ann. *Karikatur im Kontext. Zur Entwicklung der sozialdemokratischen illustrierten satirischen Zeitschrift Der Wahre Jacob zwischen Kaiserreich und Republik*. Peter Lang: Frankfurt am Main, 1992.

Rosenbaum, Ron. *Explaining Hitler: The Search for the Origins of his Evil*. Boston, MA: Da Capo Press, 2014.

Saidel, Rochelle G. *The Outraged Conscience: Seekers of Justice for Nazi War Criminals in America*. Albany, NY: SUNY Press, 1984.

Schmied, Jürgen Peter. *Sebastian Haffner. Eine Biographie*. Munich: C. H. Beck, 2010.

Schwerdtfeger, Paula. *Raum – Zeit – Ordnung. Kunstausstellungen im Nationalsozialismus*. Köln: Böhlau, 2023.

Sereny, Gitta. *Into That Darkness: An Examination of Conscience*. New York: Random House, 1983.

Sereny, Gitta. *The German Trauma: Experiences and Reflections, 1938–2001*. New York: Penguin, 2001.

Smelser, Ronald, editor. *Lessons and Legacies V: The Holocaust and Justice*. Evanston, IL: Northwestern University Press, 2002.

Steinke, Ronen. *Fritz Bauer: The Jewish Prosecutor Who Brought Eichmann and Auschwitz to Trial*. Translated by Sinéad Crowe with a foreword by Andreas Vosskuhle. Bloomington, IN: Indiana University Press, 2020.

Wachsmann, Nicholas. *KL: A History of the Nazi Concentration Camps*. New York: Farrar, Straus and Giroux, 2015.

Webb, Chris. *The Sobibor Death Camp: History, Biographies, Remembrance*. New York: Columbia University Press, 2017.

Weil, Francesca, André Postert, and Alfons Kenkmann, eds. *Kindheiten im Zweiten Weltkrieg*. Halle: Mitteldeutscher Verlag, 2018.

Weil, Francesca. *Uns geht es scheinbar wie dem Führer . . . Zur späten sächsischen Kriegsgesellschaft (1943–1945)*. Göttingen: Vandenhoeck and Ruprecht Verlage, 2020.

Welch, David. *The Third Reich: Politics and Propaganda*. New York: Routledge, 2002.

Wistrich, Robert. *Who's Who in Nazi Germany*. New York: Routledge, 2002.

INDEX

Note: Page numbers followed by 'n' denotes note numbers.

22 Lessons in Nazi-German pamphlet (Trier) 22
101st Airborne Division, U.S. Army 128
183rd Engineer Combat Battalion, Italian Army 125, 128

Abrahams, Karl "Blitz" 114
African American Military History Museum 136–8
Alexander, Hanns 114
Allen, Charles 204
   Nazi War Criminals Among Us (pamphlet) 204
Altötting, Germany 177–96
American History X (movie) 217
American neo-Nazis 215–29
Andrew, Christopher 108
Anschluss (annexation) 162–3
Anstey, John 164, 166
anti-Black racism in United States 133–4
anti-liberalism 49–50
antisemitism in Germany 12, 34, 37, 44, 49, 133–4, 184, 192, 200–1, 211, 215, 217
Antonescu, Ion 198–200
Anyksciai 1–2
Arnold, Karl 22
"As Recent as Yesterday on Proud Steeds . . ." (Schilling) 14–15
Auschwitz-Birkenau concentration and extermination camp 113
   camp for Roma and Sinti people 143
Auschwitz-Birkenau Foundation, Poland 79–80, 97, 113, 115–17
Auschwitz-Birkenau Memorial Museum, Poland 115–18

Baldwin, James 131
Barbier, Mary 203–4
Bartoszewski, Władysław 115–16
Bass, Leon 123–41
   in all-Black unit 125
   autobiography 135–6
   Buchenwald concentration camp 128–30, 132–3
   education 124–5
   in England 127–8
   first job in Belgium 127
   friendship with Waisman, Robbie 124–5
   in Intelligence Reconnaissance Section 125
   in International Liberators' Conference, Washington, DC (1981) 132
   job at George G. Meade Elementary School 131
   overview 124–5
   parents 124
   as principal of Benjamin Franklin High School 131
   racism, experience of 125–7, 131
   speeches 133–4
   as teacher 131
   in United States Army 125
Bastogne 128
Battle of the Bulge 127–8
Bauer, Fritz 150–1
Bausch, Viktor 148
Belfort, Jordan 227–8
Belzec extermination camp 73–4, 76–82
   Gerstein, Kurt in 73–4, 76–82
   Gerstein, Kurt's report on 82
   history 79

Benjamin Franklin High School,
    PA   123–41
Berger, Karl Friedrich   207–8
Bethge, Eberhard   146
Bialowitz, Philip   97
Bildungsbürgertum   41
Blatt, Thomas "Toivi"   97, 101
Blumenthal, Ralph   197, 201–9
Boger, Wilhelm   143–4, 150, 154
Bolender, Kurt   94
Bomba, Abraham   181
Bonhoeffer, Dietrich   157–8
Bonhoeffer, Emmi   143–60
    Bausch, Viktor and   148
    Bonhoeffer, Klaus and   144–7
    diary   148
    with Dieck, Charlotte   147–9
    with Diem, Lotti   147–9
    Frankfurt Auschwitz Trial
        and   151–60
    legacy   159–60
Bonhoeffer, Klaus   144–7
    detained in Moabit   146
    interrogation   146
    memorial for   147
    sentenced to death   146–7
Bonhoeffer, Susanne   159
Bothmann, Hans   119
Boy from Buchenwald (Waisman)   139
The Boy in the Striped Pajamas
    (movie)   195
Braunsteiner-Ryan, Hermine   202, 206
Brauweiler Abbey, monastery   57–8
Britain   107–8
Buchenwald concentration camp   129–41
    barracks for prisoners   130–1
    Bass, Leon experience of   129–30
    prisoner communities in   130
Burke, Peter   25

Café des Westens, Berlin   9
Call of Duty (video game)   218–19
Camp Shelby   136–7

The Campus (newspaper)   201–2
Carol II, King   198
cartoonists in 1920s Germany   7–29
    Florath, Alois   12–14
    Heine, Thomas Theodor   9–12, 19–22
    Holtz, Karl   18–19
    Krain, Willibald   16–17
    Schilling, Erich   14–15
cartoons satirizing Nazism   7–29
    "As Recent as Yesterday on Proud
        Steeds . . . ." (Schilling)   14–15
    "The German's Spring Song"
        (Heine)   19–20
    "Hitler" (Krain)   16–17
    "Munich Summer Scene"
        (Florath)   12–14
    untitled cartoon (Holtz)   18–19
    "What Does Hitler Look Like?"
        (Heine)   10–12
Central Registry of War Criminals
    and Security Suspects
    (CROWCRASS)   204
Chelmno extermination camp   119, 186
Cherche-Midi   76
Churchill, Winston   107, 128
Clark, John C.   111–13, 120–1
Clarke, Bernard   114
Comic Pages (*Lustige Blätter*)
    (magazine)   22
Confessions of a European Intellectual
    (Schoenberner)   29
Confino, Alon   160
Cook, Peter   26
Coulmas, Corinna   184–7, 189–90
    with Lanzmann, Claude   186–7
    on Nazi war criminals   187–8
Cristescu, Eugen   200
Cross, Victor   113, 118–20
Cywiński, Piotr   115–16

dadaism   9
Daily Telegraph Magazine   164
de Beauvoir, Simone   179

Defying Hitler: A Memoir
    (Haffner) 39–47
Delbrück, Justus 146
Delmont, Matthew 133–4
Demjanjuk, John 204
Destruction of the European Jew, The
    (Helberg) 180
Detlavs, Karlis 206
DeVito, Anthony 204–5
Der Wahre Jacob (*True Jacob, The*)
    (magazine) 12–14, 16, 18,
    21–2, 24–5, 27–8
Diamant, Hella 208
Diamant, Szilard 208
Die Zeitung (*The Times*,
    newspaper) 40–1
Dieck, Charlotte 147–9
Diem, Lotti 147–9
Dietrich, Otto 21
Displaced Persons Act 214
Dönitz, Karl 105–6
Dorian, Emil 200
"Double Victory Campaign" 133
Dropping the Pilot (Tenniel, cartoon) 24
Duke, David 222–3

Earl, Ruth Bailey 135–6
Ebeling, Bertha 71–2
Edelweiss Pirates 52–67
    anti-Nazi songs 54
    anti-Nazi slogans 55, 57
    in Düsseldorf 55
    festival 61, 66
    girls involved in 54
    group singing in 53–4
    Koch, Gertrud and 56–8, 60
    Schäfer, Peter and 61–2, 67
    societal status 66–7
    Thielen, Fritz and 59–60
    in Wuppertal 54–5
"Editor's Law" (*Schriftleitergesetz*) 21
education system in Nazi
    Germany 49–67
    German greeting 50

    indoctrination machine 50–1
    Montessori education 56
Eichmann, Adolf 109, 112
    trial of 209
Einsatzgruppen 188–9
Einsatzkommando 112
Eisenhower, Dwight 106
Erb, Alfons 154
Escape From Sobibor (movie) 100
Evangelical Church of Westphalia 82
Evangelism 70
Evans, Richard 4, 37, 47, 51, 72, 129,
    175, 201
Explaining Hitler (Rosenbaum) 183
expressionism 9
extremist groups 218
Eyewitnessing (Burke) 25

far-right extremism 5, 46–7, 66, 192,
    221, 227, 235
Feldhendler, Leon 91–2
Feuchtwanger, Lion 9
Field Security Sections (FSS) 105–21
    30 FSS 111–12
    64 FSS 111–12
    92 FSS 113–14
    96 FSS 110
Final Solution, The (Reitlinger)
    179–80
Flensburg Government 105–6
Florath, Alois 12–14, 22
Flossenbürg concentration camp 157
Frank, Anne 82–3
Frank, Hans 96
Frankfurt Auschwitz Trial 151–60
    Bonhoeffer, Emmi and 151–60
    learning from legacy of 156–7
    treatment of survivor-witnesses
        at 151–4
Frankfurter Allgemeine Zeitung
    (newspaper) 39, 44
Freiberg, Dov 97
Frenzel, Karl 89–90
Fullarton, Owen 118–20

Gawkowski, Henrik   181–2
George G. Meade Elementary
    School   131
German Red Cross office   151–2
German Workers' Party   8–9
"The German's Spring Song" cartoon
    (Heine)   19–20
Germany   35
  antisemitism in   12, 34, 37, 44, 133–4,
    184, 192, 200–1, 211, 215, 217
  Cabinet of Barons   17
  Great Depression and   17
  Haffner, Sebastian departure
    from   31–47
  magazine culture at turn of 20th
    century   9–10, 24
  September 1930 election   17
Germany: Jekyll and Hyde (Haffner)   38–9, 41
Gerstein, Karl   72–3
Gerstein, Kurt   69–85
  applied to join SS   72–3
  arrested and expelled from Nazi
    party   71
  in Belzec   73–4, 76–82
  Christian faith   70
  family   71
  in Nazi Party   70
  Orsenigo, Cesare and   75
  personal documents and papers   82
  posthumous reputation   82–3
  report on Belzec   82
  sister-in-law murdered   71–2
  Söderblom, Staffan and   74–5
Gestapo   59–60
Ghetto Fighters' House Museum,
    Israel   101
Gift of Our Wounds, The (Michaelis and
    Kaleka)   228
Gleichschaltung   67
Globocnik, Odilo   77, 96, 97
Glücks, Richard   105
Gomerski, Hubert   94
Graetschus, Siegfried   95

Great Depression   17
Grodno Ghetto   123–4
Gros, Frédéric   5
Gulbransson, Olaf   22
Gymnasium   56

Haffner, Sebastian   31–47
  analyses of Nazism   44
  articles and essays   38
  autobiographical book   31–7
  biographies of   40
  childhood   32
  children   39
  Defying Hitler: A Memoir   39–47
  departure from Nazi Germany   34–5
  England, experiences in   37–8
  France, experiences in   36–7
  "inner emigration"   41
  as journalist   37
  Krug interview   41
  legacy   42–3
  Life of Pedestrians, The   42
  on Nazis as enemies   33
  overview   31–2
  Pretzel, Oliver on   43–6
  Schmied, Jürgen Peter research on   40
Half American (Delmont)   133
Hamburg   112
Hanejko, Tomasz   77–82
Hannah Arendt Institute   64
Hansen, Hans Peter   114
Hareven, Alouph   179
Hartl, Albert   173
Hartl, Franz   110–11
Heiden, Konrad   9
Heine, Thomas Theodor   9–12
  anti-Nazi cartoons   9–12, 19–20, 22
  "The German's Spring Song"
    cartoon   19–20
  I Wait for Miracles   22
  "What Does Hitler Look Like?"
    cartoon   10–12
"Here There Is No Why"
    (Lanzmann)   183

heroism of resisters   100, 194, 235–6
Heydrich, Reinhard   77
Hillberg, Raul   180
Himmler, Heinrich   55, 77, 96, 105–6, 174–5, 194
Hirszman, Chaim   77
Hitler, Adolf   9
  cartoons of   18–26
  as Chancellor   17, 35–6
  fortress incarceration (April 1924)   14
  image   10–12
  My Struggle   14, 192
  speeches   26, 50
  vision   12
Hitler Youth   50–5, 58–9, 61, 67, 70
"Hitler" (Krain) (cartoon)   16–17
Holocaust   1–3, 66, 76, 78, 80, 82, 85, 88, 100, 232–6
  education in United States   66
  Hollywood narratives about   101
  museums   101–2
  name, etymology of   233
  photos of   183–4
  survivor testimonies   61, 64, 72–3, 77–8, 80–1, 98, 132, 139, 143, 155, 184, 189, 193, 195–6
Holtz, Karl   18–19, 21, 26
Holtzman, Elizabeth   207–13
Holtzman Amendment (1978)   211–12
Honeyman, Donald   164
Honeyman, Mandy   171–3
Hordenkeile   58
Höss, Rudolf   105–6, 113–14, 117–20
Huallenz, Ernst   111

I Wait for Miracles (Heine)   22
Illinois Holocaust Memorial Museum and Education Center   234
"inner emigration"   41
Inside Story of an Outsider, The (Schoenberner)   29
institutionalized racism   125–41
Intelligence Corps   107, 108
Intelligence Reconnaissance Section   125

International Bonhoeffer Society   157
Into That Darkness (Sereny)   169, 171
Iron Guard   198–201
Israel Why (Lanzmann, movie)   179

Jewish people   3–4, 73
  antisemitism in Germany for   12, 34, 37, 44, 49, 134, 184, 192, 200–1, 211, 215, 217
  demonization of   49
  deportation from across Europe   112
  in extermination camps (*see* extermination camps)
  fought in ghetto uprisings   101
  as minority in Germany   4
  resistance   56, 103, 116, 179, 215–29
  Riebeckstraße 63 as detention site for   64
Jim Crow laws   124

Kaleka, Pardeep Singh   228
Kaleska, Nina   131–2
Kaminskas, Bronius   206
Kamp, Martin   82–4
Kampffmeyer, Paul   9
Keegstra, James   140
  "Keegstra Affair"   139–40
King, Martin Luther, Jr.   224
Kittelbach Pirates   51–2
Klan, Ku Klux   228
Klassen, Ben   222–3
Klemperer, Viktor   70
Klier, Johann   94
Koch, Gertrud   56–8, 60–1
Koch, Ilse   129–30
Koch, Karl-Otto   129–30
Koslowski, Jutta   157–60
Krain, Willibald   16–17, 21
Krauthäuser, Jan   61, 65
Krug, Jutta   41
Krüger, Friedrich Wilhelm   77
Kukawski, Łukasz   87, 97–100, 117
Kurt Gerstein House   82

Langen, Albert   9–10
Lanzmann, Claude   177–84, 186–7, 189, 194, 196
  autobiography, *The Patagonian Hare*   188–9
  Coulmas, Corinna, research and work with   186–7
  commissioned to make film about Holocaust   179
  as editor of *Les Temps Modernes (Modern Times)* (magazine)   179
  family   179
  as freelance writer and journalist   179
  "Here There Is No Why"   183
  interviews with   181–3
    Bomba, Abraham   181
    Gawkowski, Henrik   181
    perpetrators   181–4
  Israel Why (movie)   179
  joined French resistance against Nazis   179
  met with Holocaust survivors   180
  on Micheels, Louis   183
  research on Holocaust   179–83
  Shoah (movie)   183–96
  visit to Altötting, Germany   178–9
League of German Girls   50–1
Lelyveld, Joseph   202
Lemkin, Raphael   233
Lerman, Miles   78
Libertatae   198–9
Life After Hate   216, 220–3, 228–9
Life of Pedestrians, The (Haffner)   42
Lill, Arnulf   111
"Little Credo" (Haffner) (newspaper article)   42
Litzmannstadt Ghetto   117
Lorant, Stefan   7
Lvov Ghetto   81

McGlothlin, Erin   193–4, 196
magazine culture in early twentieth century Germany   9–10
Maikovskis, Boļeslavs   206

Majdanek concentration and extermination camp   79–80, 98, 129, 202, 208
Mann, Thomas   38, 44
Martelange   127
Martin, Lambert   38
Maurer, Gerhard   105
Meaning of Hitler, The (Haffner)   39
Medallion, The (Sereny)   164
Mendelson, Martin   208
Mengele, Joseph   206
Metzger, Tom   222–3
Meyer, Tamara   215
Michaelis, Arno   215, 222–9
  actively collaborates with victims of violent extremism   228–9
  Centurion's albums and   225
  digital magazine   229
  Gift of Our Wounds, The   228–9
  My Life after Hate   228
  violent extremism   224
Micheels, Louis   183
Military Intelligence Museum, Chicksands, England   118–19
Minsk   87
Minssen, Barbara   151–2
Molden, Vanessa   135–8
Montessori education   56
Mühsam, Erich   22
Müller, Hilde   151
"Munich Summer Scene" cartoon (Florath)   12–14
Mussolini, Benito   14
My Life after Hate (Michaelis)   228
My Struggle (Hitler)   14, 192
Narodowe Siły Zbrojne, right-wing militia group   77
National Socialist Documentation Center of Cologne   65
National Socialist League of Teachers   49
National Union of Romanian Christian Students   199
nationalism   49–50
nationalist racism   5

Nationalsozialistische Volkswohlfahrt
    (NSV) 56
nativism 5
Natzweiler concentration camp 129
Navajos 52
Naval Academy, Flensburg 105
Nazi concentration camps
    Buchenwald 128–9
    Flossenbürg 157
    Natzweiler 129
    Ravensburg 202
    Sachsenhausen 129, 159
Nazi extermination camps
    Auschwitz 73, 79–80, 97, 102–3, 113,
        115–19, 121, 124, 129
    Belzec 73–4, 76–82
    Chelmno 119, 186
    Gerstein, Kurt's report on
        Belzec 75–6
    Majdanek 79–80, 98, 129, 202, 208
    photos of 183–4
    Sobibor 73–4, 88–9
    Treblinka 73–4, 102
    uprisings in 87–103
Nazi Germany 3–4, 8–9
    boycott of Jewish businesses 34
    civil servants in 35–6
    debasement of victims 115
    dictatorship 65
    "Editor's Law" (*Schriftleitergesetz*) 21
    education system 49–67
    euthanasia program 72
    fakery and hypocrisy 22
    Haffner, Sebastian and 31–47
    on hereditary diseases 71–2
    law for prevention of hereditarily
        diseased offspring 71–2
    Mussolini, inspired by 14
    nationwide boycott of Jewish
        businesses 34
    propaganda 22, 28–9
    reparation money for victims of 150
    restrictions on freedom of
        movement 53
    in Romania 198–9
    Soviet Army fight against 97
    surrendered 109
    war criminals, finding and arresting in
        ruins of 105–21
Nazism 4–5, 133–4, 220–5
    birth 12
    cartoons on 7–29
    in Europe 109
    gaps in research on 62
    phoniness of 13–14
    resistance against 4–5, 56, 103, 116,
        179, 215–29
    satirists alarm on (1920s) 7–29
    in Saxony 62–3
    working-class German children
        resisted 49–67
Nerac, Ellie 7–8, 28
Neu Kaliss 147
The New York Times (newspaper)
    202
Niemann, Johann 183–4
Ninth Candle, The 3, 26
Nixon, Richard 206
Norton, Edward 217
Nuremberg Laws 37, 162
Nuremberg Trials 117

Obersturmbannführer 109
Office of Special Investigations
    (OSI) 207–8
Official Secrets Act (1939) 108–9
OJ Simpson trial 155
Operation Backfire 203–4
Operation Harvest Festival 96
Operation Paperclip 202–4
Operation Reinhard camps 77, 91, 96
Operation Valkyrie (movie) 66
Orsenigo, Cesare 75
Osterfinke, Ingrun 82, 84
Oswald, Anton 111

Partisanenbekämpfung 190
Pax Christi 154

INDEX

Pechersky, Alexander   87–103, 235
   choices   102
   leader of uprising in Sobibor
      extermination camp   87–103
Pendas, Devin   154–5
Penha, Lea Judith de la   99
Peter, Janusz   80
Peukert, Detlev   4, 52
   definition of active political
      resistance   4
Pfannenstiel, Wilhelm   73, 80
Pittsburgh Courier   133
Piwko, Josef   143–4
Poland   38, 62, 71, 73, 74, 77, 79, 87, 95,
   96, 115, 117, 129, 138, 145, 151,
   153, 163, 174, 175, 180, 188, 193
Political Trials in Theory and History
   (Pendas)   155
populism   5
   in Europe   172
   rise of   184
Pourquoi Israel (movie)   186
Pretzel, Oliver   37, 39, 43–6
Punch, British satirical magazine   24

Rabinowitz, Dorothy   173–4
racism   49–50, 125–41, 217
Rashke, Richard   204
Rauschning, Hermann   44
Reder, Rudolf   77
Refuge (movie)   228
Rehbock, Ralph   231–2
Reichleitner, Franz   94
Reichstag   18
Reitlinger, Gerald   179–80
Renner, Rudolf   119
resistance   4–5, 103, 215–29, 231–6
   active political   4
   creativity as form of   235
   Jewish people   56, 103, 116, 179,
      215–29
   against Nazism   4–5, 56, 103, 116,
      179, 215–29
   spiritual   102–3

Riccards, Patrick   216–21, 225
Riebeckstraße 63   64
Ring of the Nibelung, The   11
River Elde   147–8
Robson, Felix   118
Roma people   143
Romania   197–214
   antisemitic violence in   200–1
   far-right press   200
   Iron Guard   198–9
   Nazis and   198–9
   Trifa, Viorel   198–201
Rosenbaum, Ron   183
Rosenfeld, Simjon   97
Roving Dudes   52
Rückerl, Adalbert   165
Ruhr, West Germany   14
Ryan, Allan   214
Ryan, Russell   202
Ryba, Walter   95

Sachsenhausen concentration camp   129,
   159
Sartre, Jean-Paul   179
Saxon Memorial Foundation   65
Saxony   62–4
   Nazism in   62–3
   state election   64
Schäfer, Peter   61–2, 67
Schiano, Vincent   204–5
Schilling, Erich   14, 22
Schindler, Oskar   82–3
Schindler's List (movie)   183, 195
Schleicher, Rüdiger   146
Schlingensiepen, Ferdinand   157
Schmied, Jürgen Peter   39–42
Schoenberner, Franz   7–8, 14, 23,
   28–9
Scholl, Hans   42
Scholl, Sophie   42
Schubert, Heinz   188–90
Scully, Richard   23
Sebastian Haffner Masked as an
   Englishman (Krug)   41

Second World War 38, 71, 107, 133–4, 197–8
Secret World, The (Andrew) 108
Sereny, Gitta 161–75, 194
  in *Anschluss* (annexation) 162–3
  attended trials of Nazi war criminals 164–5
  to Düsseldorf to see Stangl, Franz 165–6
  family 164
  interviewed Stangl, Franz 166–71
  Into That Darkness 169, 171
  as journalist 164–75
  making anti-Nazi propaganda for Office of War Information 164
  Medallion, The 164
  in Nazi Party Rally in Nuremberg 162
  Rabinowitz, Dorothy views on 173–4
  research on Stangl, Franz life and crimes 168–71
  in Villandry 164
  working with United Nations 164
  writer for *Daily Telegraph Magazine* 164
Shoah (movie) 1, 177–96
  as act of resistance 196
  editing 183
  Lanzmann, Claude research on Holocaust for 179–83
  McGlothlin, Erin on 193–4
  meaning 233
  premiered at Théâtre de l'Empire in Paris (April 1985) 183
Simplicissimus magazine 9–10, 18, 22–9
Singer, Bryan 66
Sinti people 143
Skarżysko 139
Sobibor (movie) 100
Sobibor extermination camp 80, 88–9
  books about 97
  movies about Uprising 100
  Nazis dismantled 97–8
  resistance group in 90–1
  SS guards in 93–6
  survivors from 100
  Underground Committee 93–6
  Uprising 96–7
Sobibor Memorial Museum, Poland 97–8
social media
  influencers 101–2
  Twitch 218
Soczewica, Wojciech 115–17
Söderblom, Staffan 74
South, Derek 109–10
Speer, Albert 194
Spielberg, Steven 183
Spiess, Alfred 165
spiritual resistance 102–3
Spycatcher (Wright) 108–9
Stangl, Franz 161, 165–6, 177–8
  Himmler, Heinrich on 175
  research on 168–71
  Sereny, Gitta interviewed 166–71
Steimle, Eugen 190–1
Steinke, Ronen 151
STET (Hilberg) 180
Stier, Walter 182–3
Suchomel, Franz 177–8, 187, 189–90
Suhr, Friedrich 112–13
Szmajzner, Stanislaw 97, 101

T4 involuntary euthanasia program 71–2
Tagore, Rabindranath 11–12
Temple Judea, Palm Beach Gardens 215
Tenniel, John 24
testimonies to the crimes of Nazi Germany
  eyewitnesses and survivors 61, 72–4, 77–8, 80–1, 98, 132, 139, 143, 155
  perpetrators 184, 189, 193, 195–6
Thielen, Fritz 58–60, 67
Third Reich 17–18, 50, 139, 202
Thöny, Eduard 22

Toller, Ernst   9
Tomaszów Lubelski   80
Treblinka extermination camp   73–4, 77, 80–1, 97, 102, 139, 165, 168–9, 177, 181, 187
Trier, Walter   22
Trifa, Valarian   198–201, 205–6, 213–14
Tzur, Yaron   101–2

United States Holocaust Memorial Museum   184

van der Lubbe, Marinus   18
Vancouver Holocaust Education Center   138, 140
Veit, Susanne   23
von Bismarck, Otto   24
von Dohnanyi, Christine   159
von Mises, Ludwig   163
von Ossietzky, Carl   9
von Otter, Goran   69–70, 74
von Papen, Franz   17–18
von Stauffenberg, Claus   3, 65–6, 145

Wagner, Erich   129–30
Wagner, Gustav   94
Wagner, Richard   11
Waisman, Robbie   138–41
war criminals   105–21; *see also* specific war criminals

Warburg, Frederic   38
Warsaw Ghetto Uprising   101
Wehr, Otto   72–3
Weimar   128–9
"What Does Hitler Look Like?" cartoon (Heine)   10–12
"White Rose" student group   3
Wiesenthal, Simon   165
Wilhelm II, Kaiser   24, 32, 34, 44
Will, Thomas   169–70
Wirth, Christian   75, 80, 96
Wirth, Ursula   151
Wirths, Eduard   183
Włodawa   99
Wolf of Wall Street, The (movie)   227–8
Wolff, Karl   194
The World at War (TV documentary)   194
Wright, Peter   108
Wulkan, Emil   150

Yad Vashem   180
Yiddish   92
YIVO Institute for Jewish Research   205
You Still Have Your Head (Schoenberner)   29

Zimmermann, Hans   27–8
Zuckerman, Antek   103
Zyklon B   73–4, 80–2